MW00906659

a

Know I had

Love

John F Miller

11 May 2012

Living the Life I Always Wanted

John F. Willey

iUniverse, Inc.
Bloomington

Living the Life I Always Wanted

Copyright © 2011 by John F. Willey

All rights reserved. No part of this book may be used or reproduced by any means, graphic, electronic, or mechanical, including photocopying, recording, taping or by any information storage retrieval system without the written permission of the publisher except in the case of brief quotations embodied in critical articles and reviews.

The views expressed in this work are solely those of the author and do not necessarily reflect the views of the publisher, and the publisher hereby disclaims any responsibility for them.

iUniverse books may be ordered through booksellers or by contacting:

iUniverse
1663 Liberty Drive
Bloomington, IN 47403
www.iuniverse.com
1-800-Authors (1-800-288-4677)

Because of the dynamic nature of the Internet, any Web addresses or links contained in this book may have changed since publication and may no longer be valid.

Any people depicted in stock imagery provided by Thinkstock are models, and such images are being used for illustrative purposes only.

Certain stock imagery © Thinkstock.

ISBN: 978-1-4502-9031-9 (sc)
ISBN: 978-1-4502-9209-2 (dj)
ISBN: 978-1-4502-9032-6 (ebk)

Printed in the United States of America

iUniverse rev. date: 4/7/2011

CONTENTS

To Barbara, my wife and soul mate

FOREWORD

In my 40s, I adopted two basic guides to life. Each is a simple idea, but neither is so easy to apply.

The first is: "All anyone really wants in life is to have someone to love, and of equal importance, for that someone to love them in return." (Herb Dever)

Herb Dever was a man I met on the road to recovery, and his simple philosophy of life helped me over many a rocky stretch. Herb was a rather rough-hewn little Irishman, with a scowl which often hid a half smile and a twinkle in his eye, when he was at his sarcastic best.

The second is a definition of success that I learned from Amway training: "Success is the progressive realization of a worthwhile goal while remaining well-adjusted."

These two ideas have been behind my drive to rise above where I started and to live a life I love.

MOTIVATIONS

What follows is my story about where I started, and the journey I took. I often wondered what my ancestors were like, what they did, and how they lived. I grew up in a family where fear ruled my days, and my parents kept secrets from their children. For reasons I cannot explain, my father threw away the scant records he had about his family as well as the diary my mother kept. My idea is to write about myself as a way of allowing my children and grandchildren to have the opportunity to better know at least one of their forefathers, and possibly to set in motion the motivation for other family members to do the same.

In Nathaniel Philbrick's book, *In The Heart of The Sea*, I came across a paragraph about a Mr. Chase, the first mate on the whale ship Essex. In 1823, in the far reaches of the Pacific Ocean, the ship was attacked and destroyed by a huge, aggressive whale. This quote helps me express a second reason for writing this memoir.

"Chase's journal-keeping satisfied more than an official obligation; it also fulfilled a personal need. The act of self-expression – through writing a journal or letters – often enables a survivor to distance himself from his fears. After beginning his informal log, Chase would never again suffer another sleepless night tortured by his memory of the whale."

These words jumped out at me. Writing this memoir would help me get free of the "whales" of my past (and besides, by coincidence, my mother's maiden name was Chase!).

One of my favorite things to do is to read biographies, especially of great characters of the American Revolutionary War. John Adams and Thomas Jefferson were close allies and then, as happens in so many relationships, they had a falling out. After many years, they reconciled. On 10 September 1816, John Adams sent a note to Thomas Jefferson that read, "You and I ought not die before we have explained ourselves to each other."

I too want to explain myself, and late in life, I acquired a strong urge to write. I have always admired writers, but felt too intimidated to refer to myself as a writer. It sounds too lofty. My only other writings are technical reports on highway planning projects, Environmental Impact Statements, and a "how to" book on citizen participation published at the University of Massachusetts many years ago.

Completed in my 78th year, the original manuscript of this book delved into my life as well as the lives of others, and was outlined as a chronological series of events much like a diary. I understand now that I had been using the first draft to parade around a lot of old hurts for the world to see. Once completed, I was shocked at the garbage I had written.

Unwilling to face the overwhelming job of beginning all over again, I resorted to my old tried and true "default" behavior, which is to run away from the problem. While I felt horribly discouraged that I could not complete the book, I was stalled, feeling like I had run smack into a concrete wall.

After a pause of many months, I decided I had to complete this book as proof to myself that I could indeed finish a very difficult project. I figured out a new route that made more sense. I would turn the memoir into a series of vignettes about my experiences and ideas, about who I am, and where I have been. The bulk of this book was written in 2008 and 2009, and I finished writing in 2010.

In writing this memoir I believe that one of the most important things for me to do is to tell my story as it happened. Everyone sees the same event from a different perspective. This book is written from my perspective. I had to rely on my own memory, on what I was told, or on what I was led to believe was the truth. I understand now that my perception of the events is my own reality. This book is as close as I can come to telling it like it is.

The stories that follow will ultimately reveal that in spite of my rather slow start, I have lived a "charmed life" surrounded by adventure, loving relationships, and intimate friends. I did not sit in the grandstand of life, but I was down in the middle of the playing field where the action is.

14 July 1993. My nine children. Front: Barbara Brugnani, Richard Gelotti. Back: Cheryl Carroll, Laura Cross, John F. Willey Jr., Debi Osgood, Linda Rousseau, Sharon Shyavitz, and Patricia DeForte. Photo taken at wedding of Richard (Rick) and Carole Gelotti.

PLUM ISLAND

Plum Island is one of my favorite places in the world, and it is there that I first had the idea to write this book. Now in the autumn of my life, even though I am happily living in New York City, I still love to spend time on Plum Island. I especially like walking the remote beach at the southern tip of the Island, which first requires driving the entire length of the federal wildlife refuge to get there. During every year spent in New York City I have managed to take at least two trips to Plum Island, winter or summer, alone or with Barbara. I always feel regenerated upon leaving my island.

Plum Island is a barrier island about eight miles long, and a half mile at its widest point. The island is actually located within four Massachusetts cities and towns -- Newburyport, Newbury,

Rowley and Ipswich. Private homes are in the northern one and a half miles in the city of Newburyport and the town of Newbury. The remaining five and a half miles are a federal wildlife refuge, except the very southern tip where there is a State-owned wildlife sanctuary. A notable historian of the region, Joshua Coffin, said in 1845: "Plum Island, a wild and fantastical sand beach, is thrown up by the joint power of winds and waves into the thousand wanton figures of a snow drift." I agree wholeheartedly with Mr. Coffin's description.

In the fall, when there are very few people in the refuge, I love to walk the lonely beaches bordering on the Atlantic. Even after so many years of visiting this peaceful sanctuary, I never tire of retracing my steps. The dune grasses, wild plum trees, cranberries, and wild flowers, set off the large areas of wind-sculpted, sandy patches, all leading up to the tops of the dunes that drop dramatically to the beaches.

The beach is constantly being eroded by the cold Labrador Current running from north to south. Here and there an oasis of scrub pitch pine, black oak, and eastern cedar flourishes, with bright red winter berry bushes, orange berries of the bittersweet vines, bayberry bushes, beach roses and wild flowers, all in concert with each other. A large area of black pine planted in the 1950s prevents erosion and gives a vivid green splash to the landscape throughout the year.

I like to put my back to the beach and walk to the marshland on the western edge of the Island, especially when the autumn winds slice through the cat tails, causing a rustling sound all their own. Towering above them all along the narrow elevated board walk is the invasive phragmites, standing 10 feet tall, their flowering tops dancing violently in the breeze. In the fall, this area is a sea of purple loosestrife, another exotic plant that has invaded the wetlands. In the summer, I look forward to the song of the red wing blackbird, the sweet high-pitched tune of the chickadee, and the ever present raucous call of the squabbling sea gulls.

Sometimes I walk from the western marsh towards the beach, crossing the park road, and continuing on the board walk on the other side, down several steps leading into a fairly deep vegetated swale, and then up the other side to continue the walk. Here there is a bench, strategically located under a magnificent eastern cedar. Sitting amidst the boughs of the cedar, their fragrance brings me peace and comfort. I feel the gentle breeze on my face, and see the scrolls left on the dunes, made by the wind moving the grasses back and forth.

Why do I love this place so much? Maybe because it is such a magical place, just like when a story begins, "Once upon a time in a land far, far away …" Plum Island is that place to me. I have had nothing but pleasant memories of being on Plum Island, dating back close to 65 years. Sometimes I imagine what it would be like to ride a horse through this wonderland of sand and ocean, landscaped with nature's 100 different kinds of trees, shrubs, wildflowers and grasses. My mind goes back to World War II when Coast Guardsmen patrolled the beaches on horseback, and huge shore gun installations were hidden in the sand.

In a recent visit to Plum Island on a bright sunny day in the cold of winter, I forced myself to stand and be quiet and wonder, "What is there about this place that gives me such comfort?" I was looking across the lower wetland in the Hellcat Trail, and all I could see was a profusion of red winter berries against a backdrop of gray shrubs and trees. Suddenly two bright red cardinals landed in amongst the red berries. The answer hit me, what brings me comfort is the absence of conflict. The gnarled, twisted shrubs, the occasional cedar, honeysuckle vines, beach heather and dried plants are at peace with each other. A feeling of contentment washes over me. I just plain feel good. That always happens here, especially when I am alone.

The John Willey that comes alive while at Plum Island is the John Willey I want my kids to know. I want them to know of my love affair with nature on this barrier island, and of the imaginary events that become possible when I sit under the cedar boughs, just *being.*

PART I

BEFORE

My life consists of three major phases:
The first, BEFORE I used and abused alcohol;
The second, DURING the time I abused alcohol; and
The third, AFTER I began recovery.

1
FREMONT, NEW HAMPSHIRE

I identify most strongly with my father's side of the family – the Willey family. My research indicates that the first Willey came to Boston in 1630 from England. The Willey name is not Irish, but of Norman derivation. There are a great many Willeys in New Hampshire and Maine.

My grandfather, John C. Willey, was born and raised in Fremont, New Hampshire. In 1891 when my grandfather was 22, he married 15-year old Florence West. One could only guess what the wedding was like. Was there a shotgun involved? Were they excited and looking forward to a long and happy life together in this tiny little village? I do not know what the customs were back then, but I do know there were shortages of mates in the rural, sparsely settled areas of New Hampshire, and women were routinely married at tender ages.

Fremont offered only a few choices for employment, and they all centered on work at the Spaulding and Frost Barrel Factory. Of course there were other opportunities for employment, but ultimately they all related to the factory or provided support for the factory. Job classifications at the mill included titles like cooper, lumber jack, teamster, sawyer, mill hand, assembly worker, and power plant engineer.

The mill produced wooden barrels, buckets and firkins for the storage of pickles, jams and jellies, dried fish, salt pork, and other food stuffs. All the barrels were made from native white pine, harvested in nearby forests. Every scrap of wood from the manufacturing process was used, including the sawdust, the cut-offs, and the pine slabs that resulted from the cutting of the logs into boards. Whatever wood did not go directly into making barrels became fuel, burned in the gigantic fire boxes used to generate steam. All the factory's machines were driven by a belt and pulley system that received its power from the main steam engine located at the lower level of the factory.

Most of the workers lived in the village and walked to the factory. Each morning groups of workers headed to their jobs, carrying black tin lunch boxes, trudging down Main Street, parallel to the Exeter River. They used the time to connect with their neighbors and share local news and gossip of the village. There were no telephones or TV and very few radios (and of course no computers, internet, cell phones, or BlackBerry smartphones).

About 90 percent of the factory workers were men, and they operated all the high-speed woodworking machinery. This was back-breaking hard labor, and you had to be very strong to carry the wood and run the machines all day. Some women worked in the mill, doing piecework, getting paid a set amount for each keg or bucket they assembled. Others were responsible for coating the inside of kegs with wax to seal the soft pine wood so foodstuffs stored in the barrels would not soak into the wood. They carefully placed a keg over a pipe equipped with a sprinkler head. Then they pulled a lever, and the perforated pipe sprayed the inside of the keg with molten wax.

The men wore bib overalls to work; the women wore plain clothes, some homemade from feed bags. Most people farmed their own gardens and grew livestock. The grain merchants sold animal feed in printed cotton sacks as an incentive for folks to buy their products. Women would re-use the fabric, sewing the feed bags into dresses.

Throughout the Village you could hear the high-pitched whining sound of the enormous band saw, NNNNEEEE-owwww, NNNNEEEE-owwww, biting into logs and spitting out boards. The band saw had teeth on both edges; it was about 60 feet long and one foot wide. The drive wheel that ran the saw was on the first floor, and the head of the band saw was on the third floor of the factory. The cutting was done on the second floor, the heart of the mill, where the logs began their journey to become barrels and other containers. Logs were locked into a carriage that ran on tracks and fed the logs into the saw. When a board was cut off, the log would kick itself over about an inch, and the saw was ready to cut another board on the return trip.

Every day of the year but holidays and Sundays, the village was filled with the aroma of pine pitch from the band saw, the heavy odor of grease used to lubricate the various woodworking machines, and whiffs of the paraffin wax used to coat the insides of the pine barrels. But the overriding fragrance throughout the village was the pine wood being burned in the power plant.

At least three generations of Willey's worked in the mill over a period of about 30 years—my grandfather, my father, and for a brief time, I worked there too.

2
GRAMPA AND GRAMMY WILLEY

At the turn of the century, my grandfather, John C. Willey, moved from Fremont, New Hampshire into a rooming house in Haverhill, Massachusetts, a center for shoe manufacturing and woolen mills. Grampa found employment in the shoe factories. Soon thereafter, he met an immigrant Irish woman named Nora Harrington.

The next important event I pieced together from bits and scraps of conversations as a young man. In early 1905, Nora Harrington, a frightened young woman, informed John, probably in a brogue as "tick" as pea soup, that she was pregnant. There she was, an Irish Roman Catholic immigrant getting pregnant before being married, and the culprit was a Protestant. She was alone except for the other Irish immigrants she met where she lived in a section of Haverhill dubbed "the Acre." Nora's parents, whom she had not heard from in years, were still in County Cork in the southwest of Ireland. Her sister, Bridget, was still in Ireland (though she moved to the U.S. years later). Her brother, Daniel, was in the English army, who knows where. The other two sisters,

Kathleen and Mary, were somewhere in Australia, never to be heard from again.

On May 27, 1905, my grandfather, John C. Willey, and grandmother, Nora Harrington, were married by a Protestant minister. The marriage certificate read, "First marriage for both." (However, those words are perplexing, because some years later I obtained a copy of an earlier marriage certificate showing that my grandfather had married Florence West in Freemont, New Hampshire in 1891. I found no record of any divorce.)

John was a Protestant, and Nora's heart was broken because she could not be married in the Catholic Church. On January 22, 1906, about eight months after their marriage, my own father, John Clark Willey, arrived to a cold and inhospitable environment. As the story was related to me, my grandmother did not bond with her baby, blaming him for the shameful position in which she found herself.

Almost two years later, on November 25, 1907, another son, Leonard Abner Willey, was born. Grammy took to the new boy with a fondness not ever experienced by his older brother, John. However, on the cold winter night of January 3, 1912, at the age of four, Leonard died of meningitis complicated with malnutrition and toxemia. My grandmother was inconsolable and went into a deep depression.

The family story as related by my father, was that his mother was so despondent that she could not attend the funeral, and good-intentioned friends buried Leonard in the Elmwood Cemetery. Apparently my grandmother and grandfather were not living together when Leonard died. I can only guess that somehow my grandmother found out that her husband was still married to Florence West. My grandmother had to face the tragedy of her child's death alone. My father told me that in a moment of torment and grief, his mother wailed, "God took the good one and left me with you." Apparently this was just one of her many acts of meanness toward my father.

Upon my grandmother's recovery, she asked to be taken to the grave site. When she found out Leonard was buried in a Protestant cemetery, she was beside herself. As the story goes, Leonard was exhumed and buried in an unmarked plot in the back of St. James Catholic cemetery. I searched at both the Elmwood and St. James cemeteries, but could not find his gravesite in either place, nor did either cemetery office have a record of his burial. To this day, there is no proof that Leonard ever existed except for his birth and death records sitting quietly in the volumes of records at the City Clerk's office in Haverhill.

My grandfather and grandmother broke apart, never to speak to each other again. Grampa was ordered to pay Grammy a stipend of $7.00 a week for the rest of her life. This bit of information I pieced together from a comment made by my grandfather when I was a youngster.

Grammy continued to live in the Acre and attended daily Mass at St. James Catholic Church. All of her life she was angry and depressed. She wore a permanent scowl, her hair pulled back and tied in a bun, and her face a map of despair. A few of her friends, including Margaret Nolan, stuck close and supported her in her world of anger and remorse. Grammy lived her entire life in abject poverty, from her birth in Ireland through her years in Haverhill.

Grammy Willey's usual lunch was a boiled potato, a piece of bread, and a cup of tea. I remember visiting her, and when lunchtime came she would give me the same lunch, with the addition of a few slices of baloney purchased especially for me. She would purposefully spill some of her tea in her saucer because it was too hot, and then slurp the tea from the saucer. Clutching the folded piece of bread in one hand, and stabbing the potato with the other, she ate her peasant meal.

Once while visiting Grammy Willey, I made the mistake of pouring a glass of water, drinking only half, and making the motion to dump the remainder in the sink. She stopped me in mid-action. "Put the glass on the side, and if ye want more have it," she said. Grammy Willey grew up in a village in Ireland where she spent many an hour lugging water in a bucket.

One day when Grammy Willey was visiting us, the old Pontiac coupe drove up the driveway with Grampa Willey at the helm. My grandmother looked out, and said in her thick Irish brogue, "Is that the sonovabitch?" She put on her coat and made a fast exit, and Grampa was never the wiser. I felt really sad, because I liked Grammy Willey and I liked Grampa Willey. When Grampa Willey walked in the door, we all behaved as though Grammy had never been there.

She died alone on March 24, 1943 after 66 unhappy years. We were told that she died by accident when a gas hose connection to a hot plate in her apartment broke during the night. The death certificate reads "Asphyxiation by illumination gas – Accidental." Her flat consisted of two rooms with sparse furnishings, and her only means of cooking was a single-burner gas plate set on the kitchen table. I loved her, and when she died I was torn apart. I could not face going to the funeral and seeing her dead. I am grateful that my parents did not insist that I go to the wake or the funeral.

Grampa Willey moved back to Fremont, New Hampshire and worked in the barrel factory as a plant engineer in the boiler room. He died in 1950.

Very little is known about my grandfather during his early years. Whatever happened with his marriage to Florence West was never revealed to me. As a result of his death notice in the paper, one of his two daughters from his marriage with Florence West, showed up at his funeral. My father claimed he never knew about his father's other children.

However, I do remember with happy fondness my Grampa Willey's occasional visits. He used to arrive in his 1932 Pontiac coupe with the rumble seat. We did not have a family car, and riding in the car with my grandfather was a special treat. He was always well-dressed in a suit, with vest and a hat--a straw hat in the summer and a felt one in the other seasons, as was the custo wore well-shined shoes and pearl grey spats with black but

3
MOM AND DAD

My father, John Clark Willey, was born in Haverhill, Massachusetts in 1906, son of John C. Willey and Nora (Harrington) Willey. My father grew up to be a handsome man of medium build and height, ruddy complexion, with dark hair parted down the middle, and the prominent nose of the Yankee Willey family. He had a natural ability to make new friends quickly. He was a great story teller, and he could take on new tasks with industrious zeal. When he was openly happy, his face lit up, but when he was in a dark mood, it was best to stand clear. He never recovered from the early days of abuse and deprivation and the abandonment by his father.

His schooling ended in the ninth grade when the school required that he attend gym sessions with sneakers. The story was that he explained to his impoverished mother that he needed sneakers. She replied, "What are ye talkin' about?" Nora lived alone and associated with only a few Irish immigrant friends in the Acre. She spoke mostly Irish with her friends, and did not assimilate with American culture. The word "sneakers" had no meaning to her. She had no idea what they were, and she did not have money to buy them. So rather than face the embarrassment of showing up without the sneakers, my father stopped going to school at 14 years old and went to work in the factories.

My mother, Frances A. (Chase) Willey, was born in 1909 in Hamilton, Massachusetts. Her mother was Henrietta (Smith) Chase. Her father, Benjamin Chapman Chase, was a railroad station keeper. My father met Frances when she was 18. She had a round face and perfectly smooth complexion, with expressive, dark brown eyes. Frances Chase came from poverty. She had fallen in love with my father, a troubled, sometimes sulky young man who was a member of the infamous West End Gang in Haverhill, a group of disgruntled and angry first-generation Irish and Irish immigrants.

On March 22, 1930, just as the Great Depression was gaining momentum, John and Frances were quietly married in Hampstead, New Hampshire. My mother and my father had to get married because she was pregnant. Here was another unwanted child to cause heart ache and shame, an unwanted marriage, another Willey arriving the same way as his dad. Several dear friends made up the wedding party, and apparently no family members attended. Five months after the marriage, a beautiful bundle of joy was delivered at the McVey hospital in Haverhill, Massachusetts. I had arrived.

My father identified with Irish Catholics, but he was never baptized. Frances was from a family of Protestants who did not take kindly to Roman Catholics, and especially the Irish. The consensus of my mother's family was "Dear Jesus, it was bad enough that Almeda, Frances's older sister, had run off and married a red-headed Irish Catholic from New York named Hugh Gillis. Here was Frances, the youngest child, getting "knocked up" by an Irish bum living in the Acre in Haverhill."

My father and mother lived in the most stressful of times. The Great Depression had begun. Bankers were jumping out of windows in despair. The whole country was scared. Everyone my parents knew was broke, and there were no signs of the economic disaster clearing up anytime soon.

Neither of my parents completed high school. With my mother a shoe factory worker and my father a laborer/truck driver, they struggled to eat and pay rent and set aside money to pay the hospital for the new baby. The cost was huge for them, and there was no Social Security, medical insurance, or any other program of assistance. The complete cost for the delivery and the hospital stay was a whopping $75.00, and my father proudly told the story many times that the bill was paid before the kid was born.

My mother was a wood heel coverer at Century Wood Heel on Essex Street in Haverhill, doing piece work for a few pennies per heel. I visited her there as a little boy and saw the way she worked. She would pick up a wooden heel, lock the heel into a holding device, reach into a basin with her bare hand to snatch a celluloid square soaking in a caustic solution to keep it pliable, quickly wrap the heel with the celluloid, and trim it with a pair of scissors. Each heel was completed within seconds, while she and her friends chatted away, making idle talk to fend off the boredom.

I can still see her cracked hands and smell the horrible caustic solution that she breathed in all day. I learned to hate those bastards who owned the factories and forced my mother to accept such working conditions. And a full day at the factory was not the end of her working day. Often when she left the factory, she walked downtown to the Mohegan Market to do grocery shopping, spend five cents to take the Main Street bus to Dustin Square, and walk home with the groceries. As soon as she was in the house, she would start cooking supper.

I do not ever recall hearing her complain about her cracked hands or the long hours she spent working each day. She did say how lucky we were to live in Dustin Square, because the next bus stop after Dustin Square was Rosemont, and then the bus fare increased from five cents to a dime.

Through thick and thin for the next 64 years, my parents stuck together in a hostile world. They made the best life they could. Perhaps the furthest they ever traveled was to Albany, New York to visit my Aunt Almeda and Uncle Hugh Gillis in the late 1950's. My parents died within ten days of each other in December 1994.

A few years before she died, my mother made her wishes known in a poem. Between the lines I can see the pain she experienced living with her "John" all these years. She had a vision bigger than all of us.

Memories
by Frances A. Willey
May I go to sleep in comfort
And dream about your love,
Wake up and find you near;
To cheer me and bless me,
And help me through the way,
That is all I ask this coming day.
To be together is one thing,
To be apart is another.
So, let us make the most of what we have –
Friendship, Unselfish Love,
Understanding and Pleasant Deeds.
Then when we are old and grey,
We can sit back and say,
"What a nice family we have today."
To feel loved and wanted is our greatest reward;
And that is all I want the rest of my days.
Merrimac, Massachusetts
April 1989

4
MEMORIES FROM THE EARLY YEARS

I was born August 13, 1930 in the McVey Lying-In Hospital on North Avenue in Haverhill, Massachusetts. I was the oldest of four children: My sister Barbara was born in 1932, Joan in 1933, and Norma in 1940. We grew up at 754 Main Street, Haverhill, a house owned by John Roach. It was a double decker, a two-family house, with a small apartment attached in the back. We lived in that small apartment. Do not go looking for the hospital, since it was demolished a long time ago. The double decker is gone too, and a bank now stands in its place.

August 1931. I am one year old, sitting atop a wood pile at Falconer Farm, Epping, NH.

My earliest and most fearful recollection as an infant is that I was lying down on my back and fighting to breathe. I struggled to draw in a breath and nothing was happening. It was as if someone had shut off a valve and stopped the flow of air. It was quiet. I remember a flame over my head and reaching up toward it. No one was there. I was terrified. I was told years later that I almost died from whooping cough, and apparently I had been in a crib in my Grammy Willey's house at 24 Primrose Street in Haverhill. The flame was a gas light over the crib. This experience is fresh in my mind. I never learned why I was there, or who was or was not with me.

Haverhill was a mill town in the Merrimack Valley about 35 miles northeast of Boston as the crow flies. Like everyone else who toiled in the mills, my parents had a mill town mentality. They had no hopes or dreams of a brighter future. They simply accepted the fact that they were drones. They lived day to day, learning to settle for less, complaining about their lot in life without any hope of reprieve.

The Merrimac River cut through the city, separating the classes. To the north of the River in the downtown area, lived most of the immigrant populations. My Dad grew up in "the Acre," a neighborhood north of the Merrimack River, home to Irish immigrants. In the center of the Acre was St. James Catholic Church. Directly across from St. James, was 24 Primrose Street, where Grammy Willey lived, alone in a small apartment in a four-family house. The Acre was a bad place to hang around if you were not Irish. If non-Irish people were in the Acre, it had better be for a good reason, and even at that, people were well advised to keep their mouths shut. There were a lot of angry Irishmen who loved to get into a fight for any reason, and someone not belonging in the Acre was a good one.

My mother lived in the poorest part of the City, on Chestnut Street, just off Water Street. Water Street was lined with pawn shops, bar rooms, and whore houses. As a child, I was warned to keep away from Water Street.

Haverhill residents included a great diversity of nationalities, ethnicities and religions. Many people in my little world spoke broken English, or spoke with an accent or a brogue. The predominant groups were Italians, Greeks, French Canadians, and Irish. Other groups around the city included the poorer Jews in the Mt. Washington area and the wealthy Jews up on Lakeview Avenue. Some French Canadians created their own neighborhood called Dodier Village several miles north of downtown. There were two Polish sections, one near St. Michael's Church, and one six or eight miles from downtown, near Snows Brook in an area called "Pollock Alley," close to where the Lithuanians lived. The Italians were centered on River Street and in the Mt. Washington section.

More affluent people lived south of the Merrimack River. Those sections of Haverhill were referred to as Bradford and Ward Hill. My parents taught me early on that Bradford Junior College was where the daughters of the rich and privileged were sent before moving on to prestigious colleges far and wide. I learned that I did not belong near Bradford Junior College. As a young teenager, I heard a rumor that the girls could go into Mitchell's Department Store and buy anything they wanted to furnish their rooms, just sign their name to a paper, and it would be delivered.

One day I went with my friend, "Pete the Greek," to the furniture department in Mitchell's Department Store to see if this was true. We saw the girls point out what they wanted, and the clerk happily hand them a sales slip, which they signed. There were no cash registers. The clerk put the sales slip in a little box that was connected to a ceiling-mounted pulley system, which whisked the little box to the accounting office where orders were processed. It was fun to watch the little boxes flying along the pulleys, carrying papers from all over the store into and out of the accounting office.

The stock market crashed in the fall of 1929, and 1930 was the beginning of the Great Depression. As a child, I was oblivious to the tragedy that struck across America. I learned to live in poverty as did millions of other Americans. However, my small world did include words like, the "poor farm," "on the dole," and "federal assistance." Evidence of the federal program called the Works Project Administration (WPA) was everywhere. Men were painting wall murals on the post office, playing in bands for the grammar school children, and repairing bridges and roads. In addition, about 10,000 men in Massachusetts alone participated in the federally-sponsored Civilian Conservation Corps (CCC). They lived in camps out in the woods, and they helped maintain and repair park trails, walkways, dams, picnic areas, and shelters.

In our family, the scariest term of all was "welfare." My father refused welfare. Everyone looked down on the kids who wore the striped denim overalls given out to families on welfare. I lived with fear about the possibility of being sent to the poor farm, where whole families would move, work in the fields, and receive City-subsidized food and shelter.

Rather than go on the dole, Dad moved the family to a back woods house on the side of the road in Fremont, New Hampshire. I learned from stories my father told me, that at age 21 he had reunited with his own father, and it was his father who had given him the use of the little house during the Depression when my father could not find work in Haverhill. There were no other houses in sight. I can still hear the lonesome, sad song of the whip-poor-will at evening time, and it always seemed to be miles away. I was told that no one could see a whip-poor-will because these birds had some magic power of not being spotted. We lived a simple life in the little house--no electricity, no plumbing, no central heating, no phone, no radio, no car, and no newspaper.

In Fremont, my father found a job at Faulkner's Farm as a laborer for about 20 cents an hour plus a quart of milk each day. He walked to the farm and back, working from 6 a.m. to 6 p.m. six days a week. Part of my father's job was to remove stumps to create larger fields for hay and other crops. My father dug each stump by hand, tied a chain to the stump, and hitched up a team of horses. The horses pulled out the stump, and my father rolled the stump onto a stone boat, which was a flat sled of heavy-plank construction, 4 feet by 6 feet in size, used to move boulders and stumps off the fields. Then Dad walked beside the horses, guiding their route to a disposal site.

It was never clear to me what years we lived in Fremont, but the time was brief, perhaps a little over a year or so. My sister Barbara was born in the little house by the side of the road on June 7, 1932. The doctor came in a Model T Ford to attend to my mother.

We had no utilities, and not even an ice box. I remember that perishables, like butter, milk and eggs, were placed in a metal pail with a rope tied to the handle, and then lowered into the hand-dug well so that the bottom of the pail just rested on the surface of the cold well water. That was our refrigeration. None of this seemed unusual, since it was all I knew. The bathroom was an outdoor outhouse. We had kerosene lanterns for light.

The little house in Fremont was at the intersection of two dirt roads called the Four Corners. One dirt road ran from Fremont to Raymond, New Hampshire. I do not know where the other road went, except that down that road was the Knowles-Chase-Leavitt Cemetery (circa 1777), where several of the Willey family members who fought in the Civil War were buried.

On the front of the house was a sign that read "The House by the Side of the Road." Samuel Walter Foss, a writer for the Boston Globe, wrote a poem in 1897 by that name. Sam was born in a little house by the side of the road, much like the one in which we lived. His was located only a few miles away in Candia, New Hampshire. Here is the first verse:

There are hermit souls that live withdrawn
In the place of their self-content;
There are souls like stars, that live apart,
In a fellowless firmament;
There are pioneer souls that blaze the paths
Where highways never ran-
But let me live in a house by the side of the road
And be a friend to man.

We were taught the first verse at a very young age. I remember with a smile that years later my mother told me that one of my younger sisters had often recited the poem, but ended the last two lines with:

"But let me live in a house by the side of the road
And be friendly to men."

The house by the side of the road where my sister, Barbara, was born. Photo taken c. 1950s.

5
GRAMPA AND GRAMMY CHASE

I am not sure exactly when we moved back to Haverhill, but it was sometime before my sister Joan was born in Gale Hospital on June 14, 1933. Now we were three kids, and the Depression was in full swing. We lived in a little attached house at the back of 754 Main Street.

My cousin, Vaughan Betty, now of San Francisco, told me that Grammy and Grampa Chase met in New York City. Grampa was working there as a railroad telegraph operator, and she was living just north of the City in Yonkers.

After their marriage in the 1880s, Grampa Chase became a railroad station agent, and they moved west to begin their family life in the Indian territories. At first, the family lived in a box car. Several of my aunts and uncles were born in the Montana and Wyoming Territories, which at that time were not within the borders of the United States. (My mother, the youngest child, was born in Hamilton, Massachusetts, after her family returned from the Indian Territories.)

I barely remember my grandmother Chase who died when I was very young. She seemed like a nice lady. I do recall that she was stout. Stories about Grammy Chase's appetite were the subject of conversation whenever my aunts and uncles got together. And for me, Grampa Chase was only a brief encounter, sort of a mystery man. I think I met him only once, and I cannot remember much other than he was tall and thin and rather handsome.

My father used to tell stories with a great deal of anger about how late in his life, the Railroad screwed Grampa Chase. After 50 years of service, the Railroad assigned him to a station in South Groveland, Massachusetts, then shut down the station, and gave my grandfather the boot without a pension. My father blamed this tragedy on the Republicans, who only cared for the rich.

I was told as a child that Grammy and Grampa Chase were so poor that they could not afford a place of their own. For a long time they were supported by my Aunt Ethel, my mother's oldest sister. Then when that was no longer possible, Grammy took turns staying with her children for the rest of her life. For awhile Grammy Chase lived with us in the little attached house at 754 Main Street. Grampa Chase moved to a home for elderly men in Newburyport.

My mother told me that before being assigned to the Groveland Station, her father was the station master in Hamilton, Massachusetts. The family lived above the station. One day when my mother's little brother, Edward, was playing around the station, he was run over and killed by a car driven by the Secretary of the Navy's chauffer. The resignation and despair came through her voice years later as she related the story to me.

According to my mother, all the government did was pay my grandparents enough money for burial expenses in the snooty town of Hamilton. My parents related Edward's death as just another case of "injustice" about which we had no control. It seemed I belonged to a clan where anybody could take advantage of us.

My mother and father visited Edward's grave every Memorial Day. I do not ever remember being asked to go with them to the grave. I knew it was important to my mother, and for that reason I wanted to go with them, to be part of what was important to her. Finally, I put my feelings about not being asked in the back of my mind, but never knew why I was not invited.

The sad story about little Edward caused me to do some research in preparation for this book. In 2007 I called the Town Clerk in Hamilton and requested a copy of Edward's death certificate. It indicated that Edward L. Chase, at age 7 years and 4 months, died on 12 December 1911. The cause of death was 'General Peritonitis from gangrenous appendicitis." Apparently my mother's family manufactured a story to cover up the awful truth. To this day, I think my mother believed the story about Edward's death, since she was just an infant herself when it happened.

I have several good memories of Grammy Chase. Grammy Chase showed my mother how to pick a certain weed that grew in the fields, which she called pig weeds. I liked these pig weeds because they were cooked with salt pork for flavoring, the same way my mother prepared beet greens. I think my mother was ashamed that we were eating pig weeds, because I learned from her that we were not supposed to talk about eating them. We also ate dandelion greens in the early spring. Nothing went to waste.

Another memory: Grammy Chase would sit for hours cutting up old clothes into narrow strips about an inch or so in width. She used old shirts, pants, or any spare woolen cloth she could get her hands on. I used to help her, and my job was to fold the strips lengthwise. Then she would take three strips and hook them together with a safety pin. She fastened the safety pin onto the latch of the kitchen cabinet, and then braided the strips into what looked like a pig's tail, much like she did with my sisters' hair. After she made a very long flat braided rope from the strips, she laid the rope on the table, coiled it around itself, and sewed the ropes together to make a braided rug.

I always felt a gap between my parents and me. I often felt lonely. From 1930 to 1935 I have very little memory of my life. During those early days I do not remember any relatives visiting us, or our going anywhere to visit them. Grammy and Grampa Willey did not like each other; I knew that. Grampa Willey lived in the village in Fremont, New Hampshire, and Grammy Willey lived in Haverhill in the Acre. (I realize now it was peculiar that neither my Willey nor Chase grandparents lived together as couples. The reasons were never discussed, and as a child, I just accepted life as it was.)

6
A LITTLE HAVERHILL HISTORY - HANNAH DUSTIN

My father did not want us to live in the Acre, and our home at 754 Main Street was in an area known as Dustin Square. Everyone in Haverhill knew about the exploits of Hannah Dustin, and a statue was erected in her honor in the park across from the City Hall.

Here's the story: Hannah and Thomas Dustin were married around 1677, and by 1697 she had presented Thomas with their 12th child, Martha. On 9 March 1697, an Indian raiding party captured Hannah, her wet nurse Mary Neff, and the infant Martha. On the way to the Indian encampment, the baby began crying and could not be quieted. The Indians were afraid the baby's cries would alert Thomas who was working in the nearby clay pits. One of the Indians grabbed the baby and bashed her head against an apple tree. The Indians then dragged Hannah and Mary to their canoes on the Merrimack River. At the canoes, Hannah met another captive, a 14-year old boy from Worcester named Samuel Lennardson.

Hannah was in shock about the violent death of her infant child, and she was planning revenge. On an island near Concord, New Hampshire a few days later, she manipulated the Indians into drinking a lot of alcohol. Later Hannah and the other two captives stole tomahawks and killed their Indian captors in their alcohol-induced sleep. Hannah, Mary, and Samuel jumped into the canoes to head back to Haverhill, when Hannah remembered that there was a bounty on the scalps of Indians. They returned to the island and scalped six or seven Indians. Hannah carried the scalps home in her apron as proof. Her husband, Thomas, delivered them to the legislature in Boston to collect the reward.

Hannah Dustin was considered a heroine, and was the first woman in the United States to have a monument erected in her honor. I always admired Hannah for her courage, read about her adventure, visited the Dustin homestead up near North Broadway, walked the old clay pits where her husband made bricks, and visited the Haverhill Buttonwoods Historical Society to view the apron that she used to carry the scalps.

In the statue, Hannah looks stern and angry, and she is pointing with her left hand, holding a tomahawk in her right hand, apparently depicting the scalping she performed. In 1946 some unknown vandals in the City managed to extract the tomahawk from Hannah's hand, probably as a souvenir. I was attending the C.W. Arnold Trade School at the time, and one of our instructors was an accomplished pattern maker named Raymond Auclair. The task fell on his shoulders to carve a new tomahawk from mahogany to be cast in bronze to replace the stolen one. The new tomahawk was attached to the old statue, and no one was the wiser (except those who read this account).

7
THE BIG FLOOD

In March 1936 the Merrimack River Rose over 25 feet and flooded a vast portion of Haverhill and all the cities and towns along the Merrimack River, from its beginning in New Hampshire to the mouth at Newburyport and Salisbury, Massachusetts. Though this was a major flood, people referred to it as a "spring freshet," a great overflowing caused by heavy rains and melted snow.

In downtown Haverhill, at the peak of the flood, the water rose to about twelve feet above the sidewalks. My father managed to work temporarily during the flood, helping some frantic merchants on Merrimack Street move their stock to higher floors. I remember that each day we waited for him to come home from this job. He brought some of the stock that the merchants would give him as part of his pay. It felt like we were waiting for Black Beard the pirate to return with his booty.

We lived from day to day with scant news of what was happening outside our little circle. I was only six years old, and I was afraid of the flood. We had no television or telephone, so we learned the news by word of mouth, newspapers at 2 cents each, and radio broadcasts from time to time.

Our house was located well away from any waterways, and we were never in any danger. However, as a consequence of the flood damage, the US Army Corps of Engineers built dams in New Hampshire to regulate the flow of water, and a huge "sea wall" was built along the Merrimac River through the entire downtown area of Haverhill.

The Willey Kids in 1937: Joan, Barbara, and John at 754 Main Street, Haverhill, MA

8
GRAMMAR SCHOOL YEARS

When I began to attend grammar school, I saw how the "other kids" lived and realized that we were poor. My father's dream come true-- we did NOT live in the Acre with all the immigrants and factories. Our house was close to an area where the rich and privileged lived, and we all went to the Walnut Square Grammar School. Actually all the children got along very well in spite of the economic differences of our parents.

It was September 1936, and my first day of school. We lived about a half mile away and were not eligible to ride the school bus. My mother walked me to school the first day. When we arrived at the school, I was impressed but scared. The school was the biggest building I had ever seen, a solid brick structure built in 1898, with a bell tower, clock, and shiny hardwood floors inside. (Over 100 years old, the building is still in use today as a grammar school.)

Mom cautioned me about coming home directly after school. Standing over me, bent at the waist with her right hand on her waist, and her left hand closed with the index facing skyward, she pointed and wagged her finger at me and said, "When they let you out of school, you come straight home." The Lindberg kidnapping incident was still fresh in everyone's mind, and parents were overly protective of their young children.

I do not remember the first class, the teacher's name, the students, or the classroom, but I do remember leaving the school yard when they let me out. I was the only kid leaving the playground at recess. All I knew was that my mother had told me to go straight home when they let me out of school. No amount of kids hollering at me or waving me back was going to deter me from my mission.

At first my mother was shocked when I arrived home mid-morning. When she understood why I had come home, she laughed. I do not remember what happened after that. But I do remember I had to listen over and over again as my parents told the story to their friends. Maybe they thought it was funny, but I felt like a fool, and I seethed inside.

In less than a month, I developed a crush on Nancy Goldberg. One day at school we dunked for apples. I dunked for an apple, damn near drowned, and came up with no apple. Nancy dunked, got the apple, and gave it to me. Wow! My world was a wonderful place.

When I returned home from school, I could not wait to tell my mother and father about Nancy giving me the apple, but again my parents made fun of me. I learned that I was not supposed to like Nancy, so I steered clear of her after that. It always hurt. Although my parents never openly said this, later I understood there were two strikes against Nancy Goldberg; she was Jewish, and from a wealthy family. What came across to me was that I was not good enough for Nancy Goldberg, and that there were boundaries that I could not cross, lines drawn by economic status and religion.

When I was about seven or eight years old my Grampa Willey and I spent some time together. He drove me in his 1932 Pontiac coupe to Kurtz, a restaurant in Exeter, New Hampshire. This was my first time ever in a restaurant, and I can still remember the meal--a small steak, mashed potatoes, and an ear of corn. When the food was set before me, my eyes were the size of saucers. Using proper table manners, I dutifully demolished the meal.

A man approached my grandfather and explained that he had enjoyed watching me eat with such great relish, and asked my grandfather if he would allow him to buy me another dinner. When the second meal arrived, I polished it off with gusto, and then topped it off with an order of strawberry shortcake.

After seventy years, I can still remember that experience. Food, or the lack of it, was an always-present anxiety for us. At the age of eight, I was given special attention and rewarded for overeating. (Maybe it's a stretch to connect that incident with my current struggles with overeating, but it feels connected to me.)

Our grocery store, Benks &Whiting, was just across Main Street on the corner of Marsh Avenue. By today's standards, it was tiny. "Joe the Butcher" was one of many French Canadians in our neighborhood. He had the usual broken English of a French Canadian. My father used to mimic Joe, and say, "Ow you can told I was a Fronchmon? By my accident?"

Directly across the street was the DuPont family, also from Canada. I liked the DuPont family. Mr. DuPont was a very soft-spoken, kind man. Due to an accident in the lumber woods in Canada, four fingers on his right hand had been cut off. His son, Joe, was a few years older than I, and he was as easy a person to like as his dad. The DuPont's Canadian relatives visited every summer, including a couple of kids my age. One year they brought me a gift of a strange-looking greenish-grey rock from Canada. If you rubbed the rock with a hard object, very fine cotton-like fibers were released. We thought it was fun to rub this rock, make the fibers come loose, and blow them up in the air like the floss from milk weed pods. (Now I understand that we were playing with asbestos, but at that time no one knew the danger.)

One of my responsibilities was to walk to the store for my mother, carrying a note listing the groceries that she wanted. I gave the list to the grocer and waited while he piled up the groceries on the counter. When the order was completed, the grocer would grab a paper bag, write the cost of each item on the outside of the bag, add the numbers in a flash, strike a line, and write the total. My mother never sent me to buy meat; that was her job. She would stand over Joe the Butcher, and point out exactly which portion she wanted, and how she wanted it cut.

We ate very little by today's standards, and the grocery store had only a few basic foods from which to choose. There were no frozen foods, no aisles of "junk" food, no instant anything, no pet foods, and very little packaging. There were no out-of-season fruits or vegetables, or prepared foods like sushi, sashimi, or other delicacies. We ate just plain New England style foods. One of my favorites was roast pork with mashed potatoes and gravy. Yummm!

When we were children, in the fall of each year my mother lined up the three of us at the rear of the kitchen stove for our daily dosage of cod liver oil. The cod liver oil came in a crystal clear rectangular-shaped bottle with a label picturing a fisherman with an enormous cod slung over his right shoulder. I think it was a Norwegian brand. It was vile, oily, nasty-tasting stuff, and we almost threw up each evening when we were given this "healthy" elixir. My mother would fill a tablespoon with the stuff, place it in our open mouths, and down it went. Yuck! Sometimes one of us would ask for another dose knowing full well that the other two would do the same to save face. My mother was only too pleased to offer the second dose of this horrid tasting fish oil.

When we were still young enough to believe in Santa Claus, my mother would sit us down at the kitchen table a few days before Christmas. She gave each of us a piece of paper and a pencil. She would "guide" us in writing a Christmas list for Santa, no doubt to help assure our list was realistic, given we were still in the Depression and money was tight. (Of course we did not know how much money they had or earned. Later I discovered that in the 1930s and early 1940s my father's pay jumped from 40 to 50 cents per hour for a yearly salary of $1,040. Mom was doing piece work in a shoe factory for less than that, which means they were living on less than $2,000 per year with three kids to support.)

When the lists were completed, Mom would ceremoniously gather them up, and with great fanfare, allow us to stand around the old black iron kerosene stove. She placed the list in the hot air space beneath the two round lid covers at the back of the stove. She usually used that space to keep food warm. We were then sent off to get ready for bed. In a few minutes we would return. She removed the round back lid on the stove, and we all peered in. She would declare the lists had flown up the chimney to Santa's workshop. We were all amazed and happy that the lists were on their way.

I was always an inquisitive kid and liked to check on things that caused me to be doubtful. One year, I pulled off a sneaky stunt. My bedroom was off the kitchen. When my sisters were getting ready for bed after the notes had been deposited, I noticed my mother was in the bathroom. I snuck out of my bedroom, quietly lifted the lid, and peeked into the air space. The notes were incinerated, and as they turned to ash they were drawn up the flue.

I quietly put the lid back in place, and scampered back into my bedroom. When my sisters arrived, I popped out to join them. We peeked into the air space, and with my sisters present, I feigned surprise. But what I really felt was betrayal. How could she lie to us about Santa?

The only extended family in our lives was on my mother's side, and without an automobile we rarely saw one another. However, I do remember getting a ride to my Uncle Ted's (my mother's brother, Theodore). He lived in the Bradley's Brook section of Haverhill near the Merrimack River. I was going to Uncle Ted's so he could cut my hair. My cousin Vaughn had warned me about Uncle Ted and his haircuts. Uncle Ted seemed to use the hand clippers to get a grip on our hair, and then rip it out by the roots. It was awful. Then we had to sit and listen to him playing classical church music on his cornet. I can still hear the cornet and feel my hair being pulled out by the dull hand clippers. But who could afford 25 cents for a haircut?

With his solo flight across the Atlantic in 1927, Charles A. Lindberg became a worldwide phenomenon. In 1935, he was still the world's greatest living celebrity, drawing enormous crowds wherever he went anywhere in the world. He and his wife Ann were living in New Jersey when their only child at the time was kidnapped. Every mother in the country was terrified about her child being kidnapped too. As a five year old, I did not understand what all this commotion had to do with me. All I knew was that I could not go out of the house unless I was in the back yard and constantly watched by my mother. Within a short time we learned that the baby had been killed. All the little kids, including me, were scared stiff.

I recall one very big, wonderful and exciting event: My father took me to Fenway Park in Boston on a steam-driven Boston & Maine train. While we were there to root for the Red Sox, I remember only one of the star baseball players, Hank Greenberg from the Detroit Tigers. He was known as Hammerin' Hank, and I was excited to see him. He is all I remember of that day.

Prior to WW II we still did not have a car, telephone, refrigerator, washing machine or dryer. There were no such things as electric hair dryers or other hand-held electrical appliances. We used so-called range oil (kerosene) for heating and cooking. When the fuel was low, my job was to walk to the store with an empty glass jug to buy a gallon of kerosene.

Trolley cars on steel tracks ran right by our front door. We kids used to play a trick on the motorman when he stopped the car to let people on or off. We ran behind the stopped car and pulled the trolley pole down from the electric wires, thereby removing the trolley car's source of power. Without the electrical connection, the motorman could not make the trolley move forward. We had to run like hell because sometimes a young motorman would leave the car and chase us, whacking any one of us he could catch. We could not report him to our parents for fear that we would get more whacks from them.

9
EARLY LEARNING ABOUT BEING DIFFERENT

Sometime in 1937 we moved from the little attached house out back of 754 Main Street and into the downstairs section of the double decker. This was a big deal for us. The rooms were bigger, and we had at least twice the space.

Upstairs lived the Gill family, Alice and George and their three children, Joe, Alice, and George. George Jr. was my good friend. The parents were immigrants and spoke with a thick English accent. Mr. Gill drove a huge tanker truck for SOCONY, the Standard Oil Company of New York. He was a hero with neighborhood kids because every week or so he would drive home in his huge shiny red tank trailer marked with the SOCONY flying red horse logo. He waved hello to us before he parked and jumped out of the truck. I felt I was really "in the know" because I had a friend as important as Mr. Gill. The other fathers in the neighborhood worked in the factories, so an enormous truck like his made quite an impression.

My father had an endless supply of derogatory nick names for different ethnic groups. He referred to the Gills as Limeys. I remember he was angry about the fact that Mr. Gill only worked four ten-hour days a week with three days off, and that he had a steady job with a pension. As a child, I never understood why my father would get mad about someone having a good job that paid well, even if he was a Limey.

I heard a lot of angry talk from my parents and their friends about those Jews, Kikes, Christ Killers that owned the factories, mean bastards always looking for ways to screw the poor sonovabitch trying to make a living. Then there were the Wops, the Grease Balls, the Frogs, Polacks, Rug Merchants (Armenians), Friggin' Limeys, Cheap Yankee Wasps, and the list went on. One fearful thought my mother inculcated in us was "The yellow race will rule the world." In the Boston University Hospital when she had a heart valve replaced, she refused to allow a Chinese doctor to tend to her.

The Bond family moved into the little attached house when we moved to the big apartment in the double decker. Mr. Bond was a musician. He dressed up in fancy clothes, had a slick mustache, slept until noon, and went to work in the evening. My father summed him up quickly: Mr. Bond was weird. Dad suspected him of all kinds of chicanery. According to my father, everyone knew that musicians like Mr. Bond were lazy and no good, not to be trusted.

Sammy Kort and his daughter lived in the house next door. My father said they were mean and complaining and nasty, being Jewish after all. Also living nearby was Mr. Esty. He was an uneducated, hardworking man who grew up in a lumbering family. He drove a big logging truck with stakes to hold the logs in place and chains hanging off the sides. He was a giant of a man, about six foot four and 300 pounds. My father simply referred to him as a "hillbilly."

This kind of talk could be found everywhere in Haverhill. We were so many different people living near each other, and competition for jobs was keen. I knew from observation that the Polacks hated the Lits. The Armenians hated the Turks, and come to think of it, the Greeks hated the Turks too. The Irish hated the English, and so did the French Canadians. It seemed routine that everybody hated somebody even though they did not always make it known.

The owner of Grammy Willey's apartment was a Greek immigrant, a rather dark swarthy looking character whose last name was Bougioukas. One day he came up the stairs while I was visiting Grammy, and in his broken English asked for the rent money. Grammy, in her equally unintelligible brogue as "tick" as pea soup, went after him with her broom saying, "I paid ye and have the receipt, ye Goddam foreigner." Mr. Bougioukas beat a hasty retreat. I asked, "Grammy how come you called him a foreigner? Didn't you come from a foreign country? She replied, "Yes but I'm in the white race." I wisely said, "Oh," and let it drop there.

I learned to judge people as wrong or weird if they varied in any way from my family's outlook on life. (Thankfully, I traveled and made friends from diverse ethnic and religious groups, and years later I gained an understanding of the harmful results of this kind of fearful thinking and behavior. To this day, I struggle to refrain from judging people, especially people I do not know.)

10
THE BIG WIND

One afternoon in September 1938 a bunch of us boys were playing football in the vacant lot next to our house at 754 Main Street. The lot was level, fairly well covered in grass, and dominated by an enormous American elm with a stately crown. Elms were plentiful, but ours was the best in the City, a guardian that provided comfort and shade and a place for the neighborhood kids to rally.

I remember throwing the football from the elm tree to my friend Walter at the end of the lot, and the ball soared way over his head. Walter was struck with amazement, and so was I. We had never seen the wind so powerful, and it was fun. We opened our jackets to catch the breeze and found we could run like

Superman. This play went on all afternoon until my father came home from work. He burst out of the house, and ordered me inside, and all the kids to go home. "You Goddam fools. Can't you see we're having a bad storm? Get in here." We all scurried home, wondering why he was so upset. (Years later I realized that he was worried that the slates on the roof of Roach's barn would come loose and act as a guillotine. Of course he never explained why he was so angry, and I thought I did something wrong.)

Later in the evening we sat huddled in the kitchen with no electricity and not knowing what was happening. This was the first hurricane any of us had ever experienced, and we were scared. Mrs. Gill came downstairs, crying and asking for a light. We had several kerosene lamps and candles, so we gave some to her.

The wind was howling like a freight train coming through the kitchen, and the house shook from sill to ridge board. The rain was torrential. We just huddled and said nothing for fear that Dad would explode. As the evening wore on we heard and felt a thunderous sound like an explosion, and we could see cracks in our ceiling and water coming down into the room. The brick chimney had been blown over and landed in the Gill's kitchen upstairs, badly injuring Mrs. Gill. We could hear the Gills crying. My father rushed upstairs to help cover the hole in the roof.

About 500 people were killed during this unnamed storm of 1938. The next day we walked around our neighborhood in wonderment at the destruction, and learned that the damage was worse in and around Rhode Island because of its proximity to the ocean.

11
MR. ROACH

An important figure in my young life was our landlord, Mr. John M. Roach. From the time I was five until I left for the Navy at 18, I had lived in his properties. He was my first connection with someone who lived in a big house. He had been a famous contractor who built many large buildings, including Haverhill High School and a number of churches.

Mr. Roach had a big barn that was mostly empty except for the fighting roosters (cocks) that he raised there. We called them banty roosters, but I think the actual name is bantam rooster. The barn was located just behind our house. My Dad worked for John Roach, caring for the birds as needed. I went with Dad to watch him transfer the fighting cocks from the inside cages to the outside cages when Mr. Roach was preparing to take them to a fight. Dad opened the inside cages very carefully. He wrapped a burlap bag around his left arm, and wore a leather glove on his right hand. When the rooster attacked his left arm, Dad grabbed the rooster with his right hand, turned the rooster upside down so he became disoriented and quiet, and quickly moved him into an outside cage.

The banty roosters often fought to their death. Mr. Roach put steel spurs as weapons on their legs. The rule was that the last banty rooster to make an effort to kill the other was the winner. A dead bird could actually be declared the winner if it made the last effort. Fighting game cocks was against the law, so games were staged in different secret places. Lowell was often mentioned as the city where they fought roosters. Lowell was a mill city like Haverhill, located on the banks of the Merrimack River. I fantasized about going to see the game cocks fight. I never did see a fight, but I felt good being with my father when he took care of the roosters.

When Mr. Roach was sick and could not get around, my father and I did chores for him. Mr. Roach had a flock of bantam hens that roamed at will in the woods around his big house. Usually hens for egg production were kept in a coop, but these banty hens were strictly for breeding his fighting cocks. When he bred a hen with a prized rooster, the hen was kept in a cage and not allowed to roam loose like the rest of the flock.

One day Mr. Roach asked me if I would like to earn some money, and of course I said yes. He said, "Go down through the woods and pick up all the banty chicken eggs you can find, and I'll give you a penny for each egg."

I was about 8 years old, and excited. I set off with a pail to make my fortune. After walking and searching what seemed like hours, I returned to the big house with a pail full of eggs, expecting to get about 25 cents. Mr. Roach said, "Well, little John, you've got quite a lot there." I felt great.

He motioned me over to a big slate sink where there was a basin full of water. I expected him to tell me to wash off the eggs, since they were a little muddy from being in the woods. But no, Mr. Roach reached into my pail and began to put the eggs in the water. I was puzzled because most of the eggs floated. Mr. Roach then said, "John, the eggs that float are rotten and not fit to eat, so you'll get a penny for each egg that lies on the bottom of the basin."

"You cheap bastard," I thought to myself, "That wasn't the deal! You said I'd get a penny for each egg I brought home." I walked away with about eight cents, feeling diminished, because in my mind, he had taken advantage of me. I never went back again to pick eggs for Mr. Roach. Instead I went back and picked the eggs and brought them home, did the water test myself, and gave my mother the good eggs.

I remember going with my father up into the loft of Mr. Roach's barn where the pigeons roosted. Dad had a coffee can full of cracked corn, as well as a burlap grain bag, also called a gunny sack. I had no idea what we were doing, but I was enjoying being with Dad. Up in the loft was a wooden box with a length of string tied to a wooden stick. Dad placed the box, open side down, on the floor. He picked up one side, and propped it up with the stick. He put a little pile of corn on the floor toward the back of the box, running a row of kernels out from the pile. I got it! He was going to trap some pigeons. He played out the string, and we went down the steps from the trap door and waited.

Pretty soon the pigeons showed up, and pecked at the little trail of cracked corn. When three of them were under the box, Dad pulled the string, and bam! We had three pigeons. Dad put the pigeons into the sack. It was 1936 and the Depression. I remember we had chicken stew that night.

12
RELIGIOUS CONFUSION

As a child, religion was a source of great confusion. For reasons they never shared with me, my parents did not belong to any church, nor did I ever have a clue as to their beliefs one way or another. My friends were Catholics, different Protestant denominations, and Jews. I was a nothing!

My Jewish friends went to school at the Temple to study Hebrew. I remember walking to Temple Emanuel on Main Street and 11th Avenue where I could peek in the basement windows and hear my friends reciting funny sounding words.

I liked St. James Roman Catholic Church on Winter Street, a big brick building with twin towers. Blue-collar folks attended St. James, with most of them coming from the immigrant Irish section called the Acre. Sacred Heart was the destination of the well-to-do Irish, the so-called lace curtain Irish from the affluent Bradford section of town. St. Josephs (mostly French Canadians); St. Michaels (Polish); St. Rita (Italian) -- these were all mysterious places to me. Catholic kids told me stories about their abuse at the hands of the nuns, Brothers and priests. Some bragged about who had been treated the worst.

Haverhill had several Protestant churches, some big, some little, some of brick and stone, and some of wood and shingles. The First Baptist Church was a sprawling brick complex across the street from the Congregational Church. Kingdom Hall was where my father said the Jehovah Witnesses performed weird rites.

The Seventh Day Adventist church was on Main Street, and they worshipped on Saturday instead of Sunday.

I had no information about any of these institutions, and I made up a lot of stories to explain why there were so many different views on worshipping God. Inscribed in stone on Temple Emanuel on Main Street were the words "The Lord Our God The Lord Is One." My Catholic friends talked about the Trinity. How could there be three gods in one?

Grammy Willey was a dyed-in-the-wool Roman Catholic from County Cork, Ireland. I never understood how an Irish woman could be a Roman Catholic instead of an Ireland Catholic.

I secretly wished I was a Catholic, because then maybe my father would approve of me. I never saw my father step foot in the Catholic Church, and that subject was "off limits." However, I knew his leanings were towards the Catholics. In later years I came to believe that he too wished he were a member in good standing with the Catholic Church. Other reasons for me to want to be a Catholic were that the Catholics had the biggest and most elaborate brick churches, impressive ceremonies, holy days of obligation, First Fridays, and priests who wore really regal looking outfits.

I do not ever recall my Grampa Willey having any connection with a religion. However, many family stories and much anger centered on the fact that my great uncle, Plum Willey, was married to a Quaker named Mary Alice. I did not know what a Quaker was, but I knew it was not good from what I could gather from listening to the adults in my family talking about Mary Alice.

My mother came from a family of devout Protestants. In the 1850s, my mother's grandfather, Benjamin Chase, was a well known and respected minister at the Congregational Church in Camden, Maine. He delivered a sermon on the Church's fiftieth anniversary which was published and is still available from the Church. My mother's brother, Ted, a preacher, started his own church, not affiliated with any of the well-known Protestant denominations. His son, (my cousin, David Chase), became a preacher in a church in Palmer, Massachusetts. My mother's brother, Benjamin Lester Chase, was a fire and brimstone Baptist.

When I was about eight years old, my mother arranged for me to attend services at the Universalist Unitarian Church at Monument Square in Haverhill. The church members were warm and welcoming. I loved it there, and I belonged. The message I heard was that we should love our neighbors, have a good life, and help others do the same. The Unitarian Church was a safe harbor from the stormy seas at home, and my mother seemed pleased that at least one member of the family was going to church.

The Unitarian Church sponsored many youth activities. A well-known music teacher, Charles Hillner, directed the choirs. I remember making a trip with the youth choir to sing at Symphony Hall in Boston, where we were all shocked at the nude statues way up near the ceiling. You could see the men's privates and the women's breasts. At the Church in later months, I participated in a performance where, dressed in pajamas, I had to set a lighted candle in a holder on the stage, then step back and recite, "Jack be nimble, Jack be quick, Jack jump over the candle stick." As I said, "Jack jump over the candle stick," I had to actually jump. I received a round of applause, and I felt really good about this. One day we made maple syrup, an old New England activity where maple sap is reduced to syrup by boiling off the water. We poured the boiling syrup into the snow where it became instantly solidified like a candy bar. Needless to say, I was enjoying going to church.

Then the fun stopped! My mother's brother, my uncle, Benjamin Lester Chase, found out I was going to the "wrong" church. Uncle Lester, as we called him, laced into his baby sister, my mother, about sending me to the Unitarian Universalist Church, telling her the Church was run by the Devil, and that I must immediately stop going there and transfer to the Winter Street Baptist Church.

I was desperately waiting and hoping that my father would rescue me, that he would intercede and tell his brother-in-law to mind his own business. But he just kept quiet and appeared to be indifferent to my plight.

My introduction to the Baptist Church was less than ideal. I sat alone in the church office, facing a small group of desiccated-looking starched-faced guys in suits with stern countenances, who asked me if I would accept Jesus as my savior.

My sisters also got roped into this, and the three of us—Joan, Barbara, and I-- were required to take the bus to the Winter Street Baptist Church every Sunday—alone. My parents never attended, and my sister Norma was too young. We would each get fifteen cents--five cents for the ride down, five cents for the collection, and five cents for the return trip. We used to play hooky, walk to the drug store near the church, spend five cents on candy, hang around, and then take the bus home.

The big day came when I was to be baptized in the tank under the stage up front by the pulpit. Each of the children being baptized wore a bathing suit, covered with a white robe, and walked solemnly down the few steps, to be greeted by Reverend Mott. He said the required words, and then he plunged each of us backward, fully under water.

13
ROTTEN TEETH

As children we grew up in an era where no thought was given to dental hygiene, at least not in my family or among my friends. It was commonplace to see children in the early grades of grammar school with noticeable cavities in their teeth.

My father had all his upper teeth removed as a fairly young man and lived without them for the rest of his life. The philosophy was simple: if you removed your teeth, you never had to experience the terrible pains associated with rotten teeth. Dental visits were impossible because of the cost, and you could tell who the rich kids were because they had wire on their teeth to correct defects.

A federal program was instituted where poor kids could get dental care. Another reason for loving FDR-- he was there for the underdog.

At the age of eight I went to the Gale Hospital on Main Street with cavities in both front teeth as well as others in my mouth. This was my first dental visit, and I was terrified.

Dr. Canary, a wizened, cranky, mean old Irishman, made it clear that he was above working with the poor kids, and he treated us accordingly. He tried to get me to submit to the drilling. I panicked and screamed, and he threw me out of the clinic.

14
ENJOYING THE SEASONS

Our playtime activities were centered on the seasons. From January through March my friends and I went sliding, tobogganing, and skating.

We had two venues where the fun on the ice was totally different. Depending how we felt, we chose either Littler River or Round Pond. If we had a January thaw and it rained, the forested areas around Little River would flood. Soon the temperatures dropped and the water froze, leaving icy pathways throughout the woods. What fun it was to skate on Little River, and then veer off into the woods and swamps, exploring places not accessible at any other time of the year. Sometimes we pretended we were arctic explorers, and we skated north up the River from Haverhill to Atkinson, New Hampshire. We explored the small inlets and tall grasses. Quite often we built bon fires on the ice to keep warm.

Round Pond was in an upscale neighborhood on Lawrence Street. On weekends, especially Sundays, hundreds of people went skating on the pond. Whole families often skated together. Over by the cove, men went ice fishing. They chopped round holes in the ice about a foot in diameter, and placed fishing lines in the holes, rigged with flags that popped up when a fish bit the line.

They continuously skated back and forth to their various fishing lines to be sure the ice did not freeze over the fishing holes.

Often, several hockey games would be played at once, each accommodating different levels of hockey-playing abilities. One of the boys would throw his boots on the ice, each one serving as a goal post.

Toward the far end of the pond, adults and older boys sailed their hand-made ice boats, which always attracted my attention. I asked for rides from the older boys. I was always welcomed because my weight helped keep the boat from blowing over in the strong winter winds. One year we built our own ice boat, from wood planks, old skate blades, and a sail made of an old sheet. We took advantage of the wintry winds, flying across the pond on our ice boat.

We also loved to skate free across the whole expanse of Round Pond, letting the wind assist us by opening our coats to act as sails. A favorite game was "the whip." We formed a long line of 20 or more boys, holding hands and skating forward together as fast as possible. When the line gained good speed, the leader at the far left would abruptly stop, causing the line to pivot around him. The person at the right end would not be able to hold on, and he would go zinging off across the lake. Then the next skater would lose hand contact, and he would spin off too, and the process would repeat again and again until everyone was flying across the ice.

Sometimes a Dad would skate real fast in a circle, towing a small child on a sled. He would stop suddenly and cause the sled to veer off on a circular orbit. The little kid would squeal with joy or fear – it was difficult to distinguish.

One year in March we tapped sugar maple trees to get sap. We walked to Polack Alley, a rural section of Haverhill where Snow's Brook traveled on its way to the Little River. Sap collection was tedious because, as we discovered, it takes about 40 quarts of sap to make a quart of maple syrup. My mother obliged us one year, and she boiled down a few gallons of sap for us. We managed to get enough syrup for one order of pancakes. We had a lot of fun in the attempt.

In April, the pussy willows bloomed. My mother loved pussy willows. Every year I would cut a bunch and bring them home to her as a gift. Also, we walked down to watch Snow's Brook, which ran in torrents in the springtime. Near the Brook was a grove of beech trees, and we carved our initials in the smooth gray bark.

Summer was the best season of all. Each day we would go out, meet our friends, play until noon, come home for lunch, and go back outside until supper time. Mom was a great cook, and one of my favorites was her doughnut holes. When she deep-fried doughnuts, she would set aside the holes, put them in a brown paper bag with a sprinkle of sugar, shake them up, call me in from play, and hand me the grease-stained bag. Oh! They were a treat. Mom was making Munchkins 60 years before Dunkin Doughnuts was even in business.

A favorite play place was "Treasure Island," a sandy bank on an unnamed stream meandering through the wetland behind Roach's barn. We dug tunnels and pretended to be pirates. Treasure Island was a place of unlimited possibilities for exploration. In retrospect, I shudder to think about the caves we dug in very unstable sandy soils that easily could have collapsed, but we all survived our Treasure Island days.

We were a creative bunch. We made rafts out of found objects like logs and rope, and we hung around at a small beach on Little River which we called "The Channel." We picked wild berries and sold them to the neighbors to get money to go to the movies. We also found junked bicycle frames in the dump and scraped together the money to buy seats, chains, fenders, handle bars and a siren activated by pulling a chain. Sometimes the bikes had two owners, until one kid could scrape together the means to get his own. We used the bikes to ride our paper routes, delivering newspapers and magazines in the neighborhood.

One summer Raynor Neilson and I were walking down Ringgold Street and we saw an extraordinary plane in the air

--- an autogiro. This precursor to the helicopter was on its way to a local airport to offer people a ride for a fee. The plane looked like a Piper Cub except that it had a rotary wing on top and a regular propeller in the front. We were amazed that it could stop in mid-air.

We also made sling shots. We found a perfect Y-shaped shrub branch and attached a sling made from rubber strips cut from old truck tire inner tubes. We could be deadly. Donald Wood ("Woodie") was so accurate that he earned a new nickname, "Plunkett." Sometimes we shot out street lights, and Plunkett (eventually shortened to Plunk) was by far the most accurate shooter.

Before I got my own paper route, Plunk let me go with him on his route, delivering the *Boston Post* in the morning. The paper cost 2 cents, and we collected our money on Saturdays. Eventually I did get an evening paper route of my own for the *Haverhill Gazette*. I also delivered *Liberty* magazines and the *Saturday Evening Post*. I remember clearly that in 1941 I skimmed an article in the *Saturday Evening Post*, written by Jack Alexander, about a bunch of men who were drunks. I was really impressed that they discovered a way to help each other avoid drinking. Some of my friends' fathers would stagger home drunk, and we all felt embarrassed for our friends. I was very moved by the article and never forgot the story.

With the coming of autumn, the walnuts and butternuts ripened, and with the first frost the nuts began to fall. We got up early to check out our favorite trees and gather the bounty before anyone else got there. We ate all the walnuts and butternuts we collected. The horse chestnuts were inedible, but there were so many things we could make from them. When they were freed from the green outer husks, we marveled at the enameled brown finish of the nut, with the circular patch of silvery white that distinguished the horse chestnut from the edible brown chestnut. We would bore a hole through the horse chestnuts to make a necklace, or cut off the top third of the nut and hollow it out to make a pipe. Or we would tie two together with about eighteen inches of string between them, creating a sling to throw into the air and wrap around a telephone wire. Sometimes it was enough to just brag about having the biggest collection of chestnuts.

The walnuts were encased in an armored shell that could only be broken with a hammer after placing the nut on a rock. We had to develop a delicate knack while employing the hammer, because too heavy a blow and the nut would be squashed and the meat enmeshed in the broken shell. The nuts were tasty and worth the work to extract the delicate meat.

The most fun was playing in the fallen leaves. It was the custom for people to rake the leaves into a pile in the back yard or in a long windrow in the gutter of streets. When folks had time, they would set the leaves on fire, and in October the aroma of burning leaves was everywhere. Burning the leaves was an acceptable way of disposing of them, and a blue hazy cloud of smoke hung over the neighborhoods. We would stand there well into the evening until the fire died out. Somehow there was a special dispensation while the adults and kids assisted in the burning. Young and old watched with fascination as the leaves burned. We would stand there as equals in the darkness of the October night, actually having a conversation with adults.

The leaves burned better if they were loosely piled, but jumping into leaves and burying each other was a lot of fun. When we were older, we used to sneakily set fire to unattended windrows of leaves and flee the scene. We would take a match and stick it into a lit cigarette at the unlighted end. Then we placed it inside the pile of dry leaves. When the cigarette burned down, the match ignited, and caught the leaves on fire. We thought we were pretty smart, pulling one over on the adults, because when the fire started, there was no one around.

15
GOING TO THE MOVIES

Haverhill had four movie houses--the Strand, the Lafayette, the Paramount and the Colonial. Louis B. Mayer owned the Colonial Theatre. As a young man, he actually started in the movie business in Haverhill. He bought a run-down burlesque house called the Gem, renovated it into a movie theatre, and renamed it the Orpheum. At one time he owned all of Haverhill's movie houses, before moving to Hollywood where he really made his mark.

By the time I was nine years old, I had seen just a few movies. We did not get to the movies very often because the bus fare was five cents each way, and the movie cost ten cents. I remembered each movie as a big event. I saw my first movie with my Dad in 1938, a movie called *Spawn of the North* with George Raft and Henry Fonda. This was a "talkie," which meant that people actually spoke (as opposed to a silent movie which had only background music and sometimes subtitles). I also saw *Twenty Mule Team*, a 1940s movie with Wallace Berry, Leo Carrillo and Ann Baxter. Wallace Berry was to become one of my favorite actors.

I had two movie experiences back-to-back that both frightened and delighted me. I cannot remember who was with me, but I saw the *Wizard of Oz* at the Strand.

I excitedly waited for the movie to begin. However, at that time, the custom in movie houses was to first show Coming Attractions, then a Pathé News film, and then the double feature, with the main attraction saved for last. When the evening ended, on the way out of the theatre, each moviegoer was handed a dish or a glass to encourage their return visits in order to acquire a full set of dinnerware.

That day, Pathé News was a clip about the rape of Nanking, China by Japanese soldiers. I did not know what rape meant, but I saw women and children running and crying and a lot of mean-looking soldiers. That frightening news report left me with an enduring fear and anger about the victimization of innocent people.

The *Wizard of Oz* finally came on. I wondered what was wrong, because normally movies were in black and white, and this one was running in a brownish color. I did not learn the word sepia until many years later. I wondered if that brown and white was "the special thing about this movie" that my parents wanted me to see. If so, I was not too impressed. I admit that seeing the house flying through space was pretty spectacular, but still not up to all my expectations.

Then Dorothy's spinning, flying house crashed. Suddenly Dorothy was in Munchkin Land, and the movie burst into color. I was astounded! I joined in squeals of delight with all the other children. Wow! A movie in color! I had no way to prepare for this miracle. Then the flying red monkeys came after Dorothy and Toto, and I was back to being scared.

16
THE FEARFUL THIRTIES AND FORTIES

I grew up feeling fearful, and with good reason. In our family, an ever-present fear was winding up in the poor house. What we kids feared most, especially in the summertime, was Infantile Paralysis, later called polio. My friend, Paul Rival, was struck down with Infantile Paralysis. The doctors propped up his arm chest-high with a metal contraption. We were all scared to be near Paul because we thought he might be contagious. We heard that other children were placed in Iron Lungs, which helped them breathe. In the summer some beaches were closed, because people believed that children caught Infantile Paralysis from the waters of ponds and lakes. No one in our family had to worry about beaches being closed, since we lacked any means of transportation to get to the beaches.

I heard my parents talking about the Ku Klux Klan which was active in Massachusetts. The Klan placed burning crosses on the lawns of people they did not like, especially Jews and Negros and some Catholics.

Father Coughlin, an inflammatory Catholic priest, invented "hate radio" long before Rush Limbaugh had even thought of it. Through his infamous radio broadcasts from Chicago, Father Coughlin railed against Roosevelt, the Jews, and anyone who did not share his philosophy. The higher-ups in the Catholic Church shut him down in 1940 and returned him to being a parish priest. However, during the Depression he had a lot of listeners. I remember seeing his framed picture on my Grammy Willey's wall in her little apartment in Haverhill.

Father Feeney, a Jesuit from Boston, cut from the same cloth, was eventually shut down by Archbishop Richard Cardinal Cushing. Feeney wound up in Harvard, Massachusetts with his own following. His clear message was that there was no salvation outside the Catholic Church.

Some people joined the Communist Party because they were hungry and had no hope. I overheard my parents talking about some friends they knew who went to Russia, became disillusioned, and were not allowed to return home.

John L. Lewis was fighting for the rights of coal miners. There were violent clashes where several miners were killed by goons hired by the mine owners.

The world was at war, and we feared we would soon be at war too. Emperor Hirohito, Benito Mussolini, and Adolph Hitler seemed to be taking over the world.

In 1933 during the Great Depression, Roosevelt was campaigning for the presidency, and he focused on helping people to not be fearful. His famous statement, "We have nothing to fear but fear itself" was used over and over again during the depths of the Depression, and I will never forget his comforting efforts to reduce our fear.

17
LISTEN TO YOUR PARENTS. LISTEN TO YOUR CHILDREN.

During the first 10 years of my life, I had some experiences, both good and bad, that have remained with me all my life. While it is sometimes difficult, I try to keep in mind that my parents had my wellbeing in mind no matter how they delivered their messages. The short story that is about to unfold is a good example of my coming close to very serious consequences because I did not listen to my parents.

On a bitter cold winter day in 1939, I was walking to Walnut Square, wearing thin shoes, with my argyle knee-length stockings tucked under the cuff of my corduroy knickers, a second-hand Mackinaw, hand-knitted mittens, and a hat with earlaps. My mother gave me a finger-shaking warning before I departed to not ever under any circumstances take a ride with anyone I did not know. She knew the temptation would arise on this particularly cold day. Only halfway to my destination I was shivering with the cold.

My mother probably never heard the word pedophile but she knew that creepy monsters preyed on little kids. As usual, she did not go into detail about what could happen if the wrong person picked me up. She just said, "Don't do it."

A car pulled to the curb and a very pleasant man said, "It's too cold to be out. Come on, I'll take you where you're going." As I stepped close to the car, the warm air hit me, and I was in the car in two seconds. Within a minute or two the man was rubbing my thighs "to make sure I was warming up," and I freaked and started to scream. He quickly pulled the car over to the curb, and I bounced out of there, and never again took a ride from a stranger. I also made sure I did not tell my mother about the incident because then I would get a whipping from my father. That little secret was going to the grave with me.

The summer vacation after my third year of high school was shaping up to be a really great time, since the guys were chipping in money to rent a cottage at the beach. Oh boy, I could not wait, because we had ideas of wine, women, beer and women. But dear old Dad came through again with a summer job, and I never did get to that cottage at the beach.

The new boss he introduced me to was a creepy old man who needed a helper on a stake body truck that delivered milk to boys' and girls' summer camps. He was a skinny, scrawny, unkempt, weasel-looking guy I will call Harry, who always had a lighted cigarette hanging out of his mouth. I rode up on the load in the fresh air to put distance between him and me. There was another reason I wanted to keep my distance. I heard from my friends that he had a son who was "strange," and my friends said he was "queer" because he liked other boys.

One day my father approached me and said that Harry offered to let me stay over at his summer house on Country Pond for the weekend. I replied with a polite, "No thank you." "You ungrateful little shit. What the hell's the matter with you," was Dad's reply. I did not dare tell my father about Harry Jr. being "queer."

The following Friday, off I went to the camp for the weekend. I was apprehensive and tried to hide it. The first night I went to bed, sure enough, during the night, Harry Jr. was crawling into my bed and telling me to be quiet while he started to play with my penis. I let out a scream, made a hell of a racket, and he hastily left. The next morning without any discussion, I was taken back to Haverhill with the excuse that the sewerage system failed and that I could visit again some other time. My father never knew the truth.

18
VISITING FREMONT

During the summer of 1939 I stayed a couple of weeks with my grandfather in Fremont, New Hampshire. I loved riding north on Route 121 with him in his 1932 Pontiac Coupe. The car had a rumble seat and something called "free-wheeling," which I think was similar to "cruise control."

Grampa lived in an old farm house located on the main road through Fremont. Marjorie Beede owned the place. He was actually a boarder, but Marjorie Beede treated me like family. She was about 30 years younger than Gramps, and until the day he died, she was very attentive to him. All I knew was my parents loved Marjorie, and she was close to my grandfather in a stand-offish sort of way. She was plain-looking and rather stout. I adored her. She had a wonderful sweet disposition, and she always treated me with kindness. In later years I thought that she was secretly living with my grandfather, but everyone in our family kept their suspicions to themselves.

Marjorie's farmhouse had no electricity or running water. Water was obtained from a hand pump in the kitchen. The farmhouse had a combination wood or coal stove. The toilet was an outhouse located in the barn and connected by an entry way between the house and the barn. The toilet was a two-holer, one being bigger and set higher for the adults, and one smaller in diameter and lower to the floor for kids. I could live to be 100 years old and not ever forget the fragrance inside the outhouse, especially in the summer. A favorite past-time of mine when I had to pee was to look down at the pile of human excrement and spot the spider webs. The trick was to hit a spider with a steady stream.

While in Fremont, I often visited my great uncle, Plum Willey. His farmhouse at the top of Beede Hill was the only one in the County that had electric power. I was really proud that he generated power from his own windmill and stored the electricity in enormous batteries. Recent photo taken in 2004.

My weekly bath was taken in the kitchen in a galvanized tin tub that was stored in the barn when not in use. The hot water was bailed out of a reservoir at the back of the stove and dumped into the tub. Usually the soap was home-made, using caustic lye and fats, and no perfume to make you feel refreshed.

Charlie Philbrick lived next door. In front of his home was a small building with about 64 square feet of floor space from which he ran a barber shop. Most all the people in the village of Fremont went to Charlie for their haircuts.

Charlie Philbrick's old barbershop in Fremont, NH. Recent photo 2005.

The Exeter River flowed east and a little north through Fremont on its way to Exeter, where it became the tidal Squamscott River, and eventually found its way to the Atlantic Ocean via Great Bay. Grampa Willey set me up with a crude fishing pole, but I do not recall ever catching anything that I could bring home for the dinner plate. In my world, no one went fishing for the sport of it. We fished to eat.

During this stay with Grampa, I visited Marjorie's relatives who lived up by Beede Hill where they had a small chicken farm. The Beedes had two daughters. I was attracted to Shirley Beede, the one about my age, and we had great days playing together on the farm. One day Shirley came running into the farmhouse crying that most all her baby chicks had been carried off by rodents. I felt so bad that I could not do something to comfort Shirley. I liked her a lot, and it hurt to see her cry. Weasels had burrowed under the chicken wire fence, they had been joined by red foxes, and together they almost wiped out all her chicks. Her

Dad fixed the fence and bought more chicks, and the disaster was quickly remedied.

Beede farmhouse on Beede Hill Road, Fremont, NH. Recent photo 2004.

Those few short days with Shirley were a high point in my life. I had a lump in my throat when I said good-bye. I had such a good time that Grampa Willey promised that I could come back again sometime. I did go back, but never again saw the Beede girls.

In the evening everyone sat in the living room around the big table, with an enormous kerosene lamp lighting up the room. Some read books, some flipped through the Sears catalog, played checkers, or viewed 3-D images in the stereoscope.

Once a week, the Beede family did the laundry, using a washing machine driven by a gasoline engine. The exhaust pipe, a flexible hose that ran outside, made an awful racket. In spite of the flexible hose, the house had to be evacuated when the machine was in use. While it was a noisy, stinking contraption, I thought it was remarkable that clothes could be washed and wrung fairly dry with a machine. My mother bent over the bathroom tub using a scrub board, and then wrung out by hand every article of clothing.

Back home after my Fremont visit with Grampa, I had an experience that has stayed with me all my life. My bedroom was off the kitchen and when neighbors came to visit my folks, they often sat in the kitchen to chat. My mother was bragging about how tanned and healthy I looked, and she and one of the neighbors peeked in to look at my tan. I made believe I was asleep, and it felt wonderful to be admired. At that moment I felt accepted and a part of my parents' life. Every year since then, I made sure I had a great tan all summer long.

19
FORBIDDEN WORDS

Certain words could not be spoken aloud. I heard my parents talking about someone who had a "touch of sugar," but not until years later did I learn that a "touch of sugar" was Irish for diabetes. One day my mother told me that I should go visit Mr. Roach because he was sick and would like to see me. She did not explain what was going on or what I could expect. She just said, "Go see Mr. Roach." He was lying on a sofa. His leg was propped up on a pillow, and it was all raw and smelled like roast pork, Mr. Roach had "cancer," another word that was not allowed to be used.

A strange thing was happening. In early 1940 my mother was gaining weight, and she had a pot belly. I learned she was "expecting." Women avoided going out in public if they were "going to have a baby." We were forbidden to say the word, "pregnant" and were told to keep our mouth shut about my mother's condition. I got the idea that there was something wrong with her having a baby. I did not know anything about the natural process of child bearing and felt sorry for my mother who had to do all the chores and lug the big belly around. I had no idea how she got that way, a mystery like everything else that went o the house.

On 10 July 1940 on a very hot day, the doctor drove up to the house in his big LaSalle and shooed all us kids away from the kitchen. Mom was in the front room awaiting the doctor. We all went out and played under the big elm tree because we did not want to be too far away from what was happening in the front room. My father had the oil stove cranking and heating water in all the big pots we owned, and it must have been about 100 degrees in the kitchen. Norma Jean Willey made her entrance and was pronounced very healthy, born in the front room of 754 Main Street.

The Willey Kids in 1942
Sitting: Joan, Norma, Barbara. Standing: John
Backyard of 754 Main Street, Haverhill, MA

1948: Grampa Willey and Norma Jean Willey
651 Primrose Street, Haverhill, MA

20
THE WPA AND FDR

One memory that I cherish was the Sundays when my father took me on the W.P.A construction job where he worked. He drove a beat-up old pickup truck (nicknamed the "jitterbug") for a company called Greenough Brothers, a road-building contractor. I rode shotgun.

The project was the re-building of Route 110 in Haverhill, Massachusetts. In the winter when a concrete culvert had just been constructed, workers placed salamanders (55-gallon steel drums cut lengthwise) underneath the culvert. Fired up with coke, a kind of processed coal, salamanders were used to warm the freshly poured concrete to avoid its freezing. My father's job was to keep the fires burning in the salamanders. Also, he kept the fires burning on "roadway bombs," steel spherical containers with a flattened bottom filled with kerosene and fitted with a wick, which when lighted, produced a flame to warn motorists at night about the construction. I really liked being with Dad in this pleasant working atmosphere, especially when he treated me like a friend and did not scold or humiliate me.

My father let me in on a secret about his salary (a big deal since he rarely shared information). He was earning 40 cents an hour, and the contractor wanted to pay him more because he was available seven days a week whenever needed. In a W.P.A. (Works Project Administration) project, laborers could work only 40 hours a week, the idea being to share the jobs with as many men as possible because of the Depression.

A deal was cooked up with an old, Italian immigrant named Pasquale. Pasquale owned land next to the job site, and Greenough Brothers stored equipment there. So Greenough Brothers put Pasquale on the payroll and split the $16 per week between my father and the non-English speaking immigrant. Pasquale's check was cashed without his knowledge, and he received $8 per week for the space to store equipment, and my father got a raise from $16 to $24 per week. Everyone was happy.

To help bring us out of the Depression that had been going on for 10 years, FDR created thousands of W.P.A. projects to make jobs for the unemployed while doing the public good. W.P.A. projects included dam construction, roadways, sidewalks, parks, buildings, and post office art to name just a few. We loved to hear the W.P.A. orchestras when they visited the schools to give a concert. Some very well-known musicians were available since there were no other paying jobs.

Here is a standard joke about why eight W.P.A. men were required to mow grass with only two lawn mowers. First they would set up an outhouse by removing a sewer cover in the roadway which gave direct access to the sewer main. Then, the story unfolded: There were two men coming; two men going; two men shitting, and two men mowing. Some folks did not like the fact that FDR was trying to create jobs for the destitute. I suspect a Republican made up the ditty.

We all hailed FDR as close to God. In addition to the W.P.A, the CCC (Civilian Conservation Corp) employed young men to perform public works in the forests and parks. They lived in barracks within camps across New England. The men were fed and paid a small salary, which most sent home. In 1940, we thought the Depression was broken and Happy Days were ahead.

21
WAR GETTING CLOSER

In 1940 war was raging in China, Korea, Europe, and Ethiopia. England was in a battle for its survival, but the U.S.A. had a "hands off" policy which most people thought was appropriate. The great British statesman, Winston Churchill, was frequently in the news asking the USA to lend a hand.

In Haverhill we kids were playing war games down in the woods behind Roach's barn. We made guns that fired elastic bands fashioned from inner tubes. At this time inner tubes were made from real rubber. Soon, however, synthetics were substituted so rubber could be used instead for the war effort.

To make a gun, first we scrounged up scraps and pieces of wood. Then we sawed a board about 12 inches long and 4 inches deep. We fastened a stick at the end of the board. The finishing touch was the trigger, a nail driven on the underside of the board, about three inches back from the stick. The projectiles were strips of inner tube about an inch wide, stretched from the front to the back of the board. The stretched rubber band was securely held between the stick and the board. Ready to wage war, we searched out the enemy and aimed the gun, wrapped two fingers around the nail, then pulled, and BAM, the elastic flew out and killed the enemy. We carried extra elastics and became quite proficient at reloading.

Being a resourceful little twit, I invented a four-shot rifle by using a board a little over three feet in length, cutting a notch about a foot from the front, then another three notches, each spaced about four inches apart. I nailed a string to the front of the rifle and laid it across the top of the rifle down into each notch. Then I stretched an elastic into each of the four notches. I could charge the Germans, and when in range, put the gun to my shoulder, lift up the string, and fire off the first elastic, When I pulled the string a little more, off went the second, the third, and the fourth.

22
ROMANTIC YEARNINGS

As a child, I used to play behind Roach's barn at the bottom of a very steep hill. There stood an enormous garage that Mr. Roach used to store his old construction machinery. He had been out of business for a long time, and the steam-driven machines were relics, but fun to play on and imagine all sorts of interesting exploits. Another abandoned barn built on piers stood close by. When we played under the barn with piers, we could not be seen by anyone.

One day I was down there with a young girl my age, and we were doing some different kind of exploring. We were probably about 10 years old. This was our first sexual encounter. While we did not have intercourse, I do remember it was a very pleasant experience and I wanted more. However, soon afterward my new girlfriend and her family moved away, and that was the end of my romantic plans for quite a while.

When the Gill family left the upstairs apartment in our double decker and moved to Somerville to be closer to the SOCONY terminal, I was disappointed to lose the Gill's son, my playmate, George, However, a French Canadian family named Gagnon moved in upstairs. Alfred Gagnon was a carpenter and his wife

Irene a housewife. The children were Alfred Jr., Helen, Raymond, and Betty Ann.

Now 12 years old, I was smitten with Helen. She was beautiful, soft-spoken and easy to talk to. I kept my thoughts about her a secret because I remembered with shame my father's teasing about Nancy Goldberg. Also, true to form, my father made many unfavorable remarks about Mr. Gagnon, including comments like "Goddam puddle-jumpers come down from Canada with a rock and a pocket full of nails, and they become carpenters."

One day I met Helen in the stairway as she was leaving her apartment, and I commented on how nice her lipstick looked. She looked at me with those big dreamy eyes, and asked me if I would like to taste her lipstick. I began to heat up instantly from my toes to my head. I mumbled something, beat a hasty retreat, and regretted my inaction for many years to come.

23
LEARNING TO WORK

In the summer of 1942 my father arranged for me to get a job at Ingaldsby Farm in Boxford. I took the first bus in the morning from Dustin Square to White's Corner where Mrs. Ingaldsby would gather up a station wagon full of kids. We were picking string beans at 35 cents a bushel. Here I met my first Black person. I was fascinated and treated him like a celebrity, and to show my interest I asked him if his parents had been slaves. He was very pissed off, and we nearly came to blows. Others interceded, and we cooled off. I kept away from him from that point on.

The best I could do was pick three bushels of string beans a day at 35 cents a bushel for a total pay of $1.05. The fields were endless and hot with snakes and bugs. Mrs. Ingaldsby was not too thrilled with our performance in the harvesting of string beans, so she changed us to strawberries. What we did not know was that the rows assigned to kids were the rows that the older farm hands had already picked. In effect, we were gleaners, and it was ... slim pickings. I noticed an abundance of nice ripe strawberries two rows over, so over I went, and was well on my way to making a pretty good day's pay. "Hey, what the hell are you doing over in that row?" screamed the field manager. My farm hand days ended abruptly. I was very happy to be fired, and I told my father that the job had ended because the fields were picked clean.

During the war, there was a great shortage of men to work on the farms since most all of them were in the service. In the summer of 1942, three of us decided we wanted to work on Mr. Scribner's farm up on North Avenue. "Pete the Greek," Al Gagnon and I approached Mr. Scribner gingerly and with trepidation. Through our own intelligence network of other 12-year olds, we knew everything there was to know about everyone in the neighborhood. We heard that Mr. Scribner was mean. However, he listened quietly as we made our pitch about the three buddies working together as a team. His reply was a disappointment, "Well, boys" he said, "I never hire three boys at the same time. You see, if I hire one boy, I get one boy to work. If I hire two boys, I wind up with one half a boy. And if I hire three boys, I get no boy to work." And off he walked.

We left there scratching our heads thinking he was crazy. On the way out from the farm house, we walked through his peach orchard and swiped a goodly amount of tree-ripened peaches. We surreptitiously entered his hay barn, climbing to the highest cross beams, and took turns jumping into the freshly stored hay. Hay in those days was stored loose, and provided a soft landing when jumping from great heights. However, if caught we would get a beating, because jumping into the hay knocked off the seeds and turned the hay into broken pieces of straw.

With the shortage of men, we were encouraged to get odd jobs around home. In the winter of 1942 after a snow storm, I joined the ranks of the kids who walked up to Lakeview Avenue to shovel snow for "rich" people. I rang the bell at one house. When the lady came to the door, she asked me how much to shovel the driveway and the front walk. I looked the job over without a bit of experience and said, "Two dollars." She replied, "O.K. Let me know when you're finished, and I'll pay you."

I really worked hard for a couple of hours, finished the job and went up and rang the bell. She came out and said, "Could you just shovel a narrow path from the back door to the garbage bucket?" (In those days garbage was deposited in an in-ground pail, and the garbage man came once a week to empty the garbage. In the summer it was a disgusting, stinking mess of rotten food covered with maggots.) I shoveled the narrow path and rang the bell again. She smiled and asked if I could just do one single path to the clothes yard. Finally I got my two dollars, and I was one pissed off Pilgrim. I felt cheated, powerless and angry. I never went there shoveling again. My father was right! Rich people were cheap bastards!

During the summer of 1942, I spent a few weeks up in Fremont, New Hampshire with my grandfather and Marjorie Beede. Given the shortage of men, I was able to get a temporary job in the mill. I worked in the kiln, which was used to cure the barrel staves cut from green pine logs. I was either loading up staves to put into the kilns, or taking out staves that were dried. I stacked the green staves, one by one, on steel racks mounted on wheels that ran on tracks into the kiln. When the racks were in the kilns, we secured the doors, and high pressure steam was applied to soften up the resins until they flowed out of the wood. Next, the steam was evacuated, and we applied high heat to dry the wood. The temperature in the kilns after the doors were opened was about 125 degrees. I sweated a lot.

The power plant is all that remains of the Spaulding & Frost Barrel Mill. When I worked there as a kid, Grampa Willey was in charge of the power plant. He let me turn on the pump to fill the Town's water tank. When the water came out of the overflow pipe, my job was to shut off the pump. Boy, did I feel important! Recent photo 2005.

After a few days I was feeling weak and woozy, but I did not tell anyone for fear that my father would find out and be angry about me being a "lazy bastard." And I guessed the hicks would think I could not keep up. After all I was 12 years old. A day or so later I collapsed. The doctor told my grandfather that I had diphtheria.

Around 1943, back home in Haverhill, my Uncle Herbert, the ice man, came to my parents to suggest that I could get a job at a local restaurant, part time, after school. All I had to do was go to Monument Square and talk to a guy at Ray's restaurant.

My mother took me to the Post Office to get a Social Security card. I was ready to apply for the job. It was a sure thing, since my Uncle had set it up, and I was a hard worker. Any men not in the service did not want restaurant jobs; they were working at defense jobs, earning good money.

I became a "pot-walloper, pearl diver," otherwise known as a dish washer and pot cleaner. Gradually I learned to work the grill and the Fryalator. *White Christmas* by Irving Berlin and sung by Bing Crosby was the hottest song for the rest of the War. *White Christmas* played over and over on the juke box; once I pulled the plug on the juke box so I would not have to hear it one more time. This restaurant was where I learned the basics of cooking, a trade that has stood me well over all the rest of my life.

24
HARVESTING ICE

When I was a child, everyone used ice boxes to keep their food fresh. For many years, natural ice was harvested from ponds and lakes. My friends and I liked to walk up to Fry's Pond on North Avenue to watch men cut and store natural ice. The Pond froze to a depth of about 15 inches. Using a gasoline-driven circular saw about four feet in diameter, mounted on steel crawlers, the men cut long slots in the ice across the whole Pond, about 10 inches deep, in parallel rows about 18 inches apart. Then they cut slots at right angles about three feet apart, which resulted in large rectangular blocks of ice.

Next to the pond was the wooden ice house used to store the ice. The men took a long steel-handled wedge and broke apart about 20 sections of ice cakes at a time. While standing on the manmade iceberg in open water, they used a pole to disconnect about 10 ice cakes at a time. They pushed these across the water toward the ice house. Then they broke the ice cakes apart with wedges, and flipped each one upside down with a hand-held hook so the uneven bottom side of the ice cake that had been underwater was exposed. They guided each ice cake onto a conveyor, which carried it up a ramp to a set of steel teeth. The teeth scraped the uneven side of the ice block, making all the blocks the same size and shape, about 15 inches wide, by 18 inches high, three feet long, and about 350 pounds in weight. At the top of the conveyor after the ice cakes had been shaved to uniform sizes, the cakes slid down a wooden chute and slipped into position with a little space between each one. When the whole first layer of ice cakes was in place, the men covered them with sawdust. Then they positioned runner boards on the sawdust, providing a raceway for the second layer of ice cakes. Using the same method, each successive layer was put in place until the ice house was full.

We used an icebox at home until several years after World War II. Each day my job was to put our "ice card" in the front window of our house to let the ice man know we wanted ice. Four sizes were indicated on the card, ranging in price from 15 to 50 cents, and I had to place the card in the appropriate position to indicate which size we wanted for that day.

The upper left side of the ice box was reserved for the ice compartment. So if we needed a 25 cent piece, then the card went in the window with the number 25 showing, and that was what would be delivered. The ice man used his ice pick to cut a 25 cent piece from his 350-pound block of ice, pick up the ice with his tongs, throw it over his shoulder onto the rubber mat he wore on his back, carry it into the house, and place it in the box.

Since no one was home during the day, we simply left the back door open and placed the 25 cents on the top of the ice box. God help me if I forgot to take the card down and the ice man came the next day and brought another 25 cent piece that we could not use.

My responsibilities also included emptying the ice pan. The melted water dripped down into a pan beneath the ice box and had to be emptied daily, or water would overflow onto the kitchen floor (resulting in an ass-chewing if discovered by my father). I noticed that we had a dirt floor in the cellar, and an idea was born. Without any notice to my parents, I drilled a hole in the floor under the ice box, shoved an old length of garden hose through the hole, placed a funnel on top, and ran the hose to a small dry well I dug in the dirt floor.

My ice pan emptying days were behind me, since now the drip water went directly into the funnel and into the dry well. No more spilled water when the pan was too full. I was so proud of my invention, that I told my dad. He was really angry, not what I expected, but I noticed that the new system stayed in place.

The business of ice-making was changing. Ice was being manufactured in freezing plants. This manmade ice replaced naturally harvested ice because it was easier to cut into regular sizes. From the tailgate of a horse-drawn wagon or truck, you could cut manmade ice in perfect cubes because it had no natural fault lines. With natural ice, pieces would splinter, and much of the ice would be wasted. Freezing ice in a plant was also much cheaper, since less labor was required and ice could be made and stored as needed.

Then GE invented its famous Frigidaire refrigerator, later referred to as the Fridge, and ice-making of all kinds soon came to an end. When the old ice houses were abandoned, they all caught fire as the sawdust deteriorated and created heat enough to cause spontaneous combustion. Ice house fires were common for a few years, as each house was abandoned and then caught fire.

25
MOM

My mother was a steadying influence for me. She constantly sought ways to counteract the negative effects of my father's anger. She tried to keep the children away from Dad because he worked so hard. She did not want to upset him or all hell would break loose. I could see that Mom was running interference between us and him. I began to feel closer to my mother and more and more distanced from my depressed father.

Mom was always in my corner, and that has never been more apparent to me than as I write this story. I realize my mother was trying to give me experiences that would benefit me in later life.

She was behind me joining the boy scouts and the sea scouts. She praised me when I became interested in collecting abandoned bird nests and learning about different birds. She encouraged me to collect sap from the maple trees, knowing full well I could never bring home enough sap to make a worthwhile quantity of maple syrup. She encouraged me to take dancing lessons when I met my first sweetheart.

One summer, my mother convened a meeting, inviting about six of my neighborhood friends, and presented us with an idea for having fun. We were going to have a new club called "The Jolly Bookworm Club." We would read books and talk about them once a week. My mother recruited the other boys' mothers to participate. Mom held the first meeting at our house, and then each week we met at a different boy's house, with the mothers taking turns providing cake and cookies. Every week my mother placed an article in the *Haverhill Gazette* about the meeting of the Jolly Bookworm Club. My mother's goal was to encourage us to visit the library, take out books, and read. I'm still remembering her efforts with a smile. (And it worked – I continue to read dozens and dozens of books each year.)

As a youngster, at her instigation, I entered the Barefoot Boy contest. John Greenleaf Whittier, the famous Quaker poet, had been the editor of the *Haverhill Gazette* in the mid-1850s. One of his famous poems was The Barefoot Boy. Here are the opening lines of the poem.

BLESSINGS on thee, little man,
Barefoot boy, with cheek of tan!
With thy turned-up pantaloons,
And thy merry whistled tunes;
With thy red lip, redder still
Kissed by strawberries on the hill;
With the sunshine on thy face,

Mom dressed me up in a pair of bib overalls with one strap undone, barefooted with one pant leg rolled up shorter than the other, a straw hat set back on my head, a little fishing pole over my shoulder, and a piece of grass to stick in my mouth just before the *Gazette* photographer took the picture. Dozens of hopeful boys made this annual trip to the *Gazette* knowing full well that whether or not we won the contest, we would get our pictures in the paper.

26
PEARL HARBOR

On a warm sunny Sunday afternoon on the 7th of December, 1941, my friends and I were out playing tag football by the Elm tree. About three o'clock, Walter Smith's mother came running out of her house, screaming, "The Japs have bombed Pearl Harbor." She ran over to our house, crying that her husband was all set to join the Army to fight those bastards.

No one could tell me where Pearl Harbor was. I had a notion it was in Quincy, a city just south of Boston. I remembered the Pathé news reel about the rape of Nanking by soldiers of the Japanese Army, and I was afraid that might happen in Haverhill.

Everyone was suspicious of everyone else. German Americans were hassled and became the subject of secret investigations. Our government rounded up Japanese Americans and herded them into concentration camps, right here in the good old USA. No one cared that Japanese Americans were placed in concentration camps. We were afraid, and we slept better knowing the Japs were locked up. This was about the time when my mother started her often-stated admonition, "The Yellow race will rule the world." Over the years I heard her repeat the warning many times.

To add to the confusion, as the War went on, we learned about the 442nd Infantry, a Japanese American division in the US Army which fought in World War II while the men's parents were imprisoned in American concentration camps. The was a self-sufficient fighting force, which served with uncommon distinction in Italy, southern France, and Germany. The unit, which included 21 recipients of the Medal of Honor, became the most highly decorated military unit in the history of the United States Armed Forces, earning the nickname, "The Purple Heart Battalion."

27
THE PHILCO RADIO

December 9, 1941, two days after the bombing at Pearl Harbor, Roosevelt made a speech. We all huddled around the Philco radio to hear it. I remember Roosevelt saying, "I ask the Congress to declare that a state of war exists between the United States of America and the Empire of Japan."

The Philco radio was the main luxury item in many of the homes in my neighborhood. There were two types: one was a table model, and the other a floor model. We eventually had a floor model that stood about three and a half feet high, two feet wide, and about a foot deep. The Philco was made of fancy stained wood and looked like a piece of furniture.

My parents would sit in the two arm chairs and we kids would sit on the floor and listen with rapt attention. Serial shows for kids lasted 15 minutes to a half hour. We could not miss: Jack Armstrong, the all American boy brought to you by Wheaties; the Green Hornet; the Lone Ranger and his faithful Indian companion Tonto; Batman and Robin; Superman; Lassie; Roy Rogers; Gene Autry; and the most important one -- the Shadow. A deep voice would open with "Who knows what evil lurks in the minds of men? The Shadow knows," followed with an evil sounding deep-throated "Heh-heh-heh-heh."

Some shows we listened to as a family, like The Jack Benny Show with Rochester, Fibber McGee and Molly, Amos and Andy,

Red Skelton, and The Grand Ole Oprey with Minnie Pearl, to name a few.

28
WARTIME YEARS

As the U.S. was gearing up for war, my father landed a job at Fort Devens in Ayer, Massachusetts. We did not have a car, so Dad joined a car pool for the long ride to Fort Devens. He told numerous stories about the confusion on the job, including one story about a union scam. Apparently new workers paid their dues weekly until they had almost enough weeks to join the union. Then they would be laid off, and a new group would be suckered in. After Dad was laid off, he worked for awhile as a truck driver at the Portsmouth Navy Ship Yard where they built and repaired submarines.

Rationing began in 1942 and was managed by the OPA, the federal Office of Price Administration. More than 60,000 employees and 200,000 volunteers ran 8,000 rationing boards in the US. They rationed meat, butter, silk, nylon, and lots of other commodities. Gasoline was a big problem for many people. Fortunately we had no problem with gasoline rationing, since my father did not own a car. People had an A, B, or C stamp on their windshield, which enabled them to buy a certain number of gallons of gas per week based on the rationing board's discretion. Truckers had a T stamp which allowed them more.

Tokens were used to buy food: red tokens for meat, and blue for groceries. Grammy Willey used to take the bus up to our house and bring her red coupon for a half pound of butter a week. We could buy horse meat without stamps, but my folks refused to eat horses. Of course we really never knew if horse meat was mixed in with the hamburger we bought. Whenever we ate hamburger, someone in the family would joke, "Please don't say Whoa when we're swallowing the hamburg."

Dad drove a milk truck for many years. When I rode with him on the truck, he sent me into every market on the route. My job was to check the floor in front of the meat display in case someone had lost a red token in the saw dust on the floor. I did find some. Picking up a red token in front of the meat counter could be a problem. I carried a jack knife and dropped it near the token. When I stooped to pick up the knife, I'd scoop up the token at the same time, and no one was the wiser. The Mohegan Market on Merrimack Street was where I had my most successful missions.

My mother came home one day with a substitute for butter called oleomargarine. It was pure white, and looked a lot like lard, packaged in a plastic bag. You peeled off a little orange pellet from the package and let the white stuff come to room temperature. Then you kneaded the orange pellet into the mass until it turned yellow. Shazam! We had butter! It tasted awful.

We ate a lot of salt cod. Most people bought cod in one-pound wooden boxes. Nice fat fillets cost about 50 cents apiece. However, we bought the scraps that were stored in an open wooden barrel, left over from trimming the fillets. Cod scraps sold for 15 cents a pound. The scraps were good, but unfortunately we never got the wooden box, which had a sliding cover and could be used a hundred different ways for storing things.

By 1943, our lives had changed dramatically. We saved cooking grease for the war effort, which was somehow used in making explosives. Old trolley car tracks were dug up out of the roads and the steel was used to make tanks and ships. We saved tin foil from cigarette packages which was used to make electrical components for the war. Women knitted sweaters, gloves and hats for the servicemen. USO's popped up everywhere. The USO (United Service Organization), a non-profit that began in 1941 in partnership with the Department of Defense, was basically a home-away-from-home for servicemen and women.

Thousands of people donated blood to be made into plasma for the war. My Mother gave a pint every time she was allowed.

She wore a pin that recognized her as a person who had given more than a gallon. The custom was to place a small flag with a blue star in the window for every member of the family in the war, and a gold star for every member who had been killed. The flags were a constant reminder of the tragedy of war.

On a trip to Plum Island we saw US Coast Guard sailors on horseback patrolling the beaches, and we noticed gigantic gun emplacements had been built. We saw what looked like black chunks of rubber floating in the surf, and we learned these were solidified oil blobs from tankers torpedoed off the New Jersey coast. Nazi U-boats were right off our shoreline, sinking our merchant fleet. We heard that a small group of German commandos actually landed on Long Island, New York

Each city and town had air raid sirens that were constantly being tested. I can still hear the piercing sound in my mind: the siren wound up to its top pitch, and then reversed as the siren shut off, gradually toning down to nothing. One day in the 7th grade, our teachers excitedly announced that German planes were spotted heading our way. We were reminded that they liked to strafe civilians with machine guns. The school ordered us to run home as fast as we could. It turned out to be a false alarm. Haverhill had air raid shelters built throughout the City; however, our teachers taught us how to hide under our school desks when the air raid sirens blasted. Hiding under the desks never made any sense to me, but we practiced doing it anyway.

During the evenings we observed a blackout. We had special curtains in every room that would emit no light. If any light showed, an Air Raid Warden would knock on the door to tell you to fix the shade or put off the light. We also had brown-outs where cars were allowed to move at night but the top half of the head lights had to be painted black. If the air raid siren sounded, the cars had to stop immediately and shut off the headlights.

Black marketeering was prevalent. A common conversation was about those lousy bastards who were taking advantage of shortages and selling things at inflated prices. Patriotism was running high, and yet some saw the war as a good time to take advantage of the conditions.

We were bombarded with constant reports about the war. Relatives and friends received telegrams from the US government telling them the bad news that loved ones had been killed or were missing in action. The fear factor was kept high by the radio, newspapers, and talk among friends and neighbors. We saw pictures of the atrocities perpetrated by the Japanese, the Bataan Death March, and the concentration camps in Borneo. We learned about places that we never heard of before, like Corregidor, New Caledonia, Truk, Palau, Guam, Midway, Mindanao, Lingayen Gulf, Okinawa, and Tarawa, to name a few in the Pacific. We read about the exploits of General Douglas MacArthur; of "Vinegar" Joe Stillwell as he built the Burma Road, and James Doolittle and his raid on Tokyo early in the war. We followed the exploits of General Eisenhower, General Patten, and the famous British Field Marshall Bernard Montgomery, who fought the German General Erwin Rommel, known as the Desert Fox in North Africa. Across the Atlantic we sent convoys of hundreds of ships with men and supplies onboard, and German U-Boat submarines were sinking them on route.

I was fortunate to land a part-time job at Benks & Whiting across the street from our house. I worked after school and on Saturdays. People called in their orders. I gathered up the items and placed the groceries into cardboard boxes for loading into the truck for delivery on Saturdays. Another task I liked was packaging potatoes in the basement of the store. In those days potatoes came in 100 pound burlap sacks. My job was to dump a 100 pound sack of potatoes into a bin located under the stairway. Using a scoop, I filled up peck and half-peck paper bags, and then tied them up with string. The owners did not know, but I would take a quart bottle of orangeade while packing the potatoes, hide it behind the potatoes, and take swigs until it was gone. Getting rid of the empty was easy since people returned their bottles; I would simply add it to the boxes of empty tonic bottles.

Riding the delivery truck was a thrill. Benks & Whiting catered to the wealthy. I remember being directed to the service entrances of homes to deliver the groceries, dealing with domestic help, and gawking in with awe at the fancy interiors. I accepted that some people had money and some did not. I expected I was going to be one of the people who did not.

Bill Herbert, who lived nearby, was the head clerk at Benks & Whiting. He and his wife lived on Ringgold Street. They had no children, and I became friendly with Bill. He had a slight build, a good sense of humor, and a deformed right foot which I suppose kept him out of the military. His wife was a knock-out, with a bust similar to Jane Russell. Funny how those things do not get lost in my memory. However she was very nice to me, as was Bill.

During these war years we moved to 651 Primrose Street, a single-family house owned by Mr. Roach's widow and her sister Mrs. Ford. We were about two football field lengths away from 754 Main Street, but it was enough to put us in a new neighborhood. From the new house we had access to a big field that was a short walk through the woods and over a stream, using a wide plank as a bridge. My father received permission to cultivate the field. We planted potatoes, corn, beets, string beans, peppers, onions, carrots, Swiss chard, lettuce, tomatoes, cucumbers and squash. Dad worked very hard, getting up at 4:30 A.M., walking to work, driving a truck all day, and then working in the big garden until dark.

I helped Dad farm the garden. Together we would walk to the field through the woods, with garden tools slung over our shoulders. I felt like I was part of the venture, and we were equal guys, off to work together. One time as we were walking through the woods along the path to the big field, I had to stop to relieve myself. Without warning he said, "For Chris' sake, you sound like a cow pissing on a flat rock." I was devastated, ashamed, disconnected, and insulted. I could not even piss right! I felt like a fool to think that I could be part of this man. Why would he say such a thing? Now in retrospect, I can see that with his earthy remarks, he was treating me as "one of the guys."

29
DAD TURNED YELLOW

When I was 9 or 10, my parents forbade me to play sports. This really upset me, and I knew they were holding something back. My father had been feeling tired. He was informed by Dr. David Zelig in Haverhill that his spleen was enlarged. One day Dad said he was going to Boston to be examined at the Massachusetts General Hospital in a famous place called the Ether Dome. He explained that this was where ether was first used in 1846 to perform an operation without pain. Dad said a battery of doctors would examine him to see what was wrong and determine why the whites of his eyes were yellow.

Sometime later I was told that I was going to be examined by Dr Zelig too. Why did I have to see the doctor if my Dad was sick? Dr. Zelig examined me, and he said that I too had an enlarged spleen. At last I understood why my parents did not want me to play sports. They feared I might be injured and rupture my spleen.

One day I was working on the milk truck with my father. We were delivering milk to the Hotel Whittier when Dad turned yellow and collapsed. The Hotel called an ambulance, and he was rushed to the hospital. We learned that his spleen had to be removed. They waited a couple of weeks to build up his strength before the operation. He needed a blood transfusion before they could operate. Although Haverhill had no surgeons experienced in performing a splenectomy, Dad was admitted to the Hale Hospital in Haverhill.

My mother went to the hospital for a visit, and I accompanied her. She was told that Dad was going to have his spleen removed that day. Dad needed a blood transfusion, and Mom was Type

O, which is what he needed. They laid my mother on a cot next to Dad. A nurse ran a needle into Mom's left arm, connected to a rubber tube which was directly connected to the needle in my Dad's right arm. She gave him her blood directly. I stood there watching, and Mom assured me everything would be OK.

A local surgeon named Dr. Chaput performed his first splenectomy that day, and the operation was a huge success.

It turned out as the years unfolded that my father inherited from his father a condition called spherocytosis, where blood cells are spherical in shape and are structurally deficient. When the blood passes through the spleen, it breaks down and clogs up in the spleen causing the spleen to become enlarged. The solution is to remove the spleen.

My father recovered at home. He returned to work at the dairy, performing light tasks for awhile. Eventually everything was back to normal.

(The latest count in the family shows that 10 family members have had their spleens removed. I prepared and gave to my children a graphic organizational chart showing all the information about splenectomies performed on our family members.)

30
CAREER PLANNING

I heard my 8th grade friends talking about what course they were going to take in high school. They actually talked to their parents about their future education and where they were going to college. I cringed every time I heard them say, "I'm taking the college course."

If you were not going to college, you could take the business course, the commercial course, or the general course. Everyone knew that the other courses were for the poor kids who should not bother to think about college no matter how smart they were. Those taking the commercial course were looked down upon because they just wanted to finish high school and go to work in grocery stores or bakeries, or work as a truck driver delivering milk.

I remember telling my father one day that I wanted to go to college. I heard the other kids talking about college, and I wanted to be able to say I was going to college too. I realize now there was no way my father could envision me going to college. He responded with anger. Dad spun on his heels with an angry outburst, and said, "Who the f--- do you think you are?"

My family did not talk about the future, let alone educational plans. Not one of my relatives had ever graduated from high school. However, my father did have a plan for me. He dared to hope that his son would become a tradesman. My father made such an impression on me about the lofty position of tradesman, that I only hoped that I could be good enough to become one.

Haverhill had an excellent trade school run by a team of dedicated men in the trades. I had the required B average from grammar school, so that was the plan. In the fall of 1944 I entered the 9th grade at The Charles W. Arnold Trade School with the goal of becoming a carpenter. On my first day of school I read the sign over the entrance, "Enter to Learn, Depart to Serve." I was proud to be a student at the School. To actually have a son who would graduate from high school and become a tradesman was a big deal for my father and the whole Willey family.

The Trade School had been established around 1929 in a small building on Winter Street. The educational program was geared primarily to then current trades--auto mechanics, printers, welders and upholsterers. A few years later the school moved to an old shoe factory on Wingate Street. Chet Spofford was the headmaster, and Thomas Garvey was the second in command. Both of these educated men and all the teacher tradesmen were committed to making a first-class tradesman out of any boy who came through the doors.

Mr. Garvey was a hard-boiled Irishman with a strong philosophy of education which he made clear to us the very first day. The School was run with military discipline. In Mr. Garvey's opening day speech he said, "I have a belief that if you put a rotten apple in with a barrel of good ones, the good one will begin to go bad." He paused. "If you are one of those rotten apples, you'll be thrown out of here so fast you'll forget that you were ever here."

The school operated 24 hours a day, teaching young men their trades during the day and teaching defense workers at night. The current trades when I attended were printing, upholstery, sheet metal, plumbing, electrical, and carpentry. Through the first three years, we rotated between a week in class and then a week in shop. The first year we were required to take a few weeks of each trade to be sure we could make a good choice about where we wanted to concentrate our efforts for the last three years.

I have very fond memories of all the teachers at that school. They helped guide me at an important time in my life. My relationship with my father was not going to serve me well out in the world. I did what my father ordered out of fear, but I followed instructions at the School out of respect. June of 1944 ended with me doing well in school, happy to be on the way to becoming a finish carpenter/cabinet maker. My Dad did not say too much, but I knew he was proud of me. I was going to become a tradesman and not a laborer. No pick and shovel for me.

PART II

DURING

Alcohol played a major role in my life.
This DURING section covers the middle 25 years when I was spiraling downward.

31
NEW FRIENDS

As often as possible, I found ways to avoid being at home. I was thirsty for friendly father-son relationships. Just a few feet from our new Primrose Street house lived Michael Sullivan, a retired Navy man, his wife and two daughters. Mickey, as he was called, became an important person to me during my high school years. He was often outside, puttering around fixing something, and he always had time to talk with me. I helped him make repairs around the house. He treated me like an equal, not a brainless kid. We had real two-way conversations. He listened to me and solicited my opinions. Mickey did not complain about the actions of others, and if someone did not like what he was doing or how he was doing it, he did not seem to care one bit. He was his own man, and he did not give a tinker's dam about what anyone thought about him. I liked that.

I met other friends in the new neighborhood. One of them was Ronnie Sylvester. He was a "State kid" and he lived with Mr. and Mrs. Caswell. They took care of about 10 kids who were wards of the State. The Caswell foster home was full of love and understanding, far more than where I lived.

I spent a lot of time at the Caswell's. I felt welcomed and a part of the family. The Caswells were renovating a big barn adjacent to the house to make room for more kids. All the Caswell kids pitched in with the renovations. One summer, I worked there, removing old walls, banging in nails, and putting up sheetrock. I felt useful and a part of a family.

Mrs. Caswell was a full-figured, heavy woman. At Thanksgiving, sitting at the head of the enormous rectangular table in the kitchen, she gave orders to about six or seven girls, all of them at work. She gave hands-on instructions to each girl, and they were peeling potatoes, cutting squash, and making stuffing, cranberry sauce, and several kinds of pies. All the girls were moving about the kitchen, and I marveled that none of the kids were "in the way." They were all part of the team, each playing a role in preparing the dinner.

In the living room, Mr. Caswell, a trailer truck driver for Wing's Express, sat reading the newspaper with kids crawling all over him, under his legs, and sitting on his lap. He tried in vain to read the paper after a 10-hour work day. Never did I hear him scowl or growl at the intrusive kids. I watched with astonishment at his loving acceptance of the kids, even with their sometimes troublesome behavior. I waited in vain for the kids to get whacked for bothering Mr. Caswell. After all, he, like my father, worked long hours and should have been left alone.

A short time after we moved to the new house on Primrose Street, I met Al McKinney. Al was a crusty old hermit who lived in an old brick farm house with a dilapidated barn. He came from somewhere in Maine, and he spoke with a down east twang. He was literally a dirty old man. He was hard of hearing, probably because of the dirt and wax built up in his ears over the years. In other words, he was disgusting to look at. I loved him.

Al was a genius in dealing with horses and their ailments. He kept his own horses in the barn and also boarded other peoples' horses. Al's house was full of collections of old harnesses, tools, saddles and tack articles. The grounds surrounding the complex were a junk yard of old wagons, hay rakes, horse-drawn farm machinery and clutter. Yet people came from miles around to have Al look at their lame horses and to leave their horses with Al for his magic cures.

I used to hang out at Al's barn. I worked for him, though not for pay. He taught me how to hitch up the single-horse wagon and drive it down to Snow's Brook. Three large wooden barrels sat in the back of the wagon. One of my jobs was to fill the barrels with water and haul them back to the barn for the horses.

One day when I told him about something someone said to me that I found hard to believe, Al said, "John, don't b'lieve northin' you he-ah, and only 'bout half of what you see."

One day I was cleaning out the stalls and started to remove a thick nest of spider webs, and he shouted, “Leave ‘em be!” On another day, a horse sustained a gash in its flank from a steel pin sticking out of a support timber and was bleeding profusely. I panicked and screamed for Al. He came to the barn, saw the situation and calmly walked over to the thick nest of spider webs. With a twisting motion, he thrust his hand into the middle of the webs, came away with an enormous swab of spider webs, and applied them to the wound. The bleeding stopped.

My parents could not keep me away from the old coot. I spent many happy hours riding horses that were boarded there as well as the horses he owned that needed exercise. I was one of a few boys he allowed to ride them.

Three times he took me to the horse auction in Brighton, a neighborhood in Boston. This was an all-day affair. We took the bus to the Haverhill depot, the train to Boston, and then the electric trolley to Brighton. The whole day had a carnival atmosphere, and I was thrilled to see the strange sights. The auction house was not just for horses-- there were all kinds of animals there. I ate hot dogs with the men, and watched the farriers shoeing horses. Men huddled together cutting deals. The auctioneer called out his sing-song chants, which I imagined everyone there understood except me.

Everyone knew Al. People came over to visit with him, asking him to look at horses in order to gain his advice before the auction. He would introduce me as his helper. I had one of the key people as my sponsor in this spectacular place. I was on top of the world.

One horse was “skitterish” and would not allow the farrier to shoe him. Al said he had tender feet, and they would have to use the twist. A man approached the horse with a T-shaped steel rod with a loop made of rope at the long end. He placed the loop around the horse’s nose and twisted the handle. I could see the rope hurt the horse, and I asked Al why they were being so cruel.

He explained that the horse became focused on his nose because it hurt so much, and then the farrier could nail on the shoes.

32
THE CHANNEL

The Little River begins in southern New Hampshire, a few miles north of Haverhill. The River is a small meandering stream which runs mostly north-south, emptying into the mighty Merrimac River. For several summers I was part of a small gang of kids from the Dustin Square area. We had our own swimming hole on the Little River, a place we called "The Channel." The Channel belonged to our gang. No adults or girls ever set foot in this area. This was a special place for us, *our* place, where the older guys ruled, and the younger guys kept out of their way.

When constructing the railroad which traversed the Little River flood plain, the builders relocated the River to the east a couple hundred feet. They dredged a new channel as a bypass, leaving a sandy berm on both banks. The new water course filled in a low section which became a swampy wetland, an excellent place for aquatic animals to live. We called this section "The Overflow."

To get to the Channel, we walked down Ringgold Street to its end, continued to the bottom of Big Hill, past the haunted house, and through the old flood plain. Between The Overflow and The Channel was a grassy section, and the first order of business was to lay down our towels there and take off all our clothes. Sometimes we sunned ourselves on the grass, or we searched for wild strawberries or blueberries, or we fished for perch, horn pout and pickerel, or we went for a swim, or explored the area around The Overflow.

Half a mile downstream from The Channel was a place we called "The Pipes," where an enormous utility pipe crossed the River, supported on concrete piers. Another gang hung around

The Pipes, mostly tough inner-city kids from the upper part of the Acre. We often challenged each other to monstrous mud fights. We would sneakily approach The Pipes by way of a trail on the edge of the River that ran through the scrub bushes and small trees. We made piles of river mud, reinforced with swamp grass. Then we naked kids from The Channel charged the naked kids from The Pipes. We threw these mud balls at each other until we were exhausted and ran out of mud piles. Our bodies were black with mud, and red splotchy bruises marked the spots where the mud hit hard on our bodies. Then we all went for a dip in the River, and if we were lucky, a passenger train would come by, and we mooned the passengers.

Upstream from The Channel was a place called "The Elms", but no regular gang hung around there. The two main attractions at The Elms were the fishing and a rope tied high in a big elm tree. We grabbed the rope, ran along the top of the River bank, let go, and zoomed out over the River, plunging into the water. I learned to swim in the Little River. The first time I flung myself off the rope into the water, I was forced to swim or sink. Many times we caught fish, brought them back to The Channel, and cleaned and cooked them over a small wood fire. Some of the adventuresome guys fished for bull frogs, tying a piece of red cloth on the hook, and casting into the lily pads. Then, wham! A bull frog jumped on the red cloth. We barbequed the frog legs for lunch.

My father told me to stay away from the Little River, but all my friends went every day, and so I joined them "on the sneak." The Little River provided us year-round good clean fun and encouraged my interest in nature. I collected bird nests, pasted twigs and leaves of trees and bushes in a notebook, and then identified them. Some of the guys trapped muskrats, and we hunted squirrels and rabbits with a .22 caliber rifle. At night, we scared the shit out of each other by seeing who had the guts to dash into the haunted house.

As I grew older and high school demanded more time, I gradually stopped going to The Channel. I could write chapters about all our adventures in and near The Channel, but the important point is that we had enough wonderful Magic Kingdom/Huckleberry Finn/Harry Potter adventures there to last a lifetime.

33
WASON-MACDONALD DAIRY

The wartime summer of 1945 was one of great scarcity of workers, and Dad got me a summer job at the Wason-MacDonald Dairy where he worked. I was not too happy to be working while my friends were going to the beach and playing. Nevertheless, I became a lumper, assigned to anyone at the Dairy who needed help. Most of the time I worked on a stake body truck as a helper. That truck brought milk and ice cream to the local summer camps.

My father's job included serving as route foreman and ice cream maker. As route foreman, he filled in for anyone out sick or on leave. If a milkman could not bring in any new customers, Dad went out with him on his route, and showed him how to increase sales. I was very proud that in the summer, my Dad was the person who made Wason-MacDonald's famous Wasmacco ice cream.

Dad had been working there for years. He worked seven days a week, and after seven weeks he had a few days off. One day I wound up working with my Dad on another guy's route whose name was Jim. I approached a lady's door with her milk order when she called out, "Come up Jim," thinking I was the regular milkman. As I rounded the hallway, I looked up, and there was a pretty lady in her revealing night gown. She seemed embarrassed, and I gave her the milk and beat a hasty retreat. I told my father what happened, and he made a remark out of the side of his mouth, "Sometimes ya' gotta' be yellow to turn it down." That's all he said, and we never discussed it further. It was not until years later that I realized that the lady was having sex with the milk man.

I worked all summer seven days a week and got paid for six days per week. The plan was to not draw attention to the fact that I was underage and could not legally work seven days a week. I worked seven weeks during that summer. When I went back to school, I received my seven days pay that had been withheld. My father saw to it that I opened a savings account at the Haverhill Five Cent Savings Bank, and I saved as much as possible.

One of my father's jobs at the Dairy was to drive a large van up through southern New Hampshire to pick up milk from small farmers who were too far from a railroad to get their milk to the Dairy. Dad usually left the Dairy at about 4 A.M. for the trip to New Hampshire. On several occasions he took me with him as a helper. After milking the cows, the farmers poured their milk into 40-quart metal jugs for storage and shipment. The jugs were stored overnight in milk sheds. Milk sheds were generally low-ceilinged, small buildings with stone foundations, built near a brook. The brook flowed freely in one end of the shed and out the other. Milk jugs were set on the foundation in the cold running waters of the brook.

The floor of the truck was about four feet off the road, and loaded jugs had to be slung up to the truck floor. The 40-quart metal jugs weighed about 100 pounds fully loaded. My Dad was not a big man, and I used to marvel at how he could grab the jugs by the two handles, swing the jug away from the truck, and then on the return swing, put his right knee against the jug, and with the added oomph from his knee, deposit the jug neatly in place on the truck floor. He did not ask me to sling the jugs into the truck. My job was to slide the jugs further into the truck body, make sure every jug had a tag identifying the appropriate farmer, and that the jugs were securely tied in place. Back at the dairy we unloaded the jugs and carefully weighed each farmer's milk. The tally was signed by both the tallyman and my father.

Those trips were a pleasure because I was working amicably with my father. Though he did not make allowances for the fact that I was only 15 years old, and I was afraid of him, he certainly taught me how to work hard, and that habit has served me well over the years.

34
1945

1945 was a tumultuous year. On April 12, 1945 Franklin D. Roosevelt died. At 15 years old, I had known only one president. Roosevelt had been the champion of the little guy. While everyone was singing, "Happy Days are Here Again," Roosevelt tackled the problem of bringing us out of the Great Depression. I worried about what would happen in his absence. Harry S. Truman, the vice-president, took over.

I learned from my father not to trust Republicans. Ours was a very strong, opinionated Democratic Party household. Of course, the only real voice was my father's, and the rest of us just agreed. Dad was a Local 25 Teamster, so we were also pro-labor and union. No one could deny that the Democrats, under the leadership of FDR, were getting the country on its feet after the Depression that had begun with the fall of Wall Street.

In 1945 the United States was firebombing cities in Germany and Japan, killing thousands of civilians on every raid. The incendiary bombs dropped on the City of Dresden, Germany were typical of the destruction. They were so effective that 150 mile-an-hour winds were created by the burning buildings, and thousands of people were incinerated.

When Harry Truman stepped into the presidency, the war was being lost by the Axis nations (Italy, Germany, and Japan). In April, 1945, Benito Mussolini, the dictator of Italy, was dethroned, murdered, and hung upside down outside a gas station in a small town in Italy. Hitler committed suicide in a bunker in Berlin in

April 1945. Victory in Europe was declared in May, and the world celebrated VE day.

Mr. Truman made it clear that he would not risk thousands of American soldiers' lives in an invasion of Japan, especially when the war was almost over. He asked the Japanese to surrender, and they refused. Without notice and without the Japanese knowing the terrible power of the atomic bomb, Truman ordered the first atomic bomb to be dropped on Hiroshima on August 6, 1945. Three days later he ordered a second atomic bomb to be dropped on Nagasaki. Then the Japanese surrendered. That day I was on the front porch of Mickey Sullivan's house talking about the wonderful VJ Day news. Sirens were blowing, horns honking, and fireworks exploding.

35
CLOPPITY-CLOP

The Clover Leaf Dairy horse knew the milk route around our neighborhood as well as the milkman. I can still hear the cloppity-clop, cloppity-clop as the horse's hard rubber shoes struck the pavement. At the same time his head bobbed up and down with each step. At the first stop, the milkman placed the appropriate number of quart bottles in his carrier, hopped out of the wagon, and walked to the front steps to drop off the milk. The horse continued along, walking to the next customer's house. There he waited for the milkman to return to the wagon to pick up the order for that customer.

All year round the milkman deposited our milk order on our front porch. In the wintertime, if we did not get to the milk in time, it froze. The expanded milk stuck up a couple of inches above the top of the round glass bottles, and we had to set them in a pan of warm water to thaw. Some dairies lent customers little insulated boxes for the front porch which would prevent the milk from freezing.

As a youngster I spent some time working around dairy barns. One of my jobs was to mix skimmed milk with ground meal to feed to the hogs. Skimmed milk was practically a waste product. No one would dream of drinking it. At home, my sisters and I were supposed to shake up the milk to distribute the cream evenly throughout the bottle. We caught hell if we were discovered, but we liked to pour off the cream for our cereal.

Who knew? Sixty years later and here we are actually *choosing* to drink skim milk.

36
RAGS

Abe Cohen was known as "The Junkman." He drove his horse and wagon through our neighborhood, letting people know he was there by calling out in a sing-song voice, "Ra-aags, Ra-aags." People made fun of Abe. He was a poorly dressed, old Jewish man who spoke with a thick Eastern European accent. He drove around town in his broken-down wagon pulled by a tired old sway-backed horse whose next stop looked like it might be the glue factory. Typically, Abe's transactions included paying a few cents for an old pot, copper wiring, a bundle of paper, rags, rusty pipes, or scrap iron.

I had never heard the words "prejudice" or "anti-Semitic." I just knew Abe took a lot of verbal abuse from insensitive people. He seemed to let it run off him as a duck sheds water. I saw Abe on the streets, but I never met him. It would seem reasonable for anyone reading this story to question why I included this short chapter about a man I really did not know.

At an early age I learned what it felt like to be an underdog, where it was OK for someone to insult me, or put me down, and I had to take it. Whenever I was present and someone made fun of Abe or tried to cheat him out of a fair price, I silently cringed and felt an angry burning in my belly. I hoped that someday Abe would stand up for himself, tell off the monsters, and return the insults.

As I grew to adulthood, I realized that Abe knew the deck was stacked against him. He experienced the verbal insults, but he chose not to respond. I now understand that Abe kept his "eyes on the prize." He did not get sidetracked by other peoples' ignorance. Abe had one goal in mind, and that was to pick up junk at the best price so he could turn a profit.

Abe never knew it, but he taught me to keep my eyes on the prize. Many times later in life, because of my own ego, I lost battles because I took insults personally and lost sight of "the prize." Later, I remembered Abe, and learned how to keep my "eyes on the prize" no matter what anyone said to throw me off balance. At the negotiating table, such tactics ceased to be effective, because I stopped taking verbal jabs personally. I like to think maybe Abe was chuckling to himself when some loudmouth insulted him, because he knew he was going to make a good living off their junk.

When the war came along, the story around town was that Abe made a fortune. He had a big junk yard full of items necessary for the war effort. Abe no longer went around picking up junk with an old wagon. People brought the junk to him. And rumor has it that Abe sent his son to Harvard to become a doctor.

In later years I was ready to adopt this pithy saying which apparently appeared on a sign in the Mayflower Coffee Shop in Chicago:

"As you wander through life, brother, whatever be your goal, keep your eye upon the donut, and not upon the hole."

37
THE WALNUT SQUARE HOBOS

My best buddies were a dozen good friends who grew up around Dustin Square. They were Ronnie Sylvester, Donald "Plunkett"

Wood, Raynor Nelson, Dick "Bunboy" Edmunds, Mike "Mickey" Shugrue, Emile "Jake" Langlois, Herbert "Herbie" Law; "Chugger" Durgin, "Jake" Leavitt; and Walter "Pee-Pee" Smith. I was John "Will" Willey.

The older guys hung out at Walnut Square, about a mile south of Dustin Square where we lived. Walnut Square consisted of the imposing grammar school building which overlooked the Walnut Square drug store, gas station, variety and grocery stores. The various gangs around the city all had names. The guys at Walnut Square decided to call themselves the Walnut Square Hobos.

We younger guys hung around in the drug store with the Walnut Square guys. Our goal was to mingle with the older guys, and someday become accepted. We listened to the older guys talk about driving around town, chasing girls, and drinking beer. We dreamed that someday we would be Walnut Square Hobos and become a part of this wonderful life. What finally allowed us to become part of the Walnut Square Hobos was that we agreed to chip in to buy handsome satin jackets like the other gangs in town wore. Each of our jackets had the owner's name or nickname on the front, and Walnut Square Hobos emblazoned across the back. We were hot stuff, no one you would want to mess with, that's for sure.

Most guys had nick names, and I remember a few. Nick names were created in a variety of ways, perhaps because of your last name, what you did well, embarrassing things that happened to you, certain body parts, etc. Donald's nickname was "Plunkett" because he could hit anything with a sling shot, Dick Edmund's name was "Bunboy" because he got pissed off one day, picked up a dried dog turd, and threw it at one of the guys. One day when we were waiting for Walter Smith to come out of his house, Walter was taking a bath, and we overheard his mother say, "Wash your pee-pee, Walter."

Ronnie Sylvester was a genius with engines and auto repair. He had an old 1929 stripped-down Whippet that he drove around in the field at the bottom of Big Hill. Ronnie was an expert driver. I was one happy kid when he taught me to drive around the field.

I met Mickey Shugrue at Haverhill Trade School. Michael (Mickey) Shugrue was a "street wise" guy from the Acre. I think what attracted me to him was that he would try anything and was afraid of nothing. I will never forget the day he showed up with a 1937 Dodge and asked me to drive him around the streets of Haverhill. I replied, "Mickey, I don't have a driver's license." His response, "Who gives a shit. Give it a try."

38
PICKING UP GIRLS

I was afraid of girls and yet at the same time wanted to have a girlfriend. The guys talked about how to approach a girl and how to "feel them up," and some guys had actually "done it." Mike had found an unhappy married woman who had a daughter. They invited the boys up to the house when the long-distance truck-driving husband was on the road. Apparently there was drinking and sex. I was so scared that I would sneak out and go home. I hated myself for being such a wimp, and would make excuses the next time I saw the guys as to why I had disappeared.

One night in August 1946 Mickey drove by in his Dodge and picked up Herbie, Jake, Bunboy, and me. We drove to Henderson's Cider Mill and bought a 50 cent gallon of hard cider. The plan was to go to the Pavilion at Angle Pond in Hampstead, New Hampshire, get drunk on the hard cider, and pick up some girls. I got drunk, got in a fight, and took a swing at Herbie. He ducked just in time, my fist hit a pine tree, and I broke my finger. Later I fell down a flight of stairs in the Pavilion, crashed into a stack of folding chairs, and ended up with multiple cuts and abrasions. To complete my romantic evening at Angle Pond, I threw up, and felt sick and dizzy. Mickey drove me home, and I snuck into bed.

The bed began to spin, and I intuitively knew to put one leg out on the floor to stop the bed from spinning.

I was 16 years old and thought I had found the magic elixir for life's problems. I escaped the "No" world directed by my father, and fled into the "Yes" world of drinking. I did not know at the time, but this evening started my 25-year run with alcohol. My drinking caused untold pain, misery, and losses for me and my family, and nearly cost me my life on several occasions.

39
THE CARPENTER

One summer, Mickey Shugrue approached me with the idea of doing some carpentry work for friends of his. We were going to build shelves for a local grocery store, put in a sky light and new front stairs for the store. Mickey would tackle any job; nothing was too much for him to try. The problem was getting the construction material.

My father was then working as a truck driver at D.D. Chase Lumber Co. He set up a charge account for us, as we were too young to open it ourselves. We could then charge for the lumber, and have it delivered. When we were paid, we could pay the lumber yard. We made good on our commitment to the customers, paid the lumber yard, bought some tools, and made a few bucks before going back to school.

Nothing is more important to a tradesman than his tools. On those small jobs with Mickey, I began to accumulate a basic carpenter's tool box. Unlike the throw-away society of today, in the 1940s a tradesman's tools were an investment for a lifetime. His tools would be passed on to the next generation, hopefully a son who would carry on the trade.

When we returned to school, I applied for an after-school job at Consentino's Furniture factory on River Street in Haverhill. The factory made inexpensive rock maple furniture for department stores. I usually worked on the gluing table where I glued and clamped the table tops together. Sometimes I worked on a joiner. I planed the edges of the table tops just before they were glued. The noise level was so high that we could not talk or shout loud enough to be heard, even if standing next to each other. Though the factory owner was a medical doctor, the concept of ear protection had not yet become routine.

In our senior year, as part of the trade school program, we designed and built a summer cottage in Seabrook, New Hampshire. One of our teachers paid for all the materials. What a wonderful experience! We built the whole house from scratch. The kids in other trades got a chance to practice their trades too. The house we built still stands today at Seabrook Beach. However, the School ran into problems with the construction unions which raised a ruckus about students taking union jobs. We never built another house.

May, 1948. Haverhill Trade School carpenters building the cottage at Seabrook, NH. Left to right: Al Paradis, John Willey, and Tom Clark

In the Charles W. Arnold Trade School, if you had a B average or better in your senior year, you were allowed to have an outside job, with the proviso that your job had to be in your trade, and you had to complete all history and English requirements. During the latter part of my senior year in 1948, I went to work for a building contractor from Plaistow, New Hampshire. I was still afraid to ask a girl for a date, and the contractor used to razz me about it. After I graduated, he finally got me to admit that I was really sweet on a beautiful young woman named Rita whom I had met at the graduation. My boss gave me all kinds of advice, "John, have you got into her pants yet?" My response was, "Of course not!" I was really angry with his lack of respect. He countered with, "If you don't nail her, someone else will." His comments caused me a lot of anxiety.

Being an apprentice, I was assigned the jobs that the older carpenters did not want. The first tool I was given was a short-handled shovel. My job was to hand-dig the footings for the lally columns which would support the building. Pretty soon I was allowed to install the bridging between joists, and other no-skill tasks as assigned. I acquired some more tools -- a hammer, two saws, a combination square, and an auger with two bits.

Sometimes I had to work with an old-school, grouchy carpenter who refused to talk to me. When he started to mark up a roof rafter for cutting, I went over to watch him so I could learn how to cut rafters. He turned his back and told me to mind my own business. With my first pay check I walked to Shoe City Hardware and bought a Stanley framing square. I read the instruction booklet, and when he was not around, I practiced cutting rafters. Over time he softened up a bit, and I learned to NEVER borrow a tool from him. I built my own tool box and prized every one of my tools. Each tool had my initials engraved on it. My tools were my life.

We built a house in Newton, New Hampshire. The people for whom we were building the house lived in a tiny house next to the new one. A young girl about my age lived there. When her family members went to work, she came outside and worked in the garden. My boss pointed out that the heavenly-endowed young cutie used to bend down a lot when I was around. He was sure she was sending me a message. He said in his New Hampshire farmer's twang, "Goddamit boy, thar's somethin' thair. What the hell are ye waitin' fer." I turned purple and ignored his advice and urging.

One day he had enough. After the young lady began her gardening wearing a halter and short shorts, he said, "John, take the Goddam pick-up downt that lumber yard and get 40 eight foot, two by four's." My reply was, "I don't have a driver's license." His urgent and terse reply was, "I don't give a shit. Take the truck and get the hell outter heer." When I returned, the boss seemed quite happy, with a half grin on his ugly kisser, busy at work laying out wall locations. I made quite a few trips in the pick-up after that, and lack of a license was never an issue.

40
DAD'S RAGE

I was confused about my father. One minute I hated him, and the next I would do anything I could to gain his approval. One minute he was yelling at me, and the next he opened an account for me at the lumber yard to help start up my new carpentry business. I hated the way he treated my mother, the names he called her, and the many times he hit Mom, my sisters and me.

He had a habit of folding his tongue and biting down on it when he went into a rage.

My mother used to stand rigidly with her hands at her side, performing a nervous ritual. She would simultaneously connect her little fingers to her thumbs on each hand, then the ring fingers, then the middle finger, then the index finger, reverse the process, and repeat and repeat until he quieted down.

41
THE LEATHER SHOP

In the summer of 1947 I had another chance to go to the beach with the guys, and get a shot at wine, women and song. I heard all the stories about getting laid, and who was "putting out." Dear old Dad came through again with a summer job at a leather shop on Washington Street in the center of the old shoe factory district. I felt really pissed off for missing out on all the fun, and relieved at the same time, because I was so scared to get close to the girls. At 17 years of age I did not have a girl friend and had never had a date.

The owner of the leather shop was fooling around with the foreman's sister. He did not have his eyes on the business. We learned that the owner was in financial trouble even though he was living high, wide, and handsome with his cute lady friend.

The leather shop was in the business of combining animal hides with cloth so the hide could be used to make shoes. We dealt mostly with cow hide, but sometimes snake and alligator skins. We ran the animal hides through a machine that applied glue to the underside. Then we plopped the hide onto a large piece of cloth, applied pressure to make sure the hide and the cloth were well bonded, trimmed the excess cloth from the hide, and tossed it into a pile where it would await shipment to another small shop nearby where the cutters would stamp out shoe parts from the hide.

Along about August we were told that we had to wait to be paid because the owner could not make payroll. By the time I went back to school I was owed four weeks' pay. I went back twice to collect my pay. On the second trip the owner said, "F--- off. I'm in bankruptcy, and you get shit."

I told my Dad. He went into rage mode, "I'll show that bastard." My Dad explained, "Bankruptcy or not, labor gets reimbursed 100 percent." Dad went to Lawrence, Massachusetts and reported the incident to the State Labor Inspector. A couple of weeks into my new school year I was visited by the Labor Inspector and asked to show up in court.

I will never forget the angry look on the former owner's face when he saw me in court. He was then working as a salesman, and he had been ordered by the judge to send a certain amount each week to the court. When he had paid the full amount I was owed, the court sent me a check. I was the only one who filed a labor claim. I felt proud that my Dad was in my corner.

42
MEETING RITA

Since I had a B average, I was able to work in my trade in the last half of my senior year. I worked for a contractor, building houses. At the end of the school year, I returned to school for final exams and to practice for the graduation ceremony. Those of us finishing Trade School would be granted two diplomas--one from the Trade School, and one from the High School. Students from both schools assembled in the High School auditorium. Each Trade School student was paired with a High School student. We were to march in pairs from the high school, down the hill to the Paramount Theatre where the graduation would take place.

My heart almost stopped when I saw my partner. Rita was tall, slender, and had a great figure. She was exotic-looking, with reddish brunette hair, a warm and genuine smile, and flashing dark eyes. Her vivaciousness was matched with her ability to engage in conversation. I was smitten upon the spot. I felt really comfortable being with her. She made me forget all about the fear I had of girls.

Rita Brugnani brought me to the highest feelings of euphoria, and ultimately brought me to the deepest depths of despair. But in 1948 it was heavenly. I could not have been happier. I was a tradesman, a carpenter apprentice with a contractor from Plaistow,

New Hampshire, learning to build houses. I was in love with a beautiful young woman.

1948: Haverhill High School Graduation.m The beginning of a lifetime relationship for Rita D. Brugnani and John F. Willey

1948: Haverhill High School Graduation. John F. Willey

However, my friend, Mike Shugrue, wanted to leave town and strike out on his own. He knew I wanted to get away from my father. He came to me with a proposition. We would move to Florida and work on a housing development. When I asked my father if I could go, he said, "No." Then I heard about the DEW line in Canada, a string of construction projects across northern Canada called Defense Early Warning. I again asked my father if I could go, and he said, "No." He never ventured a single word about why he did not want me to go. In December I visited with a recruiter to talk about joining the Navy. I brought the papers home, and my father signed them with no discussion.

Now I was on the horns of a dilemma. On the one hand, I had to leave Rita. On the other hand, I was going to escape my mean father. But Rita was the one for me. Rita was working in Boston, young and beautiful and full of life. I knew she was not about to sit at home while I roamed the seas.

1948: The Willey Family at 651 Primrose Street, Haverhill, MA
Left to right: Barbara, Dad, John, Mom, and Joan.
In front: Norma

43
BOOT CAMP

At 5:30 A.M. on 29 December 1948, I was one of the few passengers on the Boston & Maine train from Haverhill to Boston. I cannot remember how I got to the station. I must have walked as we did not own a car, and it was too early for the first bus. Upon arriving at North Station in Boston, I walked less than a mile to the Post Office which housed many federal agencies including the U.S. Navy induction center.

My first time away from home and family, I had no idea what to expect. I soon met John Molloy from Winthrop, Massachusetts, who became a lifelong friend. He was a cocky, skinny Irishman, and he knew his way around Boston. Our entire group of 20 young men walked together to South Station. We boarded the train for our 24-hour trip to Union Station in Chicago. There we boarded a grey Navy bus, which transported us to the Great Lakes Naval Training Center in Chicago. On the 30th of December, still in civilian clothes, we waited to begin our training. I remember one other new recruit telling us we would be Company 1 of 1949. We welcomed in the new year, sitting on the corners of our bunks in Camp Downes, listening to sirens blasting, and watching fireworks. As 1948 closed, I was free from the clutches of my angry father (or so I thought).

Among the new recruits, it was common knowledge that one should never volunteer for any assignment. As usual, I did not listen, but it turned out well. The first day we met Chief Petty Officer J.F. Burris, our company commander. From among the new recruits, he was forming up Company 1 of 1949. He asked if anyone had previous military training. One man raised his hand and said he had completed a hitch in the Army. Chief Burris replied, "You're the recruit ACPO" (Acting Chief Petty Officer).

Other deals unfolded. I saw some good assignments handed out. I told the Chief I was a carpenter on construction projects, and asked if there were any jobs for me. He said, "Report to the Battalion MAA office." What a deal! I was to sleep in the MAA (Master at Arms) office apart from the other recruits. Even though I was a recruit, I had a job as an all-around policeman and handy man. I wore an armband that said "MAA." I had to study the BJM (Blue Jacket Manual) and learn seamanship, and how to tie knots. But I did not have to attend the day-to-day basic training. For once, my mouth did not get me into trouble.

In January 1949 at Great Lakes, the temperatures were below zero. I was in a warm, woodworking shop, operating a lathe, turning out wooden fruit bowls for the Chief Master at Arms. I could look out the window and watch my company marching by in sub-freezing weather. I fixed broken windows, supervised some chow lines, and processed guys out of the company if they were sick or being sent to the "goon platoon." The "goon platoon" was where men who needed special attention were sent to improve their behavior and their attitude. If they did not make it through the goon platoon, they were thrown out of the Navy.

Before anyone was transferred, my job was to inspect his sea bags and remove any contraband like porn, girlie magazines, patent medicines, etc. That meant I had a full supply of all the things we were not supposed to have, especially cold medicines. When my buddy John Molloy got a bad cold in February, I saved him from getting sent to sick bay and therefore being lost from our Company 1 of 1949. I was Doctor Willey, and I nursed John Malloy back to health so he would not be sent to another company.

One night I heard a guy sniffling, crouched down by the battle lighting (a red lamp close to the floor providing subdued lighting for walking about at night). I asked him what was wrong, and he said he was homesick. I talked to him for a long time. He finally quieted down and he seemed glad that I talked to him. I thought about myself and realized that I joined the Navy to get away from my home, especially my father. I do not ever remember feeling homesick.

Rita and I kept in touch through letter-writing, but we had not made a commitment to each other. Some of the guys received "Dear John" letters that caused a lot of pain and suffering. Sometimes to help a man recover from the letter, we banded together and said worldly things like, "F--- 'em. There's plenty more where they came from."

One of our most prized Dear John letters was posted on the bulletin board,

Dear Mike:

You know how cold it gets here in northern Minnesota.

I have found someone else to keep me warm.

Your friend,

Alice

Since I had extra time the other recruits did not, I volunteered to be on the Station Drill Team. Drill practice was severe, but the reward was 6 hours liberty after each performance at sporting events and other functions off the base. While on liberty, I was attracted to the guys who liked to buy a couple of fifths of whiskey and get rip-roaring drunk. I loved the freedom being drunk gave me. No more rules. Do what I want to do, and go where I want to go. The few times I drank, from the age of 16 to Navy boot camp at 18, I always got drunk. We were fortunate on the few drunken liberties we had in Chicago to somehow get rounded up and back to the base on time and without trouble.

Until boot camp, I never realized how valuable my father's training had been. Here I was in boot camp in the frozen Great Lakes Training Center, and I managed to get myself a deal where I was given special treatment for the three months of intensive training. My father taught me how to work, how to take care of myself, and how to fit in with other people.

44
ON LEAVE

In March of 1949 I went home on leave to Haverhill. I caught up with some of the old gang and did some serious drinking. I was deeply in love with Rita, though I really had no idea how to handle our relationship. I just put one foot in front of the other and saw her as often as I could. I noticed she did not have a warm loving relationship with her Dad either.

I met Rita's fascinating family, many of whom were in show business. The whole family loved dance and opera. They spoke many languages and had traveled the world. They served exquisitely presented meals that took many hours to prepare. Uncle Eddie had been a violinist in the Metropolitan Opera. Uncle Walter spoke more than 10 languages and owned a foreign book store on Tremont Street in Boston. Rita's grandfather, Hector Brugnani, who had passed away before I was on the scene, was a chef for Napoleon the 3rd in France before coming to America and becoming the head chef at the Hotel Vendome in Boston.

They all lived in a 26-room house in Winthrop, Massachusetts which had been the summer home for the Otis elevator family. The house was directly across the street from the Winthrop Yacht Club, a place I frequented all too often in later years.

With the most beautiful woman imaginable, I had entered another world. I was feeling elated and insecure and out-of-place, all at the same time.

45
RADAR SCHOOL

After boot camp, in April 1949 I reported to the First Naval District Command at the Fargo Building in Boston. I was to attend Radar School for the next six months. I was not happy about being assigned to radar school, but it was close to Winthrop, and I was able to see Rita. I had asked the recruiter to put me in the Seabees (Naval Construction Battalion); however, with the ending of WWII, the Seabees were disbanding, and there were no billets available. Anyhow, I scored high in the aptitude test, and the Navy decided that I would be a good radarman.

Rita worked in the office of the United Shoe Machinery Cooperation on Federal Street in Boston. At first she commuted from Haverhill, but later moved in with her grandmother in Winthrop. My schedule included classes full-time, and sometimes night classes if I flunked a weekly exam. With trips to Winthrop to see Rita, there was not much time to drink with the boys.

One day while visiting Rita in her parents' house on Washington Street in Haverhill, our petting went beyond its normal course. We made love, each for the first time. On the train ride back to Boston, I was euphoric, my head spinning. I did not know how to handle my emotions.

With our six-month radar schooling completed, we were told we could have any assignment we wanted anyplace in the world! The list was tacked to the bulletin board in the passageway outside our main classroom. We all ran out to the bulletin board to view the list of about ten destroyers. "Shit" was what most of us said. Like Henry Ford said, "You can have any color you want so long as it's black." Selections were honored by the grade we received in the final examination. I selected and was given an assignment on the USS Hanson DDR 832. The Hanson was a radar picket ship. A picket ship was a converted destroyer, with the torpedo tubes removed and radar masts installed. I had heard that picket ships were the best. The truth is, none of us knew what we were talking about.

1949. The USS Hanson DDR 832 was named after marine aviator hero 1st Lt. Robert M. Hanson. He was awarded the Congressional Medal of Honor and the Navy Cross.

46
TRAINING TOUR

I was given travel vouchers and told to report to Red Bank, New Jersey to catch my ship which was docked at an ammunition pier. I arrived as ordered and looked down a half-mile long pier that seemed to have no end. Apparently years earlier an ammunition ship had exploded and caused extensive damage to a nearby town. This new pier had been built so long that if another ship exploded, the town would be safe. I looked down the full length of the pier. I did not see a destroyer, but I did spot an ammunition ship, the USS Oglethorpe. I reported to the quarter deck and turned in my orders so I would not be classified AWOL. I was directed to return to the foot of the pier and report to the Marine barracks where I stayed overnight. The next morning I was issued new orders and travel vouchers, and off I went to Newport, Rhode Island.

I finally caught up with the USS Hanson DDR 832, a radar picket ship in Destroyer Division 72, part of the 6th Fleet in Newport, Rhode Island. I arrived at 2100 hours and had to find my way to O Division in the dark. I climbed down two ladders into a black hole with "racks" stacked four deep in a space only seven feet high. When in the rack, if I rolled on my side, I hit the ass of the guy above me.

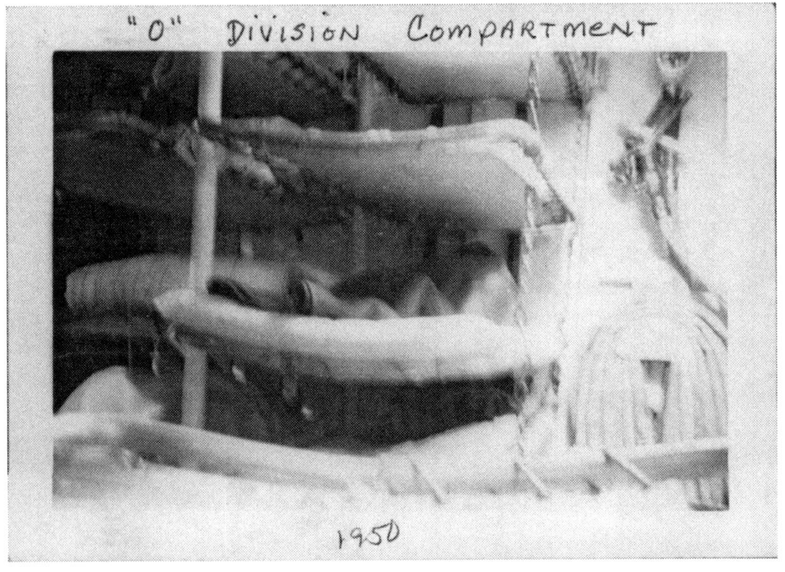

1950. Berthing compartment in the O Division on board the USS Hansen DDR 832. For three years, the middle bunk was mine.

Destroyers were dubbed "tin cans." I was proud to be called a tin can sailor. In addition to our regular jobs, many sailors had a Special Sea Detail. In addition to my radarman job, I was selected to be the Captain's talker. Located on the bridge, whenever we departed and returned to port, I had to stay within a few feet of the Captain, sending his commands by telephone to wherever they needed to go. We used sound-powered telephones between the bridge, fo'c'sle (forecastle, or the front of the ship), amidships, fantail, forward engine and fire room, aft engine and fire room, and emergency steering.

I told my shipmates that I never got seasick. I knew because I had gone out in a row boat a few times inside the Black Rocks at Plum Island. I wanted to impress the landlubbers from Kansas. However, being on the bridge about 30 feet above the surface on a fast moving destroyer plowing into the North Atlantic is not quite the same as a row boat in the harbor.

When we cleared the harbor, the Captain said "All Ahead Full. Clear the fo'c'sle."

The bow dug into a wave, and soon thereafter I began to feel queasy. The Boatswain mate piped "Secure Special Sea Detail," the signal that my duties were finished. I ripped off the phones, ran down the ladder, shot to the main deck, and puked over the side. In order to get to my bunk I had to go down another ladder, through the chow line where they were serving greasy sausages, then through the mess deck to another ladder to the O Division compartment. I reached the top of the second ladder and was overcome by the smell of the sausages. I shot back up the ladder and puked over the side again.

I finally acclimated to shipboard life, and I actually enjoyed the experience. In 1949 we headed to "Gitmo" (Guantanamo Bay, Cuba) for a few months of training and visiting ports in the Caribbean. Just prior to our arriving in Gitmo, a group of drunken sailors on liberty in Havana had urinated on a statue of a famous war hero. My dreams of the wild night life and voluptuous available women in Havana were not to be realized. All liberty was cancelled for the 6th Fleet until further notice.

We were confined to the base. At the enlisted men's club we drank gallons of Hatuey beer at the outdoor swimming pool. Highballs were 25 cents and beer was really cheap. I enjoyed the scene. This is why I joined the Navy--to escape my oppressive father and to have fun.

Kingston, Jamaica was where I experienced booze, fighting, sex, and trouble on a grand scale. Our ship was tied up to a pier close to town. On my first trip to a whore house, I was so frightened and drunk, they threw me out. A shipmate taunted me because I was scared. Here were these big black women coming on like gang busters, and McDaniels saying, "You ain't a man 'til you've split some black oak." The fight started with me swinging on McDaniels, and then the bouncer threw me out. Meanwhile there was another fight breaking out in the second floor when a beautiful Chinese prostitute showed up. Each guy thought he should go with the Chinese girl.

I returned to the ship very drunk. I saw a sailor passed out, being carried back wearing just his skivvies. One guy had a trumpet he had taken from a band in a bar, and he was making awful noises. Another sailor was wearing a pair of women's panties as a beret. The ship was sheer bedlam. The next day we talked about the fun, and we could not wait to go ashore again and repeat the process.

In Port-au-Prince, Haiti we anchored off shore. Liberty boats ferried sailors to the town dock. I heard drums in the distance, and the old timers talked about the voodoo rituals in the hills. I elected to stay on the ship. Small bum boats came alongside, with local people selling souvenirs and rum. They even secreted a whore in our ship's aft five-inch gun mount. I drank white rum, got very drunk, and never left the ship.

One of the bum boat guys sold a bottle of rum to my buddy, but it turned out to be sea water. We said, "We'll fix this bastard." We signaled him in again as though we knew nothing of his duplicity, and waved money indicating we wanted another couple of bottles. Every sailor on a destroyer is trained in fire fighting, and hoses were located along the main deck. We fitted a so-called suicide nozzle on the hose, a fitting that reduces the diameter of the water stream to less than an inch. The result is a focused stream of water that could knock a person down. We were standing on the fantail, about six feet above the water, very close to the bumboat. On a given signal, as my buddy was leaning over the rail to hand down the money, we opened up the hose, aiming at the boards on the bottom of the home-made boat. We blew the bottom out of his wooden boat. As the bum boat quickly disintegrated under his feet, the con artist jumped into the ocean. One of his buddies from another bum boat pulled him to safety.

47
OUT TO SEA

Our training tour was over. We headed north, back to our home port of Newport, Rhode Island. Within a short time, we left Newport to join other elements of the 6th fleet. We were among the 12 destroyers, a couple of heavy cruisers, aircraft carrier USS Midway, and auxiliary ships crossing the North Atlantic in early January, 1950. I was seasick for 11 days. In anticipation, I had stored crackers, fig Newton bars and candy in my locker to sustain me for the long trip across the North Atlantic. I threw up until there was no more to throw up.

As a radarman, I had to stand watch in CIC (Combat Information Center). CIC was a compartment with no lights except the glow given off by the radar screens, plexiglass plotting boards, and red night lights a foot off the deck. As a radar operator I watched the rotating sweep of the radar and identified any object that appeared. Before going on watch, the petty officer told me that he did not want any puking going on because that made others on watch get sick. I asked to be excused because I was so sick, and he refused. "Bring a bucket and Mennen's after shave" was his reply. The bucket was to puke into, and the after shave was to kill the smell. I stood my four-hour watches every day. I would go out on the gun deck and look out to sea only to see huge ocean waves breaking over the flight deck of the aircraft carrier. I was so sick I thought I was going to die, and then I became afraid I would not die. The good news was I was in good company -- there were quite a few other seasick puppies like me.

Finally as we were making our approach to Gibraltar, I stopped being seasick, and life was beautiful. Our ship was tied up, and liberty started at 1600. Off I went to drink beer and eat steamed shrimp while listening to Spanish guitar-playing and looking at the dark-eyed ladies. Much as I hate to admit it, I was still afraid of the women, and over the six-month cruise I drank instead. No moral convictions interfered with my fun. I was just plain scared, and that is what kept me away from the women. In my mind, I was thinking I should not cheat on Rita (even though the reality was that we never made a commitment to each other).

An old timer comforted me when we were getting ready to leave Gibraltar and head into the Mediterranean Sea. He said the Mediterranean was always calm, unlike the Atlantic. However, as soon as we cleared the Straits of Gibraltar, we ran into the worst storm in the Med for the past 50 years. Miraculously, after six months at sea, I began to "get my sea legs." I felt like a real sailor. I was never sea sick again.

In the Mediterranean we performed all the necessary drills for which warships are designed, including shore bombardment, gunnery practice, radar countermeasures, detection of approaching aircraft, anti submarine warfare, fire drills, plane guard for the aircraft carriers, and receiving stores, ammunition, and fuel while underway. We stopped at foreign ports including Libya, North Africa, several ports in Sicily, France, Greece, Turkey, Spain, and Italy. We had liberty in every port.

The scariest port was the eastern city of Alexandropoulos, Greece, very close to the border of Turkey and just below Bulgaria. We anchored off the beach since there was no harbor or a pier to tie up. To go on liberty, we simply beached the motor whale boats. I watched a train explode close to the center of town and elected to not go ashore. No one informed us that some sort of a civil war was going on. Yet, war or no war, all most sailors could think about was going ashore, getting drunk, and getting laid.

At the opposite extreme, we visited beautiful Italian cities including Pisa, Livorno, Trieste, and Taranto. We even took a special tour of Rome, the Vatican and St. Peter's cathedral. I again tried to begin my sexual experiences by visiting a high-class whore house. We approached the foyer and a winding marble stair case leading to the second floor. I looked up and saw three sophisticated, beautifully dressed, gorgeous women who looked like movie stars. I turned purple, left the scene, and experienced Chianti instead. I did manage to take lots of photographs and enjoyed visiting all the Italian cities, a wonderful opportunity to become worldlier.

We stopped at the Spanish Island of Majorca, and we were the first American warship to visit since WWII. The residents were friendly, the island was clean and the parks were well-cared for. The weather was sunny and clear. We received a warm welcome, and the visit was filled with wine, women, song, and excellent meals.

While in Trieste, Italy which is located practically in Yugoslavia (now Slovenia), I met a beautiful young woman at a dance held in a big hall on the pier where we were docked. She could not speak a word of English, but we had a great time together. Later I indicated that I was going to walk her home. She smiled, and off we went for a short walk. Soon she waved me back toward the ship. She was quite adamant about me leaving. Suddenly I found myself standing next to a guard box on the edge of the sidewalk, a soldier with a machine gun staring at me. I had crossed into Communist Yugoslavia with the beautiful young lady with the teal blue and black striped sweater. I tipped my white hat and bid a fast withdrawal. She left me with a knowing smile that said, "I would have liked you to walk me home, but you might get shot."

One day I was on the bridge watching the crew trying to march in formation on the adjacent pier. They were a disaster, totally out of alignment, and out of step, bumping into each other on turns. I heard the Captain say, "What the hell are we going to do with this rag-tag bunch." The Captain with a contingent of the crew had been invited to a very important Military Review at

Montebello Stadium. Also attending would be crack elements of the British Army, the Royal Marines, and the Black Watch. The Captain had ordered the First Lieutenant to select about 30 men and have them practice on the dock so that he could make his entrance without being embarrassed.

I said, "Captain, I was on the station drill team at Great Lakes." He replied, "Get below and report to the First Lieutenant and stay with them until they are squared away." I reported to the Lieutenant and told him I was the Drill Instructor assigned by the Captain. "Go to it." was his reply. First, I assigned each man to a position according to his height, went through a few simple commands, and I was feeling right at home as though I was back at Great Lakes. Attention! Dress right, dress! Forward march!

And I began the cadence call:

G I brush an' G I comb
G I wish my ass was home
Sound off. 1-2.
Sound off. 3-4.
Cadence count, 1-2-3-4
1-2. 3-4.

A miracle happened. They all began to move as one. We stayed out there practicing until they were ready for the big event. The day we marched into Montebello Stadium, the Captain was puffed up with pride as we marched in perfect formation and took our assigned seats. That's how, as a half-assed Drill Instructor, I got to attend the military review at Montebello Stadium in Trieste.

In its totality the Mediterranean cruise was a great experience, but I looked forward to going back to Newport and seeing Rita. In May 1950 as we were headed west to Newport, the Captain announced that our home port would soon be changed to San Diego, and we would be joining the 7th Fleet. We arrived in

Newport around the first of June 1950. I headed straight north to see my folks and spend as much time as possible with Rita.

48
OFF TO WAR

The North Koreans started shooting on 25 June 1950 while I was home on leave. Forces were working to assure I would get all the adventure I needed for a lifetime.

I stayed too long with Rita and arrived back in Newport about 15 hours AWOL (Absent Without Official Leave). I figured this would be OK because I was the Captain's talker at Special Sea Detail, and he knew me, and he would understand that I was with my sweetheart and could not leave. However, with the Korean War starting, we were on wartime status and missing a ship was a very serious offense. I had "gone over the hill." Consequently, I was nailed, and ordered to attend a Captain's Mast, a hearing by the Captain to handle disciplinary problems on board. I lost my 3rd class petty officer rating and was given 20 hours extra duty. What I did not know, was that we were scheduled to get underway the next day for the Panama Canal on our way to San Diego. If I had missed the ship, I would have received far stiffer punishment.

The trip through the Panama Canal was a once-in-a-lifetime experience. I stood in awe on the ship's deck, watching the lines of freighters, tankers, and warships making their way through the Canal, admiring the dense, steep jungle vegetation growing right down to the water's edge, and thinking of the hundreds of men who died building the Canal. After negotiating the locks, we traveled through Gatun Lake, an enormous man-made lake created by damming the Charges River. As soon as we docked in Balboa on the Pacific end of the Panama Canal, we topped off with fuel and immediately got underway for Hawaii. I said to no one in particular, "What happened to San Diego where our dependents are waiting?" None of my shipmates had had time to contact their families, and they were worried about their wives and families in San Diego who did not know where we were.

Our assignment was to escort the U.S. Marines to Pusan, Korea. We headed first to Honolulu. The trip was uneventful but full of activity. Everyone in CIC was scrambling around for charts for Hawaii and Korea. Where the hell is Korea? We stripped the ship of all the loose gear and brought on a full load of ammunition, food and fuel. We instituted war-time berthing, splitting up the men by their skill ratings to avoid losing all of one skill set in the event of a hit in a berthing compartment. Off we went to the mid Pacific to meet the marine troop ships. Everyone's mood was changed. I was frightened and excited at the same time.

While tying up at the pier in Honolulu, I looked down from the bridge and saw a whole company of additional sailors standing on the pier. They were the extra crew that would bring us to a wartime complement of over 300 sailors. I could not believe my eyes--I saw Tom Clark, a young man who was in my carpentry class at the Charles W. Arnold Trade School in Haverhill. Later when we had a chance, we talked about how excited we were about actually going to war.

By the time we landed the Marines at Pusan, the North Koreans had almost pushed our forces off the South Korean peninsula. The USS Hanson DDR 832 became part of Task Force 77. Our missions included shore bombardment, and seeking out enemy radars. Also, we performed plane guard duties for aircraft carriers during flight take-offs and landings, staying close to the carrier, so that if a plane ditched, we were on the spot, ready to rescue the pilot.

Sometimes we were detached from the Task Force and sent alone to a forward area to act as a beacon (bird dog) for the returning aircraft to direct them back to the aircraft carriers. When naval aviators took off, their "airport" was moving and could end up 100 miles away from where they took off. When returning from a strike, the pilots would head for our ship. With a coded radio beacon, we could direct them back to the Task Force.

We were part of the Inchon invasion which included over 300 war ships. We provided pre-invasion bombardment to clear the beaches, helping to land thousands of American troops behind enemy lines. The tides dropped 30 or 40 feet at each change, and currents were fierce, making our landing of the troops very difficult.

While operating off the coast of Korea, several ships were damaged or sunk after hitting floating mines. We always had extra lookouts on watch. As soon as we spotted a mine, our 40 MM gun crews would detonate it. Mines were hard to see because they were set to ride low in the water. Sometimes the North Koreans tied two mines together with several hundred feet of cable. When a ship ran into the cable, the mines swept down and smashed both sides of the ship. Floating mines were constantly on my mind when I hit the sack because my bunk was just below the water line in the bow section of the ship.

The Geneva Convention prohibited mines floating free on the open seas since they could drift into friendly shipping lanes and harm innocent non-combatants. However, the North Koreans did not follow any laws about anything. They put mines in fishing boats and loaded the boats with people who appeared to be refugees. Their plan was to use the so-called fishing boats to set mines adrift near our ships. On a couple of occasions we spotted what looked like a boat load of refugees. The captain ordered us to open fire with 40 mm guns. From the explosion, we knew the boats had been loaded with mines. I was 20 years old. I felt sick watching us blow to bits a boat full of 20 or 30 innocent people.

Our home port was Sasebo, Japan. We were there in 1950, only about 5 years after the Atomic Bomb was dropped not too far away. I went ashore once with a few guys to get drunk. Suntory whiskey and Nippon beer became my beverages of choice.

On Thanksgiving morning 1950, we left Sasebo at dawn and steamed off for Korea. We did not return to port until the middle of January 1951. Sundays at sea off the coast of Korea were replenishment days. We knew we would hear the bos'un's pipe call, "All hands working party. Muster on the starboard side."

We came close aboard to an ammunition ship and replenished our 5-inch casings and projectiles for our main batteries. We pulled alongside a provisions ship, and using a high-line transfer, brought on net-loads of frozen and canned foods. We lined up like the old fire brigades, passing from one man to the next man the projectiles, powder casings, and boxes of food, until they found their home in the lower decks.

The fleet oiler would be the last ship to visit us. We could "stand down" then, because this was a job for the deck crew. They rigged up the high line and connected the large diameter fuel lines to replenish our 196,000 gallon fuel tanks. Our ship had a range of 5,800 miles at 15 knots, but quite often we ran full speed to reach assignments on both the east and west coasts of Korea. We had to be topped off weekly. To connect the high line cable while the ships were making about 15 knots and running parallel courses, each ship had to contend with the bow wave of the other, mindful of maintaining proper slack for the steel cable that connected the two ships.

1950. Refueling at sea in the Mediterranean. At bottom, my ship, the radar picket ship USS Hanson DDR 832, is refueling from the USS Salamonie AO 26 (Tanker). The tanker is also refueling the USS Newport News CA 148 (Heavy Cruiser). At the same time, the cruiser is refueling the destroyer USS Powers DD 839.

1950. My ship, the USS Hanson DDR 832, at right, refueling from an aircraft carrier off the coast of Korea in the Sea of Japan

Every day we had General Quarters at dawn and at dusk. At 0530 the bos'un's pipe would sound its shrill, high-pitched, piercing call over the loud speakers located throughout the ship. "Now hear this. Dawn alert. All hands, man your battle stations. All hands, man your battle stations." Quite often a bos'un's mate would stand at your battle station with a stop watch. If you arrived a moment late, he would ream your ass, which means he hollered and yelled at you so fierce you were never late again.

At the end of 1950, the ship's office sent out a mini-report that documented all the ports we had visited during the year. The USS Hanson DDR 832 had spent 254 days at sea. I felt proud of those stats. I was finally a real deep-water, salty "Tin-Can" sailor.

49
WEDDING BELLS CHAPEL

In April of 1951 when we arrived back in San Diego, I was grateful to be all in one piece.

I had missed Rita and could not wait to use my 30-day leave to get home to see her. Rita and I had been sending love letters back and forth the whole time I had been in Korea. In my mind, I was committed to her. However, time flew by, my leave ended, and I found myself back in San Diego. I had not dared to pop the marriage question.

As soon as I returned to San Diego, I received a letter from Rita telling me that if we did not get married, "it was all over." I was frightened and surprised because we were not even engaged. Rita told me she had gone to the Arch Bishop of Boston and received special permission for her to marry a non-Catholic. I told her to come to San Diego, and she arrived in June of 1951.

Looking back on that time, I am appalled at our lack of maturity. We had no plans for the future. We knew I was going back to Korea for at least another year. I was making less than $100 a month. For a couple of months we rented a little shack from a Chinese immigrant some distance from downtown San Diego. I had to request permission from the ship's captain to get married. I was promptly met by the First Lieutenant and a Chaplin. Their job was to talk me out of the marriage.

Rita and I went to a local Catholic church, presented the priest with our plan, and asked him to set a time for the marriage ceremony. His reply in a thick Irish brogue was one I'll never forget, "I don't care about the Arch Bishop of Boston's permission. I'm not going to marry a Catholic woman to a non-Catholic, and that's that!"

We put Plan B into action. We were married at the Wedding Bells Chapel on 26 June 1951. Lead Petty Officer, Jack Sheridan, and his wife Lillian, acted as the best man and the maid of honor.

In less than two months I was standing on the port wing of the bridge complete with sound-powered telephones as the Captain's talker at Special Sea Detail. I waved a teary farewell to Rita who was standing on the dock. I had a lump in my throat as the Captain said, "Single up all lines," which was followed all too soon with, "Take in all lines." My response was, "Aye, aye, sir." Then I repeated the order to the proper stations, "Fo'c'sle, amidships, fantail. Bridge - take in all lines." Off we went on our journey across the Pacific for another tour in Korea. After two months ashore, we were on our way back to Korea.

My wife of less than a month drove back to Haverhill with Lillian Sheridan, whose final destination was New York City. Rita moved into an apartment in Haverhill, which my parents said was located in an unsavory section of the City. By September 1951, Rita had discovered she was pregnant. I worried about her being alone and pregnant.

50
BACK TO KOREA

This second trip to Korea was different. I knew how quickly life could be snuffed out. We lived with constant anxiety and fear. The Hanson's primary mission was shore bombardment, blowing up bridges, tunnels, trains, and gun emplacements on the Korean coast. Most nights we carried out H&I gunfire, meant to harass and interdict and create psychological havoc among the enemy troops. We shelled enemy front lines, firing at random times, on and off all night long. As radarman, I gave directions to our planes on where to drop napalm to wipe out whole villages or enemy troops. At sea, our own mine sweeper ships were being blown up. We continued to fire on wooden fishing vessels full of innocent people posing as refugees in need of food and water, while the vessels were actually laying mines in the ocean. Every time we did this, I was just as upset as I was the first time. I could not get these people out of my mind.

We rescued men from the battle at the Chosin Reservoir, referred to as "The Frozen Chosin." The temperatures plunged as low as 35 degrees below zero. Some of our soldiers and Marines froze to death there. Some of those we rescued removed their feet from their boots, but their toes remained frozen inside the boots. We had a special detail constantly chipping ice from the ship's superstructure to guard against being top heavy which could cause the ship to capsize in heavy seas.

As part of a detached unit from Task Force 77, the heavy cruiser Helena, the Battleship Missouri, and two destroyers, the USS Small and the USS Hanson, were sent on a gun strike in Hungnam harbor. The Missouri and the USS Small stayed a few miles offshore. The Missouri was lobbing 16-inch projectiles, weighing over a ton apiece, into targets 15 miles inland. The Helena and the Hanson were firing at targets close to the harbor, taking instructions from spotters on shore.

As evening approached, our gyro compass broke down, which meant we could not locate our targets and accurately direct our fire. Our sister ship, the USS Small, was ordered to take our position, and we were ordered to take its place escorting the Battleship Missouri. The Small steamed toward Hungnam Harbor to assume our position, and the Hanson steamed out to sea to rendezvous with the Battleship Missouri. Less than five minutes later, at 1801 hours on 7 October 1951, the USS Small hit a floating mine, blowing off its bow, over a third of the length of the ship. Nine men were killed; 51 were wounded.

Photo # 80-G-708456 Bow of USS Ernest G. Small breaking off, October 1951

The sister ship to my ship the USS Hanson DDR 832 was the USS Small DDR 838 (Above) was ordered to change stations with the USS Hanson on 7 October 1951 while engages in shore bombardment off the coast of Hungnam, North Korea.

Shortly after we changed stations the Small hit a mine that tore a 50 foot hole on her port side. Nine men were killed and 51 wounded. The bow tore off about 110 feet from the prow.

We could see the Small and were shaken to think that had we not changed stations the mine would have hit my ship.

All four photos of the USS Small DDR 838 taken from the web site of NavSource Naval History: Photographic History of the United States Navy. All four photos contributed by Joe Radigan

Photo # 80-G-708458 Bow of USS Ernest G. Small floats away after breaking off, 1951

The 110 foot long bow section finally broke loose on the trip back to Japan as the Small made the trip backing down all the way to Japan. The Bow section had to be sunk as it was a hazard to navigation.

All four photos of the USS Small DDR 838 taken from the web site of NavSource Naval History: Photographic History of the United States Navy. All four photos contributed by Joe Radigan

Photo # 80-G-708460 USS Ernest G. Small after losing her bow off Korea, 1951

The USS Small DDR 838 all engines astern heading back to Japan for temporary repairs. One third of the ship finally broke away due to rough seas on her way back to Japan.

All four photos of the USS Small DDR 838 taken from the web site of NavSource Naval History: Photographic History of the United States Navy. All four photos contributed by Joe Radigan

In November, 1951 at the Yokosuka Naval Base, Japan the Small received a false bow for the trip back to Los Angles for a permanent one. The Small was sent back to Korea with her new bow.

All four photos of the USS Small DDR 838 taken from the web site of NavSource Naval History: Photographic History of the United States Navy. All four photos contributed by Joe Radigan

I was really shaken. If it had not been for the faulty gyro compass, we would have taken the hit. My General Quarters station in CIC was right above the spot where the bow broke off. With her bow missing, the Small backed down all the way to Sasebo, Japan where she was outfitted with a false bow, returned to Long Beach, California, and fitted with a new bow. Within months she was back on duty in Korea with most of the original crew still on board.

One day we were steaming off the east coast of Korea in the Sea of Japan, with extra lookouts positioned all along the ship, watching with binoculars for floating mines. The port lookout was a young sailor from south of the Mason Dixon line. Suddenly we heard him scream, "There's a mine! There's a mine! There's a mother fucking mine!" The Captain was shocked to hear such landlubber language on board. He appropriately replied, "Where away?" expecting a proper Navy report, "Bridge! Port look-out. Mine portside. Close aboard, two points abaft the port bow." This kind of precise nautical terminology would have given the Captain immediate and exact information about where the mine was and what evasive action to take. But in response to "Where away?" the port lookout replied, "Over here! Over here!" Although I was terrified, it was all I could do to keep from laughing. The bos'un's' mate of the watch turned purple and threatened to throw the lookout off the bridge, calling him names I had never heard before. All's well that ends well. We located the mine, and the gunners mates blew it up with 40 MM deck guns.

Sometimes we received messages from Navy reconnaissance planes about a train heading either north or south along the coastal rail line. We would team up with the Helena, and head for a particularly long seaside tunnel, waiting until the supply train entered the tunnel. When the train had completely disappeared inside the tunnel, the heavy cruiser USS Helena CA-75 would blow up the northern portal, and we would blow up the southern portal, trapping the train inside. Out of nowhere thousands of laborers, called "coolies," came streaming down the slope to dig out the train. Then we called for carrier-based planes to come over and drop napalm at the top of the slope, causing this inferno to destroy every "coolie" on the slope.

On the way to R&R (Rest & Recreation) in Hong Kong, we spent a couple of weeks on the Formosa patrol between Quemoy Island and the northern tip of Formosa. The seas were unbelievably rough, with 30 foot waves coming in a north/south direction. We would head north for a certain time at about 6 knots, and then come about. For a short time, we were broadside, in the trough of the enormous waves. The inclinometer on the bridge rested on its pegs, indicating that we were close to capsizing every time we turned to head either north or south. I was terrified, but as the Captain's talker, I was expected to act like there was nothing wrong.

In these high seas, one afternoon a call came to the bridge from sonar, explaining that they had located a stationary vessel resting on the relatively shallow bottom of the Formosa Straits. We knew there were no submarines operating in that area, so we sent the exact location to the Navy headquarters in Washington for evaluation. Upon investigation and examination of the location, we were advised that we had discovered the remains of a very famous WWII submarine named the USS Tang SS-563. During WWII, while a Japanese fleet was heading through the Straits of Formosa, the submarine USS Tang sank an extraordinary number of Japanese naval ships. Upon firing its last torpedo, a malfunction caused the torpedo to circle around and come back to sink the USS Tang. The Captain of the boat was Commander Kane. He, along with several others, was rescued by the Japanese. They were severely beaten and shipped to a prisoner of war camp. Commander Kane survived and was returned to active duty after the war. He retired as an Admiral.

We reached Hong Kong and R&R. To a young sailor at sea in a war zone, R&R really meant B & B, Booze and Broads. I had developed a plan for dealing with life. I lubricated myself with as much booze as I could take. I did not get near the women, but had a lot of fun drinking and sight-seeing. Hong Kong was an experience I will never forget. We saw thousands of boat people close up in Hong Kong Harbor, living in rickety boats, most never setting foot on solid ground. With a shipmate, I made the trek across the harbor to Portuguese Macao which was actually in mainland China. We were drunk, and we nearly got on a wrong train which would have taken us on a trip to the interior of unfriendly Red China.

When our Hong Kong R & R tour was over, back we went to Korea for more shore bombardment assignments. As a radar picket ship, we also received detached duty assignments because of our additional ECM (Electronic Counter Measures) gear and extra radar and other surveillance equipment. We rendezvoused with members of the Army Rangers, who would come out to the ship in a little pumpkin seed-shaped boat that skimmed across the top of the water, powered by an outboard motor. These men lived by their wits behind the enemy front lines. They gave us information about targets that they gathered while working in enemy territory. Sometimes they gave us coordinates to targets that we bombarded at night, with them acting as spotters from the shore. Each time they visited, the first thing they did was to take a hot shower. Then we gave them 100-pound bags of rice, sugar and flour, so they could survive behind enemy lines.

At Christmas of 1951 we were in Sasebo, Japan. The ship's crew decided to give a Christmas party for kids living in a Catholic orphanage. Each of us was assigned as a big brother to a little boy, and we spent the day together on the ship. The children enjoyed a turkey dinner. We gave them presents, and watched a movie together. Each boy received the same gift, a little blue sailor suit with gold buttons, shoes, and socks. The clothes were purchased by the nuns, and paid for by each sailor. We felt really good about helping the children. They were especially excited about the ice cream and pumpkin pie.

During a conversation at the party, one of the nuns told us about the shortage of blankets for the orphans. One of my buddies asked her the name of the orphanage and where they were located, and explained that we could probably get a few blankets. The next day we went to the naval base with a requisition for a jeep to pick up supplies. We scouted around the base and found a warehouse that stored supplies for the Marine Corps. We stole two big boxes full of blankets, drove to the orphanage, and asked for the nun we had talked with earlier. We told her that we had explained her plight to the Captain, and that he had sent the blankets for her use. We were blessed many times for the stolen blankets. We made a hasty retreat back to the base, turned in the jeep, and hustled back to the ship.

In two days we were back on the bomb line providing shore bombardment for an army unit at the front lines. I was on watch in CIC, manning the tactical network, a voice radio between ships. On April 4, 1952, a radioman came into CIC and dropped a clip board at my desk. I picked up the clipboard and signed for the message. It was a telegram informing me I was the father of a baby boy. He and his mother were doing well in the Chelsea Naval Hospital in Chelsea, Massachusetts. I did not know what to do. I was on watch. I told everyone nearby and continued to stand my watch. Here I was 10,000 miles away from my wife and son, a scared 22-year old sailor in the Yellow Sea off the west coast of Korea. I could not call anyone, and I felt lonely and disassociated from the birth of my son. For many years after John's birthday, we wondered why I thought John's birthday was on the 4th of April when he was born in Chelsea, Massachusetts on the 3rd. Finally, I realized that I was in the eastern hemisphere (April 4) and John and Rita were in the western (April 3).

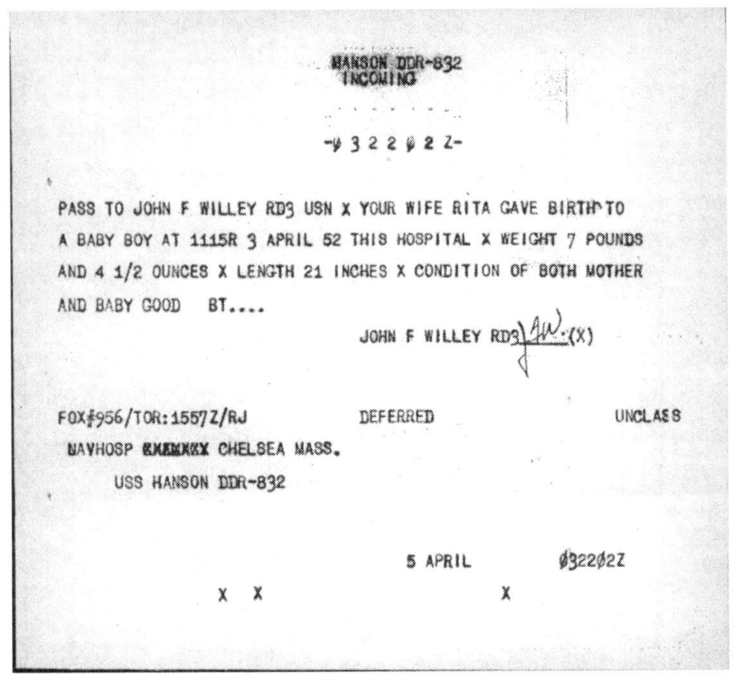

HANSON DDR-832
INCOMING

-Ø322Ø2Z-

PASS TO JOHN F WILLEY RD3 USN X YOUR WIFE RITA GAVE BIRTH TO
A BABY BOY AT 1115R 3 APRIL 52 THIS HOSPITAL X WEIGHT 7 POUNDS
AND 4 1/2 OUNCES X LENGTH 21 INCHES X CONDITION OF BOTH MOTHER
AND BABY GOOD BT....

JOHN F WILLEY RD3 (X)

FOX#956/TOR:1557Z/RJ DEFERRED UNCLASS

NAVHOSP XXXXXX CHELSEA MASS.

USS HANSON DDR-832

5 APRIL Ø322Ø2Z

X X X

3 April 1952: Copy of telegram announcing the arrival of John F. Willey Jr., received while I was on patrol in the Yellow Sea off the coast of Korea

Our second tour was supposed to end in May 1952, but luck seemed against us. Just as we were getting ready to go home, we were assigned to strike against onshore enemy gun installations in a new location. We expected trouble, because we were in range of the shore batteries. It was only a week until we were scheduled to leave, and all we could think of was, oh shit, here's where we get it. However, we emerged unscathed. We gave coordinates to aircraft carriers, and then our planes demolished the shore batteries. Our shore bombardment responsibilities were completed, and we left for Sasebo, Japan. Shortly thereafter, we headed back east across the Pacific for the fourth time since 1950. We were going home, and that was my last trip to the war zone.

51
SAN DIEGO SPLENECTOMY

Late in 1952, we arrived at our home port of San Diego. Because my enlistment of three years plus the one year extension by President Truman would end on December 28, 1952, I was assigned to shore patrol. In four years I made Radarman 2nd Class. I probably could have made Radarman 1st Class if I had not been AWOL back in Newport in 1949.

Rita and baby John were coming out to live in San Diego. At the Navy housing office, a southerner from Alabama assisted me with the housing application. The southerner gave me a house assignment in one of three eight-unit apartments laid out in a "U" shaped configuration. A Chief Petty Officer from Fall River, Massachusetts was in the office at the same time, and he was assigned to the same building.

The Chief and I drove to the assigned units. We discovered that we were the only two white families out of 24 units. We both vowed to settle in, and we got along fine with our black neighbors, though it was a culture shock to be the minority. Many nights Rita felt scared to be there alone, especially on weekends when lots of partying was going on and I was on the 11 P.M. to 7 A.M. shift at the Shore Patrol Headquarters. The Chief and I had a plan to make as many friends as possible while we were there, and we did that. This was a new experience for both families, but a successful one despite the efforts of our southern "friend."

One day I reported to sick bay because I twisted my ankle on a gantry crane track that ran along the pier. At the completion of his examination of my sprained ankle, the doctor asked me how long I had had a yellow cast in the whites of my eyes. I told him I had not noticed any color problem in my eyes, and that they always looked like that. Within a short time, I was admitted to the Naval Hospital in San Diego for a complete blood evaluation. I felt healthy as a horse, having no symptoms other than yellow eyes.

I imagined I might have contracted some dreadful Korean disease, and that I was going to die. After a week of blood tests and examinations, I learned that my spleen was enlarged to the size of a football, when it should have been about the configuration of a banana.

The medical terminology I was hearing began to sound familiar. I remembered Dr. Zelig back in Haverhill, and my father's splenectomy. I imagined I might be in trouble if the Navy found out I knew something had been wrong with me all along. I kept my mouth shut and let the doctors do their thing. I was not going to call my parents; I was in this alone.

After what seemed like dozens of blood tests, and conversations with numerous doctors, I was told to report to an operating room where doctors would take a sample of my bone marrow. Were they going to cut off a finger? How would they get access to the inside of my bones? My imagination was working overtime. Two tall Navy corpsman and two doctors were waiting in the operating room. I slipped onto the table. One of the doctors explained that this was going to hurt really bad for a few minutes. They placed an apparatus on my cheat that looked like a small drill press, including a handle to make the drill move downward, but with a very stout-looking needle protruding, aimed directly at my sternum. I do not recall getting any anesthesia.

The doctor explained that he would pull the lever which would allow the needle to puncture through the bone in my sternum. He explained, "When I pull out the plunger in the needle to draw out the marrow, you will feel excruciating pain. The corpsmen will hold you down." He did not exaggerate. When he began to draw out the plunger, I felt like a giant was ripping the ribs out of my chest.

A week later I was informed that several Navy doctors were meeting in the auditorium to examine me and discuss my health. When I arrived at the auditorium there were also several civilians from the famous blood laboratory at La Jolla, California. I was told to stand in front of this group while the chief Navy doctor described my symptoms and the results of the past weeks' tests. Later he asked me to lie down on the examining table. Each of the 15 doctors came up and prodded and probed the area under my left ribs where the spleen is located.

The diagnosis was spherocytosis. My red blood cells were shaped like spheres rather than oblongs, which made my blood structurally unsound and fragile. Rather than pumping through my spleen and becoming rejuvenated, the blood was breaking down and clogging in the spleen, causing its enlargement. The doctors decided that my spleen had to be removed (just as my father's had been 12 years earlier).

October 1953. John Jr. and me at the Navy Hospital, San Diego, CA before my splenectomy

In October they removed my spleen. The next three months were a horror show. Because the enormous spleen left such a large cavity after its removal, my intestines became entangled and blocked. The doctors installed a Miller-Abbot tube which was supposed to work its way through my intestines, but it failed. Emergency surgery was required. They opened me up again, removed my intestines, and placed them in a basin as the surgeon straightened them out and put them back into my body. A week later the incision had to be reopened again due to infection. They decided to leave the incision open. I was given a hot plate to keep next to my bunk. Using a pan of heated saline solution, pads of gauze, and a pair of forceps, I soaked the incision several times a day to cleanse the infection.

During this time I developed a fever and was feeling nauseous. They performed more blood tests and put me under close watch.

Late one evening a Navy doctor visited and reported that I had acute appendicitis and was going to be taken to the operating room immediately. What really bothered me was a visit from a Catholic Chaplin who said he was praying for me. I think I received last rites. The operation was a success, but the drama continued.

For over a month I bathed the splenectomy incision with a warm saline solution to fight the infection. I lost 21 pounds, down from 150 to 129 pounds.

In December 1952 I pleaded with a surgeon to sew up my 11-inch long incision. He agreed to do so on a Saturday, even though this interrupted his golf game. After three months in the hospital, I was moved to rehab and placed on a special diet designed to help me gain weight before being discharged.

I met a Corporal Wagner from the US Marines, and we became fast friends. He was close to certifiably crazy. He had been caught on a troop ship as a stowaway, trying to make his third trip to Korea. One night when I was out drinking with him, he told me the reason he stowed away on the troop ship. "Jesus, John. I love war." After a couple of close calls with him in barroom brawls, I realized I'd better avoid his company. With my incision still unhealed, one punch and I could be a dead duck. Anyhow, the people at the rehab found out I had been drinking, and I was confined to quarters until discharged.

In the middle of January 1953, I left the US Navy with an honorable discharge and a very freshly sewn-up incision. At my discharge meeting, the Navy representative told me that by legislation, my military obligation was eight years. I had completed four years of active duty. He explained that I could be called back into any service--the army, navy, marines, or wherever they needed me—unless I was committed to the Navy reserve. He told me that I could join either the Navy active reserve or the Navy inactive reserve which would guarantee that if called back, I would be in the Navy. I guessed the Korean War was going to be going on for a long time, and as a Navy man, I sure did not want to be an infantryman waging war on the ground. I chose the inactive reserve, which meant I would not be paid, but I had no obligations unless called up for duty.

Little did I know as I embarked upon the trip east that the Navy surgeon, Commander Miller, had insisted on sewing up my inner gut with wire sutures, which would soon provide me with a whole lot more health problems.

52
GOING HOME

Upon release from the Navy hospital, Rita and I planned to drive back to Winthrop, Massachusetts. First I had to get a driver's license. I found a 1940 Ford with a 1948 engine for $100. I scrambled around, studied the book, filled out the application, took the road test, and waited for the license to arrive in the mail. At 23 years old, I was granted my first drivers license. Rita and I packed the car, making a special space in the back seat for 11-month old John Jr.

We headed cross-country to Massachusetts, taking southern Route 80 to avoid the winter weather. We stopped in Americus, Georgia to visit an old shipmate, Ken Watson and his wife Joan. We also stopped at West 76th Street in New York City to visit Rita's Aunt Jackie and Uncle Ed Brugnani. We arrived at the Brugnani house on 105 Cottage Avenue, Winthrop, Massachusetts in the winter of 1953.

Our new marriage was rocky, and the trip home was full of stormy and emotional conversations. We had been married two years but had lived together only a few months, with lots of trauma built into that short time together.

I found a job at Raytheon in Waltham, Massachusetts as an inspector of cathode ray tubes. One day I noticed an itch where my incision was located. Later I could feel something sharp sticking through my tee shirt. Sure enough, two of the wire sutures had come loose and were sticking out through my side.

I remembered that in 1951 while on leave in Haverhill, my father had introduced me to John Sullivan, the Commander of a local VFW post. At his suggestion, I joined VFW Post No. 29 in Haverhill. I called John Sullivan and explained the situation. When John realized that the Navy had not afforded me a medical board review, he was furious. He told me that I should have received a medical discharge because of my physical condition. He asked me to give the VFW power of attorney to represent me regarding my medical condition, and I gladly signed the document.

Within a few weeks, Raytheon lost its government contract, and I was laid off. I was without a job, had a wife and a baby, and wires were sticking out of my side. I reported to the Veterans Hospital in Jamaica Plain, Massachusetts. Another surgery was performed to remove all the wire sutures placed there in 1952 by Commander Miller.

I was discharged and began a job search without any results. Rita and I discussed a plan where I would go back into the Navy on active reserve. In desperation, I went to the First Naval Headquarters at the Fargo Building in Boston and asked them how long it would take to reactivate me to active duty. The personnel officer replied that I could come in the next day, process the paper work, and start active duty immediately.

Upon arriving home that very day, Rita told me I had received a letter from the federal government. I opened the letter and learned that I had been designated 100 percent disabled, and a check retroactive to 19 January 1953 was enclosed. The VFW had come through. I will be forever grateful to the VFW and my Dad for his guidance.

53
THE BRUGNANI FAMILY

We lived in the Brugnani family home at 105 Cottage Avenue in Winthrop, Massachusetts. The 26-room house was beautifully located on a corner lot overlooking Winthrop Bay, with a panoramic view of historic Boston Harbor and the city skyline. Many of the Brugnani family members had been active in the musical and literary worlds. For a Haverhill meat-and-potato guy like me, this was a truly fascinating world. I was in love with Rita's family and the way they lived.

I never met Rita's grandfather, Hector. Apparently he emigrated from Italy to France where he had been a Chef for the family of Napoleon the III. Hector met his wife, Eugenia, when he was a chef in France. When they moved to Boston, Hector was the head chef at the prestigious Hotel Vendome. Hector spoke Italian, and Eugenia spoke French, and each had learned the other's language. Eugenia was known by the family as Nonna. She was the dominant grand dame, mother, and grandmother, and she presided over the Brugnani house.

Their son, Edward, had been sent abroad as a child to study violin. He returned as a young man, and became a well-known violinist with the Metropolitan Opera. He lived in New York City with his wife, Jackie, a lovely red-headed woman from the mid-west. Nonna did not hide the fact that she did not approve of Jackie, and Jackie was always unhappy in Nonna's presence.

Nonna had a live-in maid and cook named Celina Destugue, who came from France. She spent most of her days in the basement kitchen. She had a doughy face, with about three teeth, and hair that looked like it needed to be degreased. Her matronly dress always needed washing, as did the apron she wore over it. Her BO was earthy, plus she smelled of snuff and beer. She was a heavy woman with ample jowls and a permanent scowl. She was bent at the waist, walked with a limp, and looked like a character from a

Charles Dickens novel. I liked her because she confronted Nonna. Their arguments were legendary. I spent many an hour drinking beer with Celina in the ground-level kitchen where she performed culinary miracles on a regular basis. Nonna used the ground-level dining room for family dinners which were usually attended by fascinating family members and their guests.

Dinner guests often included a mysterious family friend, Madam Cassani, a woman of royal bearing; Walter Dumas, Rita's uncle, who spoke a dozen languages fluently; Rita's two brothers, Hector and Edward; her mother and father, and many others. Some spoke in German, and Nonna could carry on in either French or Italian. Most of the conversation centered on music, opera, and famous Broadway shows.

Having dinner with the Brugnanis was like being transported to an elegant villa in a European setting. We gathered upstairs and drank high balls and cocktails and had wonderful conversations. Then down we would go to the dining room, with Nonna at the head of the table as befits the grand dame. An oval-shaped Tiffany lamp hung over the table, which was large enough to seat a dozen people. The meal began with a large serving of delicious pasta. (At my first Brugnani dinner, I was in the process of filling my entire plate when Rita nudged me and informed that that this was just the first course.) The pasta was followed by a scrumptious leg of lamb, French style string beans, roasted potatoes, and glazed carrots, accompanied with warm crusty Italian bread purchased from the North End of Boston. Next we were served an elegant salad with white wine. Then we made selections from the cheese plate, served with small glasses of brandy. Dessert was Italian pastry including cannolis from the North End of Boston. By then we would be drinking Benedictine and Brandy, and I would be feeling like a king. Usually, these large dinners were ended abruptly when Nonna started to sing the French national anthem, La Marseillaise, the signal that we all recognized meant it was bed time for Nonna.

When I first met Rita I was excited to learn that there were some really talented musical people in her family. As a youngster growing up in the '30s and '40s, I loved to listen to the radio. I remember very well the famous Jewish American Tenor, Jan Peerce, and how he sang "The Bluebirds of Happiness." Later there followed the golden voice of Thomas L. Thomas, a Welsh baritone on the program called "The Voice of Firestone." How could I ever forget America's Sweetheart, the beautiful soprano, Jeannette MacDonald, and the baritone, Nelson Eddy. To this day when I hear an old movie and listen to them sing "Ah! Sweet Mystery of Life" or "Indian Love Call," I am transported. They were my introduction to opera.

For about 50 years Texaco sponsored "Live from the Met" every Saturday afternoon for the entire opera season. Rita's grandmother, Nonna, listened, and I joined her whenever I could. Nonna explained the story of each opera, and I really enjoyed those Saturday afternoons with her. She would translate the words so I could appreciate what was happening. Milton Cross was the voice of the Met, and he gave lectures about each opera. He also authored a book called "Great Operas," edited by Karl Kohrs. Rita's Uncle Eddy was a personal friend of Karl's. One evening I met Karl Kohrs when Eddy invited Karl and his wife for dinner. This was a new lifestyle for me, and I enjoyed every minute.

54
SEARS & ROEBUCK

It was early 1953, and I had a new outlook on life. I landed a job in the Display Department with Sears & Roebuck on Brookline Avenue in Boston. Sears offered good benefits and a career ladder in display and window decorating. I had the opportunity to use my creative abilities, and I liked the job.

However, I was having a tough time with my boss. One day I finished decorating a display case advertising women's stockings.

Within the case I had suspended a woman's leg wearing a sexy, black silk stocking. Encircled at the top of the leg was black lace. High on the thigh I placed a diamond necklace. The bottom of the case was covered with free-form shapes with black lace in between. I thought it looked pretty classy. Mr. Kiley, my boss, came by and made a sarcastic remark, "What the hell are you doing? This is Sears & Roebuck, not Tiffany's." Just then the store manager, Mr. Rodriguez, happened upon the scene and said; ""Now that's more like it. I hope to see more of this in my store." I swelled up with pride. Although I was right there standing at his side, Mr. Kiley replied, "That's what I'm here for, to bring up the standards of the store. I've been giving them instructions on how to make displays more classy."

I went ballistic, and I lost my temper. Mr. Rodriguez ordered me to report to his office. Once there I told him what had happened. He tried to calm me down, but to no avail. I quit the job, storming out of the store, thereby blowing an excellent career opportunity.

Kiley was ultimately fired. We learned that all the while he was behaving like a demanding monster toward me and the other employees he had been busy stealing merchandise from Sears.

55
THE G.I. BILL

It was Christmas 1953. I decided to take advantage of the G.I. bill and go back to school. Given my trade school education, first I had to take some accelerated courses to prepare for college. I enrolled at Newman Preparatory School on Marlborough Street in Boston's Back Bay. Named after Cardinal Newman (1801-1890), the school was founded in 1945 by a group of alumni from Boston College. The Jesuit teaching methods used by the lay teachers were very effective, and Newman had a good reputation.

I was carrying a heavy scholastic load because in six months I had to complete what was equivalent to two years of high school. First I studied Algebra I, Plane Geometry, English, and Physics. Then I moved onto Solid Geometry, Algebra II, Trigonometry, and Calculus. The school expected students to perform at least 25 hours of home study each week.

Again I was an absentee father and husband, only this time I was not available because of school. I also worked as a part-time bar tender at the Winthrop Yacht Club weekdays and weekends, and I was a roofer with Supreme Roofing in Winthrop on Saturdays. I retrieved my tools from my parents' home in Haverhill after returning from the Navy, and they proved useful when working with the roofing company. The boss discovered I could do carpentry, and many jobs required replacement of wood gutters or rotted cornices. I even branched out on my own to work little projects in Winthrop for a carpenter/contractor named Paul Facella. My tool box expanded.

During this time my drinking came to a screeching halt as I attended school full-time, crammed to meet the scholastic requirements, and worked two jobs. Then Rita informed me she was pregnant. I was broke and a full-time student. I was worried about the additional responsibility a new baby presented. On 23 November 1954, Patricia Ellen arrived, a beautiful baby girl.

One day the placement director at Newman Prep approached me excitedly, "John, we've made inquiries, and you are all set to go to MIT." My reaction was visceral. I shook my head, "No! No! No!" There was no way I was good enough to attend MIT. It was out of the question, and I adamantly refused to even consider trying. I enrolled at Wentworth Institute, which at the time was a top-rated two-year technical school. I started in the fall of 1954, using pretty much the same school and work style I had developed at Newman.

I attended Wentworth full time, arriving home late in the afternoon to study. Sometimes I studied until the wee hours of the morning, often falling asleep at the table. Even while working two jobs nights and on weekends, I was able to maintain a 3.3 average. I ran for class president but lost by a close margin. Usually the class president served as valedictorian. However, I was honored by being selected as class valedictorian that year.

Attaining an education from Wentworth Institute turned out to be one of the most important accomplishments of my life. No one else in my family had ever attended college. My father, who had only dared to hope I could get a trade school education, was extremely proud and pleased. I remember how upset I was at President Harry S. Truman for extending my enlistment an extra year and sending me to Korea. However, now I look back and thank good old Harry for making the GI Bill available for millions of veterans to attend college and for giving me a chance I would not have had otherwise.

56
TRAVELING MAN

At the time, one of the premier engineering companies in the world was Stone & Webster. When they offered me a job, I was really excited and brought the good news home to Rita. When Rita found out I would be assigned to a power plant project in the Po River Valley in Italy, she was very unhappy. We scrapped that idea. Stone & Webster had a training program that would have afforded me an opportunity to earn a Master's Degree, and turning down this job was a terrible disappointment for me.

In retrospect I can see why Rita would not consider the move. She would face more of the same behavior--husband John not at home. We did not have the skills to communicate or negotiate. We did not know how to discuss reasonable career options for me to explore. I did not realize at the time that Rita was very much a part of my quest to acquire an education, and any victory I achieved was partly hers.

I finally settled on working for Factory Mutual Engineering Division in Norwood, Massachusetts as a fire insurance surveyor. I was really pleased at the starting salary of $75.00 per week or $3,900 per year. I went to Luby Chevrolet in Boston and bought a new 1955 Chevrolet for my daily travels to Norwood, Massachusetts.

My choice of Factory Mutual was unsound. Factory Mutual was a destination for engineers looking for a stable company for a lifetime career. I found the job appealing because I was unsupervised on the road and could drink the way I wanted. I had no drive to "be" anything in particular.

The policy at Factory Mutual was to assign new surveyors to close-by assignments until they became more proficient, and then gradually send them further afield across the United States and Canada. When I first went on the road, I was assigned to a wire manufacturing plant in Pownal, Vermont, which borders on the state lines of Massachusetts and New York. I arrived in Vermont at a motel the night before I was to begin work. I found a road house just over the State line in New York. Returning to the motel at three in the morning, driving drunk on the curvy mountainous roads, I sideswiped a guard rail at the edge of a steep ravine. Luckily I managed to get the car under control. When I removed my new charcoal grey suit coat jacket from the back seat, I noticed burn holes from my cigarette and thought nothing about it.

I was moving further and further away from my marriage and my responsibility as a husband and a father. I was on the road examining factories for two or three weeks at a stretch. I resumed my drinking habit and learned to live alone and be self sufficient.

On an assignment in Pennsylvania, I drove 13 hours to Latrobe, checked into the hotel and went out to drink. It was St. Patrick's Day. I found a VFW and was a celebrity because they saw me as an Irishman from Boston. I had my VFW membership card showing that I was from Post No. 29, one of the oldest in the country. That really clinched the deal; they bought me the drinks. I got so drunk that I do not remember going back to my hotel. When I awoke to get ready for work the next morning I remembered I had two bottles of the famous Rolling Rock beer "bottled on the banks of the Monongahela River" sitting on my bed side table. Thank God for my foresight, as I really needed them to start my day.

As a traveling man, I updated fire protection plans for fertilizer plants, steel mills, coal mines, slaughter houses, dye works and all kinds of other nasty places. The exciting places I traveled included Zion, Illinois, where much to my consternation I awoke on a Saturday morning to discover that Zion was a dry town, and I had to spend the weekend there. I visited places like Janesville, Wisconsin; Sandusky, Ohio; Americus, Georgia; and Altoona, Pennsylvania.

57
HEAVY CONSTRUCTION

I could see that I was heading for trouble with this Factory Mutual nationwide never-at-home job, but I hated the idea of sitting in the home office. After one year, I quit to find a job in the construction industry. In 1957 I started working for Thompson & Lichtner in Brookline, Massachusetts, with the same mind set as I had when I went to work for Factory Mutual: I needed to be "in the field." I wanted no structure, and I wanted excitement.

Thompson & Lichter was a construction management company, and I hired on as a field inspector of cement and bituminous concrete plants where hot-top paving was made. I expanded my expertise to cover inspections at cast-iron pipe foundries and structural steel fabrication plants. I also carried out field inspection of all phases of construction projects.

Now I lived full-time at home with Rita and the kids, but I moved around each day on different construction jobs. I had no structure, no office bullshit, and I was free to be me. Consequently,

I fell in with a heavy drinking crowd. I had car accidents and barroom brawls, and lots of fights at home with Rita.

I would be half drunk while working on structural jobs 200 feet above the street level, carrying a torque wrench to check bolted connections. When I was an inspector on the midnight shift for the construction of the Prudential Tower in Boston, the construction site was all action, just the way I liked it, with cranes swinging overhead, muck a foot deep, and drill rigs boring caissons. At the construction site for the Globe newspaper building, I stood on the rims of 18-inch mud buckets and rode down 80 feet below ground in order to inspect the bottoms of 30-inch caissons to be sure the ground was solid and ready to receive concrete. I loved the thrill of being in a dangerous place, and I felt justified in drinking with the sand hogs or iron workers because we had just been in a dangerous work place together. I loved the "I don't give a shit" attitude. I floated through life on a river of beer and whiskey, letting come what may.

Sometimes in a moment of reflection I would talk to myself. "John, what is this irresponsible behavior all about? What about your wife and kids?" I was sincerely perplexed, but to be honest, I was not thinking. All I knew was that booze was my friend, and I could not live without it. My attitude was -- I don't care, and don't tell me what to do.

I developed a varied and well-rounded resumé by teaching myself whatever I needed to learn. Each time I was sent on a new assignment, I studied the job specifications and the engineering principles involved, and asked question of the old-timers about the specific operation to which I had been assigned. I was always well-prepared and knowledgeable. This philosophy served me well. Construction is a seasonal business, but I never suffered a lay-off in the winter. Because I had acquired so many skills, I could be moved to some other aspect of construction, such as inspection of the manufacturing of cast iron water pipes, or inspection of the fabrication of structural steel elements, or giving new workers welding tests.

Because of my drinking, I was numb to the world around me. I made sure there was food on the table and the bills were paid, but being a husband or parent was not a priority. However, in February 1960, Rita informed me that she was pregnant with our third child. Barbara Jean, a beautiful baby girl with jet black hair, arrived on 25 October 1960. By then Rita was fed up with me, and I cannot remember too many good times.

58
CHARLES RIVER PARK APARTMENTS

I liked to work with the geotechnical engineers, solving problems associated with construction of foundations. I took adult education night courses at Harvard to learn about the basics of geology, petrography, and soils mechanics.

I spent a week or so working in the West End of Boston at the Charles River Park apartment construction project. The entire West End was being demolished to make way for Urban Renewal. The area looked like a desolated no-man's land with nothing but razed buildings, piles of construction timbers, and idle excavation equipment. The ground was Boston blue clay, which when wet, turned into one to two feet of mud and muck, and pulled at our boots as we walked around the site. On the night shift, we had to be careful because rats were running loose, having been dislodged from the demolished buildings.

Foundations for some large buildings are supported by driving hundreds of piles into the ground and then building a concrete cap on top of the piles. To test the strength of the piles, we drove a pile into the ground and then applied incremental loads to the pile to see how much weight it could take and to assure that the geotechnical engineers' design calculations were correct. I was a site engineer in charge of load testing, and I shared a small field office trailer with a union man. The union guy operated the hydraulic jack in order to apply prescribed loads according to my direction. I observed the testing and recorded the pile settlement.

Frequenting the local bars and restaurants on the fringe of the demolition area, I heard many horror stories about people who had been unceremoniously kicked out of their homes. People were comparing the Boston Housing Authority's tactics to those of the dreaded Robert Moses of New York City who demolished thousands of homes to make way for his road and bridge-building programs. I noticed a little three-story brick building standing all alone among the demolished buildings. Upon inquiry, I learned that an elderly woman lived there and refused to leave even after the eviction notice.

I had completed the load test and was now overseeing the driving of the 13-inch pipe piles. Everything was moving along routinely, until late one afternoon, I heard a huge commotion on the edge of the site, complete with police cars, newspaper photographers, and television trucks. Sherriff Fitzgerald and two goons carried out the elderly woman sitting in her kitchen chair. Before noon the next day, the house was gone. A home and a lifetime of memories, and all the old lady warranted was a few seconds of time on the 5 o'clock news.

This scene was a common occurrence in the heady days of urban renewal and the interstate highway construction program. The elderly woman being carried away in her chair left an indelible imprint in my mind, and in later years caused me to make a major change in my career.

59
WENT OUT TO HAVE A FEW

I was a consultant engineer working on a pile driving job in Clinton, Massachusetts with Franki Foundations. The more difficult the site, the better I liked it. The project in Clinton turned out to be a tough one with lots of technical problems to overcome.

When we finished the job, I went out to "have a few" at O'Hara's Pub with a laborer named Jim Crowley. I felt comfortable in Clinton, because much like Haverhill, there was a section of town called "The Acre," home to the Irish Immigrants. While playing cards in O'Hara's, I provoked a fight, and Crowley flattened a guy. We ran for our lives, jumped into my car, and drove off, sideswiping several cars along the way. Within several minutes, I crashed my Chevy into a statue on the lawn of a Catholic Convent. Crowley crawled out of the car and told me he had been arrested the previous week for putting a guy in the hospital after a drunken brawl. He said, "John, you do not want to be caught with me," and he escaped before the cops arrived. I was pinned in the car. When the police arrived, they extricated me from the car and drove me to the local hospital.

Two days later, two cops showed up at the hospital. They seemed like nice guys, and I thought they were going to take me to my car so I could assess the damage before getting a ride home. They drove me to a junk yard so I could see my car was a total wreck. One cop looked at me with disgust and said, "You're lucky to be alive. Now get back in the cruiser." They took me to the Clinton jail and locked me up. I made the allowed one phone call to ask one of my drinking buddies at the Winthrop Yacht Club to come and take me home.

I remember walking into the kitchen and whimpering to Rita about how I would never drink again, and how sorry I was, and how things would be different from then on. That's the day when I learned the opposite of love was not hate but rather "indifference." Rita looked at me and said, "John, I don't care if you drink. I don't care if you don't drink. I don't care if you come home, or if you don't come home. I'll take care of the house and the kids, and you do whatever you want." It was over. I had killed whatever love there was or could have been. That was the loneliest I have ever felt. An enormous hole in me could not be filled, no matter how much booze I consumed.

Subsequently I hired a politically-connected lawyer to help me with the car crash problems, and we plea-bargained "no lo contendere," neither guilty nor not guilty. The plea was accepted by the court, and I thought I was off scot free.

60
LOSING IT

Rita and I were still together in spite of our feelings or lack of feeling for each other. We lived under great stress and had horrible fights. My drinking continued, and Rita's indifference continued.

In 1959 my youngest sister, Norma, was married to a wonderful man named Arnold Horsch, who came from a well-established and respected local family. His dad, a former Haverhill High football star, owned Horsch Aluminum, a window and door company. Arnold worked there all his life, first as a salesman, and later as the owner.

Arnold and Norma invited us to Thanksgiving dinner at their apartment on 17th Avenue in Haverhill. My father and mother and sisters were also invited to share this festive occasion as a family in their new apartment.

My relationship with my father was at an all-time low. I expected some trouble with him, but I was determined to make every effort to be pleasant, especially for Norma's first big social event in her relatively new marriage.

My father could never be cordial during any holiday family event, and this day was no exception. He started to find fault with people, places and things. His negativity was causing a pall to settle over the table. The Thanksgiving scene in the movie *Scent of a Woman*, where Al Pacino is an obnoxious, argumentative, fault-finding, nasty bastard, was way upstaged many years earlier at Norma's beautifully decorated dining room table that Thanksgiving.

I leaned over to Rita and whispered, "If that sonovabitch starts picking on me, I'm gonna cold cock the prick right where he sits." Sure enough he started to pick on my sister Barbara. My mother commenced her nervous ritual that we all knew so well. She alternately placed her little finger against the fleshy part of her thumb, then the ring finger, the middle finger and the index finger, and then reversed the process, all the while wearing a frightened worried look on her otherwise peaceful face. Sometimes she did this with both hands simultaneously. My sister, Barbara, was taking his abuse, and no one was speaking up for her.

I erupted like a man shot from a cannon, flew over the corner of the table, and grabbed him by the throat. His chair tipped over, and he landed on his back with me on top. I had my left hand on his throat, and my right hand cocked back, ready to deliver a smashing blow to his mouth. Thankfully, I realized what I had done. I let go, packed up my family, and left the scene. My biggest regret is that I subjected Rita to this terrible state of affairs and brought our children into an environment of disrespect, drunkenness, and conflict.

I told Rita that I would try to stay in the marriage and correct my behavior. I will never forget Uncle Eddy's talk with me. He was astonished at my wild reaction to Rita's indifference. Uncle Eddy was brought up in Paris, and had another view of life. He was really puzzled that I would consider making payments to a former wife when we could just kiss and make up and go forward. In Eddy's world, an unhappy marriage was no big deal.

Rita insisted that I visit our family physician to see about getting "help." Doctor Traunstein recommended I see a psychiatrist in Lynn by the name of Doctor Maletz. I was drinking heavily, and each time I visited Dr. Maletz, I became angrier with him. After all, I was a good guy and deserved to have a few drinks. I was not hurting anyone but myself. Dr. Maletz, nor anyone else, could force me to look at my part in this horrid drama.

61
MASSACHUSETTS DEPARTMENT OF PUBLIC WORKS

My days at Thompson & Lichtner were drawing to a close for the same reason they drew to a close at Factory Mutual. I decided the job was causing my problem with booze, and I would be okay if I worked in a better environment with more decent people.

I had taken an open exam to join the Massachusetts Department of Public Works as a Junior Civil Engineer. My pay at T&L had risen to $4,600 per year, but the State engineer pay, civil service benefits and pension looked better.

In February, 1961 I started work in Danvers at the Massachusetts Department of Public Works. I was assigned to the Projects Office, designing roadways. I worked at the Department for 21 years, until 1982. I enjoyed the work, and studied hard to meet the requirements of each more demanding position. The 21 years were split close to 50/50 between engineering design/ construction and what was then a new field called environmental engineering.

As a soils engineer in the mid 1960s, I was working on I-495 in Methuen, Massachusetts. An incident occurred that triggered my memory of the elderly woman forcibly carried out of her home at the Charles River Park project in the West End of Boston. The section of I-495 construction I was working as a soils engineer cut through a well-established farm. This highway was going to take all the fields, but leave the barn and homestead. The Resident Engineer stalled clearing the land until mid November so the 80-year old farmer and his field hands could harvest all the late vegetables.

The farmer and his wife and 60-year old son had owned and operated the farm all their lives, and they were heart-broken about the loss of their precious farm. One of our right-of-way people said, "What the hell's he worrying about. We're going to pay him fair market value for his land." I wanted to wring the guy's neck. I explained that the farm was their life and livelihood, and that in a matter of hours they would witness the destruction of three generations of their family's work.

On the day the earth moving machines showed up, I was on site to check the soils after the scrapers had removed the top layers of earth. The 80-year old farmer, his wife, and the 60-year old son stood there watching the scrapers wipe out their fields in just a couple of hours. They had tears in their eyes, and I left before anyone could see the tears in my eyes. The following morning an article appeared in the local paper, covering a story about the 60-year old son who had committed suicide later that day. That, coupled with the elderly woman in Boston, was etched deeply in my mind.

62
MAKING MONEY WHILE YOU SLEEP

While working in the Project Office in Danvers, I met a quiet-spoken, likeable man named Louie Wax. Louie was transplanted from somewhere in New York City to Beverly, Massachusetts. Like me, he was fairly new to the Department. Louie was totally focused on making money through his investments. He was slight of build, and looked the part of a clerk at an accounting house in a Dickens novel. All that was missing was a high stool, spectacles, green visor, and sleeve protectors.

We were as different as day and night, yet I gravitated to Louie, because he fascinated me with his talk about investing in the stock market. He was focused on his goal of investing, and he never bothered me by mentioning my drinking. The idea of investing really resonated with me. "John" he would begin, "If you invest a small amount in Dreyfus on a regular basis, you could be a millionaire by the time you retire." He explained dollar cost averaging, which meant regularly putting away a certain amount of money no matter what.

I often think about Louie because he started me on the road to investing. Louie used to say, "John, you should be making money while you sleep instead of always working for money." He reminded me that money never sleeps. I chuckle now when I think about the very similar words that Warren Buffet uttered as he became the richest man in the world.

63
DAVE WILLIAMS

The Department of Public Works offered me a much envied position with the Real Estate Division. I was really excited, ready and willing to report for duty the week following my acceptance. A few days before I was to report to my new position, I received a notice from the Massachusetts Registry of Motor Vehicles instructing me to turn in my driver's license because of the drunken crash I caused two years previous that I thought was "taken care of." Now I really had an excuse to feel sorry for myself, so I increased my drinking. "They screwed me," I thought. Not for an instant did I say, "I screwed me." It was always, "They."

A driver's license was a requirement for this statewide job. Without a license, I was reassigned to a construction job in Lynnfield, Massachusetts. Dave Williams, another engineer who lived in Winthrop, agreed to drive me to and from work. I knew nothing of him or his history, only that he was willing to give me a ride to and from work. On a cold January morning in 1962, I was standing at Mugford Circle in Winthrop, a scant few feet from the ocean, hung over and nursing a black eye gained in a barroom brawl, waiting for the new guy, Williams, to pick me up. Poor me. Here I was, a married man with a wife and three children, having to walk to a pick-up point, and stand waiting in the freezing cold. At 6:30 A.M., Dave pulled up in his white Lincoln Continental, with a stogie stuck in his Orson Well's kisser. He rolled down his window and his first words were, "You look like shit. What's the other guy look like?"

Obviously, he saw that I was hung over. He popped the trunk of the Lincoln, and he said, "Get two." I saw a case of Ballantine Ale. At that point, I realized I had a new best buddy, a drunk like me. Off we went, reporting to the job site in Lynnfield. Dave was the drainage engineer, and I was his assistant. Our favorite greeting each morning was, "Where ya' goin' drinkin' after work?" The response was always the same, "I don't know but I'm going somewhere."

Dave was a handsome, 275-pound, six-foot-three hulk of a man. He worked out regularly, and he was strong as an ox. He had been a lineman on the championship Boston College football team in 1942. Sometimes he acted like a tough, wild character out of a Damon Runyon novel.

Dave was a top-notch drainage engineer. He was a hardworking man who even took on extra jobs during his free time, working for contractors on the side. Between the two of us, we laid out and designed drainage systems for the entire Lynnfield/Peabody Route 1 and 128 interchange project, keeping at least three drainage crews working full time.

One day, after drinking all day on the job and keeping up with our drainage crews, we stopped at Mangini's in East Boston to pound down a few more. By then, my driver's license had been returned. When we left Mangini's, on the road home to Winthrop, the car in front of me slowed, and I rear-ended him. The guy got out of his car, and I realized he was drunker than me. I reached my head out the window and said, "Get back in your car. Take off, and I'll say nothing." He drove off without a word. I then stopped off at William's liquor store on Shirley Avenue, bought three quarts of Ballantine Ale, and proceeded home to finish off the evening.

The stories of my drunken escapades with Dave could fill a volume. Dave had been known to subdue three cops at a time.

He was mean when drunk and aggravated. Years later when I read Kerouac's "On the Road," I thought it was a rather dull average story, until I realized I was comparing it to the story of Dave and me.

64
A ROOM IN SALEM

Along about February 1963, Rita told me she was pregnant with our fourth child. My emotions were getting out of control because for a long time I had suspected that Rita was seeing someone else. When my suspicions proved true, I reacted like a wild man. I visited a priest who advised me to leave home because of my angry attitude. The booze was calling the shots for me. I could not reverse the damage I had done in the past few years. I also knew there was no way Rita could continue to live with me and my drinking problem. Rita and I agreed that I should leave home.

When I left Winthrop, I found a room in Salem, Massachusetts, a one-room studio apartment at 15 Winter Street, a short distance from the Witches Statue, the historic Hawthorne Hotel, and the corporate headquarters of the company which made the Monopoly Game. I brought my carpenter's tool box with me to Salem. Somehow I felt comforted to come home and see the tool box; a connection to a more orderly life.

The first place I settled into was a bar on Bridge Street called the Cove. I made friends with other confused, misdirected drunks also bent on their own destruction. I pushed out of my mind my wife, the kids, the 26-room house, the yard, the yacht club and everything else.

At the Highway Department I was shifting to construction management, working in the Projects Office as a Junior Civil Engineer. My job included performing simple roadway design projects. I spent all my spare time acquiring the new skills expected of me. My old study habits served me well.

One day I was visiting my children in Winthrop. Rita was cordial and glad I had come to visit the kids. As I was getting ready to leave, my three-year old daughter, Barbara, came out to the front door with me to say goodbye. She looked like a little porcelain doll, all dressed up for my visit, her jet black hair in bangs, with a white short-sleeved blouse, a black and white checkered skirt, long white stockings, and patent leather Mary Jane shoes. She stood in the doorway looking at me with expressive dark brown eyes that found my heart. She sobbed, "Daddy, please don't go away." I gave her a hug, and said, "I gotta go." I drove down Cottage Avenue and got as far as Mugford Circle, stopped the car, and cried until I could get it together enough to go back to the Cove and tell my sad story. Years later I realized I left because drinking was more important to me than anything or anyone else. I did not say, "I gotta go." Booze said, "You gotta go."

I found myself with three major demands on my salary—an estranged wife and children, the apartment in Salem, and the booze. I had to get a part-time job to supplement my income.

65
VICLIFF'S

As a teenager I had some experience as a dishwasher and a cook, and I decided to look for a job as a waiter in a restaurant. I walked into ViCliff's Steak House in Danvers and asked the attractive hostess if I could talk to the manger about a job as a waiter. Soon I saw a tall black man striding across the rear dining room, making his way to the lobby, impeccably dressed in a conservative suit. With the look of someone accustomed to giving orders, he said, "Good afternoon. I'm Cliff Crawford, the owner of ViCliff's." We hit it off well and became good friends for the next couple of years. Shortly after starting work as a waiter, I heard Cliff swearing and muttering something about, "Goddam drunks." Apparently the first cook was off on a bender. I said. "Cliff, I can cook." In a tone of disbelief, he said, "What? Well, Goddammit. Go get on your whites." From that day forward, I was no longer a waiter.

I noticed a rather heavy-set rugged woman who was lead waitress. She had a build like a linebacker and was very much in command. So apparently wanting to make my life more complicated, before long she and I were spending off-hours playing house.

I was drinking pretty heavy and was not much of a partner. She soon saw that I was not a candidate for a future life together. She and I had very different agendas. Not long after we started this awkward affair, I called her one night from a gin mill, and drunkenly told her I wanted to see her. She told me to "screw" or words to that effect. About an hour later I arrived at her house too drunk to walk. I could hear a guy say, "Do you want me to get rid of the bum?" She replied, "No, I'll tell him to leave."

I was a State highway engineer by day and a half drunk cook at night. Life went on. I was promoted to broiler man, and each night I put on a show at the broiler, impressing the customers, with flames roaring as high as my tall chef's hat.

There were times when I'd show up for work half drunk, and was told there was a party, and I needed to prepare 30 Lobsters O'Neil, a baked lobster stuffed with the claw meat in the body cavity, covered with stuffing. I snapped the claws off the live lobster, tossed them in a pot to boil, laid the lobster on its back, and using a large French knife, split the crustacean from the head to the tail, snapped it open, and removed the innards. When the claws and knuckles were boiled, I opened the claws with the French knife and removed the meat. A lobster is a very thorny critter. In my state of intoxication, I was sometime less than skillful. I sustained numerous cuts, punctures and scrapes. Sometimes I had to wrap my left hand in a kitchen towel to stop the bleeding.

One Saturday evening a new waitress showed up for work. I was surprised because breaking in a new waitress on the busiest night of the week was unusual. She was drop-dead gorgeous, blonde, shapely, blue eyes, and in her mid to late 20s. When she walked across the dining room floor heading for the kitchen, I lost my concentration and almost burned my right hand on the broiler.

I was lonely, angry, discouraged and desperate for someone to care for me. Toward the busiest time of the evening, the new waitress became befuddled while serving a large party of about 10 people. The restaurant was a mad house, and she was on the verge of panic. She had filet mignons, sirloin strips, club steaks, T bones, lamb chops, and she did not know one from the other or how they were cooked. I smiled at her and said, "Sally (I had read her name on her dupe order), don't worry. The end of the night is bound to come." She looked at me like I was her knight in shining armor. I showed her the different cuts of meat. She survived the night, and thanked me for the kind words of encouragement. Sally was on my mind from that day forward.

One night she said to me, "John I need a ride home. I was dropped off at work today." I replied quickly with, "I'll be happy to give you ride home." She lived in Peabody, close to the very busy Route 1, and near night clubs, motels, restaurants and other retail outlets.

I was on cloud nine during the short ride from Danvers. I nervously said good night as she exited the car at the end of her driveway. I knew she was a married woman with four children, and I was treading on forbidden ground. My needs were so great that I was blinded to any moral reality. Some nights we left work early and drove on a detour to romantic Essex and Gloucester. The sparks flew in the front seat of my 1957 Ford. I had dreams of a better tomorrow without a thought to the consequences. We were attracted to each other, and unfortunately self-respect did not cloud my vision.

About this time a friend of mine opened a restaurant in Salem Willows and asked me to help with prep work for an Easter Sunday. I explained that I was scheduled to work at ViCliff's from 10 A.M. to 10 P.M. on Easter. I did both. I started working at Salem Willows at 4 A.M. and left there in time to get to ViCliff's at 10 A.M. Naturally, we started drinking at 4 A.M. when we began work. Then I reported to ViCliff's for prep work, getting ready for one of the busiest days in the restaurant business. I worked through until early evening, having been nipping and sipping all day.

I left the restaurant about 6 P.M., tired and drunk, having put in a 14-hour day. I crashed my car into a 30-inch oak tree on Route 1 and totaled the car. I knocked out several front teeth, dislocated my shoulder, broke my wrist, and blood was all over my whites. When the State cops showed up, I was out directing traffic, acting as though I was O.K. The cops rushed me off to the Hunt Memorial Hospital in Danvers where I was patched up. I spent a few days there recuperating. No charges were brought against me. I was just having another one of those bad luck days and probably should not have worked all those hours. The thought that booze was the culprit never entered my mind.

(I'm still paying for my drunken behavior. As I sit here 47 years later, I am in the process of again replacing those teeth with a new permanent bridge at a cost of $10,500.)

66
FLOUNDERING

I was transferred to I-495, another interstate project in Lawrence, Massachusetts, and I took a room at the YMCA on Common Street in Lawrence. Just across the street from the Y was Ford's Tavern. I met a lawyer there who drank the way I did, and we became friends. For the sake of the un-informed, in Massachusetts at this point in time a "tavern" was a drinking establishment where only men could drink. Women were not allowed to step foot in the place for any reason.

Ford's Tavern was located in the shadow of the court house. The barber shop next door had a rear exit that led directly into the Tavern. So the lawyers and court officers could walk into the barber shop at any time, and enter the Tavern without anyone being the wiser. Ford's was also the only tavern I ever drank in that had champagne on hand for the special "back door "customers, some of whom enjoyed champagne cocktails.

I was seeing Sally on a regular basis. Somewhere in this timeframe it became obvious, even to me, that I was not going to repair my marriage, and that divorce was inevitable

In early November 1963 I received word that Rita was in the Winthrop Community Hospital delivering our fourth child. I mustered the courage to visit the hospital. I was full of shame. This would be the forth beautiful child that I would lose due to the use and abuse of alcohol. I never got to know Laura Ann. I was not there when she was growing up. With the birth of Laura, I was forced to look back from where I had come and where I was going, and it could be summed up in one word -- loss.

From a work perspective, things were looking pretty good. I was learning a new profession – civil engineering – including the basics of highway design, drainage engineering design, and construction management. I was promoted to Resident Engineer in charge of construction projects. For my first job as a resident engineer, I was assigned to a small construction job on Route 1 in Peabody. We ran into quite a few problems, but I managed to solve them to the satisfaction of my supervisor, the District Construction Engineer.

However, my personal life could best be described as "floundering." Actually, many men on construction projects believed that a really good "construction man" lived a messed up personal life. I continued to work as a chef at night. Sally also worked at the restaurant. Although Sally had a husband and four children, we were seeing each other as often as possible, and we were feeling closer.

In October of 1964, Sally approached me with news that she had not expected. She hesitantly choked out the words, "John, I'm pregnant." We decided to stick with each other. We had dreams of being together in the future, and our intentions were to provide a good home for her family. The foundation of our relationship was built on my guilt about abandoning my family, Sally's guilt about getting pregnant, and my terror about a new baby and my drinking.

My former wife and four children were struggling along with only the court-dictated child support payments. Rita was going through her own maelstrom of relationships as well as the confusion and disappointments of our failed marriage.

On 21 May 1965, Rita and I met at Suffolk Probate Court for our divorce hearing. Uncle Eddie accompanied Rita to Court. I remember being upset by the wording on the divorce papers: ..."was guilty of cruel and abusive treatment" ......"that the libellee was guilty of gross and confirmed habits of intoxication caused by the voluntary and excessive use of intoxicating liquors." I watched the woman I was so much in love with just a few years before walk away just as scared as I was. I realized that I was still in love with her.

Although the ink was not yet dry on the divorce papers, I was already involved in a drama with another woman whose marriage was unraveling. I was a confused man, with two unhappy women in my life, not to mention my mother and father, and eight children wondering what was going to happen next. I used to say, "No wonder I drink. If you had my problems, you'd drink too." It's remarkably that it never occurred to me that I had these problems because I drank.

On 18 June 1965, a month after my divorce papers were submitted, Sally delivered by her fifth cesarean section a beautiful baby girl, Linda Jean.

I was now an Assistant Resident Engineer on a section of the interstate highway system in Lawrence, Massachusetts. I had moved to a one-bedroom apartment at 499 Haverhill Street in Lawrence. When I was not building highways or cooking, I lived and drank in my alternate home at the Cozy Café, one block from my apartment.

Somewhere about this time, I left ViCliff's and got a job at the Margery in Ipswich. The Margery was a classy restaurant with an upscale clientele. I worked the charcoal broiler in the dining room and put on the same show as I had at ViCliff's.

One evening while on the charcoal broiler, I spotted Sylvia, a very beautiful brunette who had also left ViCliff's soon after I did. She was dressed in a plaid skirt with a white wool blazer, and she looked very attractive. She informed me she was applying for the hostess job at the Margery.

We agreed to meet in the parking lot when I got off work. We met in my car. I could not help but think of my ridiculous situation--recently divorced, Sally in my life, and here was the beautiful Sylvia making it clear that we could connect. I was in over my head, and I chickened out! Sylvia left.

I heard a horn beep and a light flash on and off in a dark corner of the parking lot. Sally was parked there with her girl friend Jeanie. Sylvia had been visiting Sally earlier in the day, and revealed her plans to seek work at the Margery. Sally called her girl friend and decided to check out what she suspected would happen with Sylvia's visit to the Margery. I was entangled in a soap opera and I did not have a clue.

One Saturday night I was operating the charcoal broiler and had a shallow pan of lamb chops finishing off in the oven. Being half drunk, I opened the door to check on the lamb chops. I pulled out the pan too quickly, and when the pan came to a stop, the molten hot pan grease slopped out onto my right knee. I was severely burnt, but I finished off the night and then went to the hospital.

My thinking at the time was, it's a good thing I was half drunk so I could not feel the pain of the third degree burn. It did not occur to me that if I had not been half drunk, the accident would not have happened. Now 44 years later, I can still see the outline of that burn just above my right knee.

My tour at the Margery did not last too long. They did not approve of me bringing in a six pack and a half pint of whiskey to get me through the night while I was working behind the broiler. My last night at the Margery was a short one. I stopped at a joint in Ipswich and got really loaded. On the way home I crashed my nice little Dodge Dart into a deep drainage ditch. The car straddled the ditch such that when I opened the door, I fell about six feet to the bottom and found myself looking up at the underside of my car.

The ditch was in front of the VFW in Andover. The bar tender, who was closing up, heard the noise. He came running out to see what happened and heard me moaning in the ditch. He yelled to me, "Stay quiet. I'll be right back." In a minute or two he returned and placed a folded up stepladder down in the ditch so that I could crawl out.

He gave me a hand and pulled me to the top of the ditch where I got on my feet. He helped me walk back to the club. I told him I was a member of VFW Post number 29, the oldest Post in Massachusetts, and that I was kind of shaken up. He said, "You need a drink." And he got me a shot and a beer. Then he called a friend with a wrecker and I had a few while we waited for the wrecker to arrive. The wrecker pulled the car out from the ditch. I thanked them both, and drove home to Lawrence.

Sally was living in Peabody under a lot of stress with divorce proceedings underway. We had great plans that included Sally eventually moving to the Lawrence area. In retrospect, the whole idea was driven by desperation, especially when I consider Sally was willing to throw herself and her five kids in with a drunk.

My "floundering" period was a nightmare of negative emotions, work and whiskey. I frequented a barroom in Lawrence called Conn (Cornelius) Donahue's, where we social drinkers used to meet at six o'clock in the morning for a wee taste before heading off to work. It was the custom at the time to close barrooms on Good Friday from noon to 3:00 P.M. At Conn's, Conn would lock the door at 12 noon, pull the shades, and we were trapped and therefore had to drink until three.

This kind of thinking caused me to live in three different worlds at the same time. By day, I had a responsible job building state highways. I was now a half-drunk cook at night at the Lamplighter Motel Restaurant in Lawrence. And I was a juggler of my personal life, with four children from my past marriage, and a new family on the horizon.

Sally and I decided I should meet her four children. We went to the beach for a picnic. Children compete for their parents' attention, and Cheryl, Sharon, Rick, and Debi were no different. They all set out to hook my attention. My feelings of inadequacy were soon replaced by feelings of embarrassment. The kids did not know what to call me. "Dad" or "John" was inappropriate, so they all yelled "Mr. Willey, Mr. Willey, Mr. Willey," whenever they wanted my attention.

At the same time, I was occasionally visiting my own children in Winthrop. When I left my children, I felt like the lowest form of life on the planet. Visiting them was a constant feeding of my guilt. Here I was trying to be a father to someone else's kids, while abandoning my own children. I do not know what I would have done without alcohol to deaden the feelings.

Sally's girlfriend was seeing a man who was a pilot. One weekend we all met at the Beverly Airport and flew down to Martha's Vineyard. We landed on a grass strip near Gay Head. We pulled out our picnic baskets and enjoyed a wonderful sunny day of adventure on the Vineyard.

Sally looked beautiful. She ran free on the beach, laughing and shouting. She wore a two-piece bathing suit of white and blue checks that showed off her great legs and exquisite figure. My eyes could not believe my good fortune in being there that day with her. Later we flew to Provincetown and ate lobsters and clams at the Lobster Pot before flying back to Beverly Airport.

I had developed a saying that I used constantly, a handy way to not accept life as it was. The saying was, "Wouldn't it be nice if ..." Wouldn't it be nice if Sally were not married. Wouldn't it be nice if I didn't have four kids from a failed marriage. Wouldn't it be nice if I'd never gotten married, etcetera. That mantra was just another way of being dishonest with myself. What I was really saying was "I don't accept the results of my actions, and if the world would just do things my way, everything would be great."

One day in my field office, my office manager said "Hey John - phone." Eddie Glickhouse knew of my travails, and upon handing me the phone, he discreetly left the office. Sally was calling to talk with me about our plans to get married and her plans to move to the Lawrence area where I lived and worked. Sally had an opportunity to rent a full-sized two-story house on Oakside Avenue in nearby Methuen, Massachusetts, which was temporarily under the control of a Lawrence attorney for whom Sally's girlfriend worked. The house had ample room for Sally and the five children. We were planning our wedding, yet Sally was not yet divorced, and my final divorce was less than a year old.

Rita informed me she was moving away with the four kids. She planned to marry a man named Lyman McKay who had relocated to Michigan to work in the auto industry. I knew Lymie. I went to school with him at Wentworth, and I drank with him at the Winthrop Yacht Club. I was surprised, because Lymie was a quiet, confirmed bachelor, who lived with his mother.

Our divorce decree mandated that Rita live in Massachusetts so I could continue to visit with the children. I met with my new lawyer friend at Ford's Tavern to explain the situation. He suggested we amend the divorce agreement to accommodate this change. We moved from the bar to a booth with a pad of legal paper. Between champagne cocktails for the lawyer and Budweiser for me, he explained the gist of what the agreement should say. I wrote it up, using phrases like heretofore, notwithstanding, thereby, and pursuant. He took the rough draft to his office where it was typed up for signature. Basically, my drunken lawyer and I wrote the agreement in a barroom.

My fourth child, Laura, was about six years old when Rita moved to Michigan. I did not know Laura, since I had not been living at home for most of her young life, and my visits with the children were not frequent.

67
SALLY

Thinking as a foundation engineer, signs were abundant that Sally and I were constructing a building on shifting sands instead of well-compacted glacial till. We were having fewer and fewer peaceful moments together. Our lives were full of unhappy people. Rita had dropped her bomb about moving with the kids to Michigan, my parents were angry because I wanted to marry Sally, Sally's former in-laws were angry, my sisters were not speaking to me, Sally's folks were upset, my friends thought I was insane, and on and on it went. While all this was going on, I was trying to get to know Sally's children, all the while aware that my kids were without a father.

We were married on August 18, 1967 on the back porch of the City Clerk's house in Lawrence. Sally designed and sewed her own wedding dress, and she looked beautiful. Bob and Shirley Keefe stood up for us. Bob was a close friend of mine and a fellow State engineer. We went to dinner at the Red Tavern in Methuen, Massachusetts and then drove to the White Mountains to an upscale resort called The Brick Yard.

We had a standing joke about the honeymoon, because it seemed we each had different goals. Sally wanted to swim in the pool, play shuffle board, go for a boat ride, go horseback riding, have drinks in the lounge, and walk the trails. She seemed to want to do anything she could to avoid being close to me. I had other ideas.

I moved into the house in Methuen. We tried to provide the best home we could for Sally's children. I sent child support to Rita for my kids in Michigan. I was an Assistant Resident Engineer on I-495 in Lawrence. My second job was as first cook at another restaurant, The Country Squire Inn in Middleton. Sally worked part-time. For about a year, I kept my drinking on the job to a minimum.

1986. At left, John and Sally Willey at dinner with friends while vacationing in Aruba

68
BACK TO HAVERHILL

We heard from Sally's friend that our rented house in Methuen would soon be sold. The kids were enrolled in the Methuen school system, and our family was coming together. But we had to find another place. The pickings were slim, considering we needed a house in a decent neighborhood, large enough to accommodate five kids. We began looking in my old hometown, Haverhill.

I was really worried about being able to afford to buy or rent a big house, support a wife and five kids, and pay child support every week. We spent a lot of anxious moments trying to figure out how this would work. Sally reminded me that I had G.I. benefits for buying a house with no money down. We found a house in Haverhill that was perfect, eight rooms with a basement and an attic, on a quiet side street in a very good section of the City. We paid $16,000 for the house; I was earning about $8,500 a year.

We had just a few weeks to plan the move. Sally's parents took care of the five kids. We scrambled around on short notice to find a mover. The mover showed up on the morning of the 29th of December, 1967, and the head guy said, "Which floor?" My reply was, "Whadda' ya mean, which floor? Both floors have to be moved, and I made that clear to the guy in the office." He said, "I hafta go get some more guys." And he left with the truck and the two lumpers. I turned to Sally and said, "We're screwed. He's off to a barroom, and we are screwed!" And sure enough, they did not return.

I made some calls, first to a contractor friend of mine to borrow a truck. However, contractors take their trucks out of registration when not in use, and none of his trucks were registered at that moment. I called Sally's father, and he borrowed his brother's pick up. Then I called my Trade School friend, Mickey Shugrue, and he said I could borrow his pickup but he wanted no part of moving. I picked up the truck, took him to a barroom in Haverhill, and returned to our old house in Methuen. Now I had two pickup trucks, Sally, Appie (Sally's father), and me. I called a man who had advertised in the Yellow Pages, and he said he could not help because his son was home on leave from Viet Nam. I prevailed upon him with my sad tale of woe and suggested that he bring his son along. I sighed with relief when he said he would bring his son, but only to move the heavy stuff which would be one trip to Haverhill.

We busted our collective asses and moved as much as we could the first day, collapsing in our new home that night. The next day we continued the move, but toward the end of the day it began to snow. We must have looked like a band of Gypsies to our new neighbors, with our two pickup trucks, and our meager crew, moving into a decent middle class neighborhood where most peoples' belongings no doubt arrived in big Atlas Moving vans. I felt like Jed Clampett, head of the TV Ozark Hillbilly family, moving into Beverly Hills. But by early New Year's Eve of 1968, we finished moving in. We sat exhausted on a crate, Sally with a glass of champagne, and I with a bottle of Bud. Thus began the Haverhill adventure.

We were now proud home owners of 21 Minot Avenue, a house of eight rooms with a big attic and a basement, and a small back yard, all on a lot about one quarter acre.

We were in a middle-class neighborhood on the border of the area where the wealthy folks lived in Haverhill. We were up to our limit financially, my drinking was escalating, and we were not getting along very well.

I put my Haverhill Trade School education to good use in making repairs to the 100-year old house. One day I received a frantic phone call from Sally telling me that the family room ceiling was sagging and leaking water. I arrived home, looked up at the tin-covered ceiling, and could see the problem. Today, tin-covered ceilings are considered a plus by people who love old Victorian houses. However, tin-covered ceilings were popular in the 1920's because they covered up old lath and plaster ceilings that needed repair. Embossed tin squares were simply nailed over the old damaged ceilings. I inspected the upstairs bathroom and found a leak from an old lead water pipe. I shut off the water to the toilet, then went downstairs and punched a hole in a tin panel. Water gushed out, and the ceiling fell into the family room. More work to add to the list of needed repairs. I am grateful that I had the experience to make all the repairs including the plumbing.

One day during one of our seemingly constant battles, Sally told me for the umpteenth time that she wanted a bow window in the family room. She had been asking for months, and I had been telling her it was too expensive. One afternoon Sally was off shopping or visiting, and I tore a four foot by eight foot hole through the side of the house and installed upright temporary supports in the living room. What always amazed me was why this could not have been a fun project instead of my being pissed off. Anyhow, I installed the bow window, and it made a pleasant addition to the house.

69
FIGHTING THE POUNDS

As if the alcoholism (which I denied) was not enough, I was overeating. I overate and then hated myself. These feelings were worse than the feelings when I woke to find I had done it again with booze.

I visited Dr. Wheeler, a quack doctor in Haverhill, whose office was at Currier Square in the Mt. Washington section. Dr. Wheeler gave me a shot of speed every week. I was losing weight at a great clip. I was so spaced out and goofed up with booze, I could not see that I was playing serious games with my health--but I looked great!

In order to secure life insurance, I had to have a physical examination. The insurance company required me to visit a Dr. Constantino for the exam. My weight had dropped from 250 pounds to 175 in a relatively short time. The doctor put the stethoscope on my heart and jumped back and said, "What the hell are you on?" I explained about Dr. Wheeler. He went ballistic and swore, "That sonovabitch should be in jail."

My eating disorder could not be corrected by getting weekly shots of speed from a quack doctor. I promised Dr. Constantino I would stay away from Dr. Wheeler and return for my exam a month later. My heart was healthy when I returned to see Dr. Constantino, but I had been gaining back the weight. Within a week after the exam with Dr. Constantino, I returned to see

Dr. Wheeler. His office was closed, and his license to practice medicine had been revoked.

70
POLICE ACTION

Our fights at home were increasing in frequency and intensity. I began to wonder about my "problem drinking" which had been going on close to 25 years. On more than one occasion Sally called the police. While I never hurt her physically, I could not deny the adverse effects on our marriage my heavy drinking caused. I was an angry, belligerent, argumentative, negative person. Our relationship had become acrimonious and dangerous, each of us making threats toward the other almost every day.

In January 1970 Sally met a woman from Plaistow, New Hampshire named Joan She explained that she had lost her marriage and nearly her life from alcoholic drinking but was now sober and living a new life. She explained to Sally that she had found a group of people who were helping her to stay sober. Joan told Sally she would be glad to talk to me. She gave Sally some pamphlets and said I would have to call, which would indicate to her that I was willing to talk. Sally came home quite excited and said, "John, I think there is an answer to our problems." She described Joan's offer. I roughly told Sally that I had heard about do-gooders who were supposedly helping drunks, that I was not a drunk, that I might have had some bad luck along the way, but I worked hard and I deserved a few drinks after work to relax. I told her what she could do with the pamphlets and continued drinking.

In 1970 I began a new job as the Resident Engineer for the rebuilding of a section of Route 97 in Groveland. As Resident Engineer, it was my call as to how many traffic police I needed each day. I was a resource for the Chief of Police of Groveland to keep his officers on paid detail. I became very close with the Chief of Police, and life was going OK, at least on the job.

One night soon after starting the new job, Sally and I went out to dinner with another couple at DiBurrow's restaurant in Haverhill. As the evening wore on, I became drunk and obnoxious and caused a disturbance. The owner took me aside and explained that he would have to call the police if I did not calm down. Because I was drunk, rather than piping down and behaving appropriately, I convinced the owner to let me call a good friend of mine to vouch for me. The friend was a State cop. I made the call, and my friend convinced the owner that I was good guy, and I calmed down. Sometime later that night, I crashed a wedding party in the function hall at the restaurant. I tried to convince the bride to dance with me, and of course the groom and others were very upset. This time the owner did not waste time talking to me. He called the Haverhill police, and after a brief scuffle, I wound up in the Haverhill jail.

I arrogantly asked for my one phone call and called the same State cop. I knew he had the clout to spring me. I had forgotten that earlier that same night he had helped me get out of trouble, I asked him to talk to the Haverhill Lieutenant. As I turned the phone over to the Haverhill police officer, I could hear my State cop buddy's voice respond to the Lieutenant. To my shock and amazement, I heard him say, "F--- 'em. Let 'em sleep it off." I was escorted to the cell, and the door clanked shut.

The next morning when I was released, I had the hubris to call the Chief of Police in Groveland and ask him to send a Groveland cruiser to pick me up at the Haverhill Police Station for a ride to my field office. As I left the Haverhill police station feeling like a big shot with my Groveland police chauffeur, I could see the duty cop shake his head with a look of disgust. At my request, I was deposited at the Cedardale Health Club for a steam bath and a massage before returning to the job.

Denying the damage alcoholic drinking was causing became more and more difficult. The evidence mounted about its effects on me and my family. I experienced paralyzing fears that I could not explain. I lived each day with thoughts of impending doom. My mind was focused on all manner of unpleasant things that could happen to me. Fear was how I lived, day by day. I was afraid to answer the phone or the door bell. And I was terrified that someone would find out how fearful I was, throw a net over me, and toss me in the loony bin.

How did I respond? I drank more. Many of my friends and acquaintance in the barrooms and taverns used to joke about D.T's (Delirium Tremens) and wet brains, and I knew you could not stop drinking too quickly. When guys had the D.Ts, they saw things like spiders and rats that were not really there. Some of them developed a "wet brain" which meant they would never return to sanity. And yet I continued to drink.

PART III

AFTER

A miracle not asked for and without my consent—I stopped drinking in a black-out in 1971. I traveled from the depths of despair and hopelessness to a wonderful life I could not have imagined. This section describes my life AFTER I began recovery.

71
APRIL 7, 1971: THE AWAKENING

When I began work in January 1971 as the Drainage Engineer on I-95 in Danvers, I was drunk just about every day. I was a Senior Civil Engineer at a salary of $14,000 per year, and I no longer worked as a chef.

In this decade, all the kids were teens, experiencing their teenage challenges. Our family dynamics were exacerbated by the comings and goings of my children from Michigan. My daughters, Patty and Barbara, came to live with us, and then later John Jr. lived with us for awhile.

In March 1971 Sally went back to visit her friend, Joan, in Plaistow, New Hampshire to discuss my "so-called" problem with alcohol. Only this time she came home with another brochure and a new phone number for me to call. Joan had called a friend in Haverhill to aid her in this endeavor. I reacted the same way I had the year previous; I told Sally what she could do with her pamphlets and the friends who gave them to her. After all, I had talked to my buddies in the bar rooms. They said this was a bunch of crap, and that I was a hardworking guy who was not hurting anyone, and I deserved a drink after work to unwind. I was not going to hang around with a bunch of do-gooder losers who could not handle their booze.

In spite of my friends' words of comfort, I could not stop thinking about my alcohol-induced escapades. I had totaled at least four cars and had been in at least four hospitals with serious injuries from the accidents. I remember the night in early 1971 when Sally called the cops because I was threatening mayhem, and I ran from the house before they arrived. On that rainy night, I was running through my own neighborhood like a common criminal. I ran neck-high into a clothes line, effectively garroting myself, and my feet went out from beneath me. I landed flat on my back, banging my head on the ground, nearly unconscious, soaked in the pouring rain. As I laid there momentarily unable to get up, rain driving into my face, I shouted to no one in particular, "What's happening to me?"

Then there was the time I asked Sally what happened to her elbow because it was bruised and skinned. She replied, "You should know, you lousy bastard." Seems I chased her from the house in broad daylight while wearing nothing but my underwear. She slipped and fell on the pavement. I was in a black-out and had no recollection of the incident. The neighbors remembered, Sally remembered, but I did not.

On April 7, 1971 I left for work at 6 A.M., nursing a monumental hangover. Upon settling in behind my desk in the construction trailer, I reached into the bottom drawer and took out an almost empty fifth of Seagram's 7. I usually left a little corner at the bottom of a fifth for the next morning. I learned to have "a little hair of the dog that bit ye," as the saying goes. It was 6:30 A.M., and I was just pouring the whiskey into an empty coffee cup when the Resident Engineer, Gerry Donnellan, walked by my office. He looked at me with disgust and said, "You gonna start that shit so early in the day?" My reply was, "F--- you!" I finished off the fifth, rounded up three of my drinking buddies, and off we went for "coffee," where I explained to them what happened. When we returned, our pay was docked. At noontime, the four of us left the job and went to the Sky View in Danvers for a day of drinking.

This was going to be the second biggest day of my life. The biggest day was my birth in 1930. This was going to be the day of my rebirth. This was going to be the day that the monkey finally got off my back. This was to be the day that Sally gave me my life.

By early afternoon I was in the Sky View bar and very drunk. I was talking to a young woman, when I noticed a rather big guy walking toward me. My paranoia kicked in. I imagined that the woman I was talking to was probably his wife or girl friend and that he was going to kick the shit out of me. I immediately began to brag about my wife so that he would not think I was being inappropriate with his lady. As it turned out, he was simply a guy on the way to the men's room. However, as he passed by, he casually remarked, "If your wife's so Goddam great, why don't you go home to her?"

I walked to the telephone booth. I dialed Sally and said in my drunken state, "Hi, Sally, it's me. Remember last year when you went to Plaistow to your friend about my drinking? Well, I think I'd like to talk with someone now." "Screw you," was her angry reply, and she hung up.

My next memory was sitting in a living room talking to a stranger, befuddled and confused. My first words were, "Who are you? Where am I? How did I get here? Then I told the man I could use a drink. He said, "I'm Irving Cleary. You're on Arlington Street. Your wife dropped you off. And I don't have any booze in the house." Later in the evening, Sally came to drive me home. Irving and I agreed to meet in a day or so, and he promised to teach me to live without alcohol.

That's all I remember of that afternoon, and I never drank again.

Having "blackouts," or more correctly, alcoholic amnesia, had been a common occurrence for me for the past 20 years or more. Drinking alcohol can cause the brain to malfunction so that short-term memories are not recorded, and therefore cannot be remembered because they were never recorded.

I started off on a journey with Irving for which I was ill-prepared. I soon realized that while I was 41 years old by the calendar, I was still 15 years old in my emotional maturity, the very age at which I began to drink alcohol. It is probably a blessing that I did not know how sick I was. Soon after meeting Irving, he insisted that I get a full medical exam, follow up to get the results, and take the doctor's direction. The good news was that my liver was slightly enlarged, but otherwise I was in pretty good shape. The doctor told me to see him from time to time to check on the recovery of my liver. Thus began a new habit of taking better care of myself.

Soon after I stopped drinking, I was at war with the world. Life was worse without the booze. I called Irving at all hours of the night. He listened to my insanity and encouraged me not to drink no matter what. When I craved booze, he explained that my body needed sugar and suggested I carry a pocketful of hard candy. This went on for a few years.

Working on the construction job where I had been drinking, I was constantly in the company of my old drinking buddies, which was really difficult. I had been sober a few months, when I was having lunch at the Green Barrel in Danvers, Massachusetts, one of my old drinking haunts. I was with Ernie Munroe, one of the four of us who had had our pay docked on 7 April 1971 because we had been drunk. Over many years, Ernie and I did some very heavy drinking. Out of the blue, Ernie put his arm across my shoulder, looked me straight in the eyes, with a breath that was ignitable and said, "John, if I ever see you reach for a drink, I'll break your arm." Ernie had lost a drinking buddy, yet he was on my side. With loving words like that from Ernie, I knew I could make it. He was proud of me and really cared about my wellbeing.

72
SELF-HELP

A few years later, Irving Cleary moved to California. I found another mentor. Don Carroll was a big affable Irishman from Lawrence, Massachusetts. He was dedicated to helping guys like me. I was taken aback when he explained to me that all my problems were of my own making, and that I needed to get my mind right if I were to live a normal life. He also indicated that the road back to reality was a long one, and that I would need to put some serious work into my new life in order to succeed.

Practically from the day I quit drinking, I was looking for answers to the mystery of living a good life. I became a self-help fanatic and started to accrue a library of books about the human condition. I was excited. I was a hungry student. Many people make light of self-help, but it worked for me, helping to keep me on the road to uncovering my truth.

I said to Don, "You don't understand. All my problems were caused by drinking booze. So all I have to do is stay away from booze, and everything will be great." His big Irish kisser lit up like a Christmas tree, and he smiled as he put his arm around my shoulder. "John" he said, "Are you willing to go to any lengths to stay sober?" Of course, without knowing what I was committing to, I said, "Yes."

His next instructions seemed rather weird but I said I would do what he told me to do. "I want you to read a book called *Psycho-Cybernetics* by Dr. Maxwell Maltz." He left it to me to figure out whether or not to take his suggestion. I read it!

This book began a lifetime journey of "self-help" through reading, researching, attending seminars, workshops, and retreats. A day never went by when I was not reading and trying out new ways of relating with my wife, children and fellow workers. I thought I was a miserable flop because no matter how much I read, I still could not mend my relationship with Sally. So I decided I needed professional help.

Thus began a long string of visits to therapists. Both Sally and I were in individual therapy, and we went to couples therapy. We also went to group therapy together. We attended seminars. Progress was discouragingly slow, or actually non-existent, but I did not drink.

I realized that the way out of financial or mental poverty was through education. By the time that message finally hit home, I was on my second marriage with nine children for whom I was responsible. I could not very well head back to college for an education. I needed a practical education that would lead to a well-paying job. At the same time, I had to work and bring home money for the family. At night I took classes in philosophy, geology, and soils mechanics. I read biographies of outstanding people. I learned that there are many reasons for getting an education. Some people go to college because their parents make them, some go because they want to, others go to gain prestige and attain status. I wanted education because I saw that it was the only road out of poverty. Education was an opportunity to get better jobs, make more money, and save for the future.

I was able to pass civil service exams, and by age 50 reach the top of my profession as a Civil Engineer in the Massachusetts Department of Public Works. When I went to work in the private sector, I managed to pass the requirements to become a Registered Professional Civil Engineer. Now I could sign my name with the letters P.E. following.

I was driven by necessity. I did not want to be a poor laborer like my Dad nor do piece work in a factory like my Mom. I wanted to learn how to appreciate art, music and become familiar with the finer things of life, simply to make life more enjoyable. I saw very wealthy people who had no appreciation for the finer aspects of life. They simply plowed through life using money as their shield, and they became colossal boors and acted stupidly

One of the disadvantages of self-help or self-education is there is no status attached. You do not get to be a Doctor, or have MBA after your name, and that has to be recognized and accepted graciously. Getting an education is still the most important thing humans can do for themselves. It was not enough to get an education to just make a better living. It was necessary to get an education in the appreciation of the arts and to acquire the ability to be overwhelmed with the appreciation of the wonders of nature.

I became aware that my wife Sally suffered from the stigma of not having graduated from high school. I saw her pain, understood the reason, and I was motivated to help her do something about it. Sally had several different jobs as we struggled to bring up our large family. One thing became abundantly clear; Sally was very bright and could take on difficult jobs and do really well in spite of the fact that she did not have a high school diploma. She was becoming frustrated and disappointed about the job market. One day while we were discussing this problem, she mentioned again that she had to leave high school in her senior year and never received a high school diploma.

Being a rescuer, I called the Principal of the North Reading High School and explained the situation about Sally not receiving her diploma. The Principal was apologetic. Sally and I met him in his office, and he ceremoniously presented Sally with her diploma. The look of satisfaction on Sally's face was another reminder for me of the importance of an education.

Probably the most important subjects were those that allowed me to learn how to work well with others, especially the difficult ones who are abundant everywhere. The measure of intelligence upon which our country relies is I.Q. (Intelligence Quotient). I noticed that many people with high I.Q's were miserable and could not get along in the world. Through study I learned about the importance of a person's E.Q. (Emotional Quotient), their ability to be comfortable in their own skin and to work well with others, which could sometimes be more important than the I.Q.

I do not need to defend self-help. Benjamin Franklin, a brilliant mind during the time of the American Revolution, was the father of the self-help philosophy. He was a self-educated man. I simply want future generations who read this book to realize that an education is our most important asset as we travel the road called life. If you cannot afford a formal education, then start reading and educate yourself.

73
GET RICH QUICK

Shortly after World War II, a couple of veterans from Michigan created a multilevel marketing scheme for selling cleaning products.

People could invest a small amount of money and instantly go into business for themselves. The company was called Amway, and the craze went across the country. Getting rich was going to be easy, all for a small investment, and a little effort selling good merchandise to family, friends, and colleagues.

After 24 years of drinking alcoholically, I had not saved any money. I was living from paycheck to paycheck. The idea of "getting rich quick" appealed to me. My buddy, Marty Killourie, introduced me to Bestline, a marketing scheme similar to Amway. Marty and his wife, Brenda, Sally and I, along with other friends, rushed to sign up with Bestline.

We were going to be rich capitalists and live like kings and queens. We could not lose. We looked over the business plan from every angle. We drew sketches, and figured percentages. We could not see any flaws in our new business venture. Of course, the reality was that none of us had ever done any direct selling, and we were about to embark in competition with billion dollar giants like Procter and Gamble, not to mention Amway.

Our best friends Marty and Brenda became our Direct Distributor. We confidently bought a couple of thousand dollars worth of cleaning supply products which we stored in our basement. In addition to our regular full-time jobs, we attended training classes, and we worked nights and weekends selling the soap.

Sally and I knocked on doors and made cold calls. We held house parties to recruit new members, who would in turn become salespeople. I read up on biodegradable cleaning products, studied eutrophication, and became an expert presenter. We met a new circle of friends, all dedicated to becoming rich.

We worked hard and had a lot of fun. But we did not become rich. We were damn lucky to break even or maybe make a few bucks. This quest went on for a few years until our cellar was pretty near empty of the cleaning products called Zif, LC, Phosphate 7, and other names I have forgotten. The good news is that we all stayed friends as we returned to earning a living at our regular day jobs and let go of our get rich quick schemes. We had to settle for being normal.

Then somehow, Sally and I got hooked on the Amway promise "to walk the beaches of the world," free of financial worries. This time we were going to do it right. Bestline had been sued and went out of business. The Amway organization was legitimate, so how could we lose? Again, we both worked full-time, and at night we schlepped soap, attended training classes and pep rallies. We were at the task seven days a week. We put in unreasonable hours to see our dream come true.

Sally and I agreed on one thing, we were not going to buy a cellar full of soap on speculation. We received the orders and then drove to our distributor to pick up what we had already sold. We carried little to no inventory. We were not going to get stung again.

In retrospect, as Friedrich Nietzsche once said, "That which does not kill us makes us stronger." Our getting rich experience did not kill us, but it certainly made me realize that a life based on slow but sure accumulation is far superior to one based on listening to slick-talking personalities about get rich schemes. All my time in Bestline and Amway did give me an education. I even adopted the definition of success from an Amway motivational speaker which is in the opening of this book. However, we gradually realized we were not getting anywhere. We dropped out of Amway.

I learned a valuable lesson, namely, that there are no short cut paths to riches.

74
BAILEY ISLAND, MAINE

An unexpected and pleasant event happened shortly after I became sober. Sally was a consumer; I was a saver. She wanted us to buy a summer cottage on a lake in New Hampshire. I was dead set against the idea. We were discussing this dilemma with Dave Chareth, a friend of mine who was also a State engineer. Dave said his father was managing a summer cottage on Bailey Island, Maine, for a very elderly woman. He described the place as "run down" but in a quiet secluded location within 50 feet of the ocean. We cut a deal, sight unseen. We would pay $75.00 per week and contribute my labor to make repairs. My tools were coming in handy again, only now I had power tools too.

In July we excitedly loaded up two vehicles with the five kids, food, linens, toys and tools. Sally drove the station wagon, and I drove the pickup truck. Off we went to Brunswick, Maine, where we then headed south to Bailey Island, the last in a string of islands in Casco Bay. Our driving directions consisted of a pencil sketch showing that we should drive past Great Island and Orrs Island, cross the famous crib bridge, and continue down the main road onto Bailey Island. We turned left at the volunteer fire station. Every way we looked held beautiful open ocean views. Then we turned left again at the bottom of the hill, and drove carefully onto a two-track rutted unpaved lane, the bushes scraping against the car as we bumped along.

We could hear the waves crashing against the rocky shore, and we breathed in the sea air and the fragrance of wild roses. We were mesmerized with the drive down the lane, and we fell in love with the place before we even caught a glimpse of the cottage. When we arrived at the clearing, to our right was the weathered gray-shingled run-down cottage. A pole was stuck up against the doors of the detached garage, holding them closed. The porch and the steps were rickety. The exterior as well as the interior rooms of the cottage were constructed with boards nailed on two by four inch studs. The tiny kitchen had a small gas stove and a cast iron sink. Even a cat could not walk across the floor without a wave of creaks following. Upstairs were three or four bedrooms. The front room had an old fireplace and a direct view of the ocean out of the picture window. Beyond the goldenrod, Queen Anne's Lace, lupine, and wild roses, we could see the waves crashing against the solid granite coast.

For many years, we returned each July. Bailey Island became a very special place for each one of us, full of memories of good times together. We walked the footpath from the cottage through the wildflowers and a patch of evergreens down to a little sandy swimming beach. We hiked the Giant Steps, a natural rock formation with enormous steps leading down to the ocean. We visited a clothing and souvenir shop at the very end of the island, called Lands End Gift Shop. We watched the lobstermen motoring through Jaquish Gut, a passage between Bailey Island and Jaquish Island, an uninhabited island about 200 feet off shore. We also hiked to Mackerel Cove, a picturesque well-protected cove lined with cottages and evergreens. Several restaurants were located there, as well as Glen's Lobster Pound where all the lobstermen dropped off their catch, which Glen then sold at retail at the dock, and wholesale to restaurants. We also drove to Cundy's Harbor, where we ate lobster in the rough at picnic tables on the docks.

I brought my table saw and carpenter tools and made repairs to the cottage steps, the fireplace, the flooring, shingles on the exterior, windows, screens, doors and cabinets. Sally and the kids cut back the wild vegetation so we could drive in without scratching the car.

One summer, Linda was about 11 or 12, tall, slender, beautiful, and vivacious. A local fisherman's son fell madly in love with her. I was really nervous watching the sparks fly between Linda and Warren. Warren visited frequently, bringing tubs full of fresh fish and lobsters. We enjoyed many seafood cookouts. I stood at the water's edge, filleting the fish. Sally and the kids shucked the corn. The kids played "lobster races," placing lobsters on the floor and urging them into competition.

Once when Rick was in the Marines, he drove all the way from Virginia to spend a few days with us on the Island. One summer Linda was in the US Navy, stationed in California. She made a surprise visit, flying from San Diego to Boston where we picked her up, so she could spend a few days with us in the old cottage. She also arranged to have a couple of her friends from Haverhill visit at the same time.

Long after the cottage was unavailable for us to rent, Linda, Rick, and Cheryl spent time on Bailey Island. Cheryl moved to Portland, Maine and made many trips to Bailey Island. Shortly after I met Barbara Greenberg, I took her to Bailey Island, Cundy's Harbor, and Mackerel Cove. I would like to go again (and again).

75
THE PILOT HOUSE

Our time at Bailey Island was a reprieve from the chaos of our daily lives. The kids were in the difficult teen years. I was beginning to understand the devastation caused through my use and abuse of alcohol. Sally was finding her way in the business world.

During the later years of our summers at Bailey Island, I realized my need for connections, for a meaningful relationship, a peaceful and respectful life. I saw what had happened and where I was, and did not know what to do about it. I felt lost and hopeless.

In August 1985 while we were at Bailey Island, I wrote a short story with a pencil on notebook paper. I happened to be alone in the cottage, feeling melancholic. I felt comfortable at that moment in the cottage, and I dreamed of having a pleasant caring relationship.

Here's the story I wrote that day.

The Pilot House

The island, third in a chain, reaches out into the North Atlantic for quite a few miles. Its environment is typical of coastal Maine. The wildflowers are abundant as are shore and sea birds. The island is a granite outpost with sharp cliffs defying a mighty ocean. But the ocean wins. Ever so slowly, the granite erodes and the ocean wins.

This is a place of strange-sounding Native American and nautical names like Merriconeag Sound, Will's Gut, Bigelow Bight, Quahog Bay, West Cod Ledge, and Mackerel Cove. This is a place far removed from my work-a-day routine of the train ride to Boston, the walk to the office, and the never-ending bureaucratic games.

I'm looking out to the sea, and the day is rainy and lightly overcast. The lobstermen are everywhere, reminding me of a colony of bees collecting honey as they flit from flower to flower in a seemingly random pattern. The lobstermen flit from lobster buoy to lobster buoy, hauling in the traps, and heaving back into the ocean the crabs, undersized lobsters and seaweed, keeping a lobster or two, re-baiting and re-setting the trap, day after day. Do they dream of wearing a business suit and traveling on the train to Boston day after day? Where do they go on vacation? I come here to play. Maybe they would like to try the city for a while. That's another story.

I sit here in an alcove at the living room window, and I feel like I'm sitting in a pilot house on an oceangoing ship. However, to my left the fire place is sputtering to let me know it's alive and providing comfort and warmth. My coffee cup is steaming. The incessant sea is working away at the granite coast, which for the time being protects us from the sea. Someday the sea will triumph, but not in my lifetime.

The mixture of ocean air, salt spray, wood smoke and freshly brewed coffee is the elixir of romanticism. If I could share this with another person, someone who sees and feels the beauty, that would be the very essence of intimacy. To walk along the rock-bound coast hand in hand in the rain, laughing, with feelings soaring, two people united in an uplifting experience -- is that too much to ask? Is it too lofty a dream? I think not.

I'm grateful for my ability and courage to set feelings and thoughts on paper as a way of seeing their reality. If that's the only way this can happen, then I'm content to let it be so for now.

I never tire of observing the sea as it creates its own symphony, wave after wave, each one different, dashing against the sturdy coast. Today I notice the brightly colored lobster buoys dancing up and down, to and fro, not struggling against the sea, as does the shoreline, but taking each wave as it comes. Their small world is charted by the ebb and flood of the tide, and the wind and the waves. They have quiet times, and they have wild times, tethered firmly to their charges.

I see the buoys as though they are living beings like me. Their chore is to keep watch over the traps, to let the lobstermen know where to seek the treasures of the Atlantic. They do not resent their limitations, even though they are not free to roam the ocean at will.

They are tied to their responsibilities, and in turn, the lobstermen care for them. The lobstermen repair them each season with new fastenings, and from time to time they are set in new locations. During the winter they are dried, cleaned and painted. Because of their responsibilities, they that are kept tied to the traps have a feeling of worth, an unspoken contract with their master. What of the ones that break free? The buoys that break free are no longer responsible, they no longer answer to anyone, no longer serve a purpose, and for a time they wander unfettered. Oh, the glorious feeling of just fleeting with no purpose and no direction. But then the winds take over, and some of the unfettered buoys are dashed against the unyielding granite.

The rope that binds also provides security and safety. Once bashed against the stone, they set out to sail again, no vacation, no safe storage at the lobsterman's shack, no serving the master, and no new coat of paint. They will ultimately be reduced to tiny splinters on the shore, or perhaps picked up as a souvenir to be taken to a place of honor, or perhaps used to start a bon fire.

But what of the faithful buoy that silently performed the tasks assigned by others. What's its reward? Probably the same in the end; when they have served their purpose, they may be sold as a souvenir or be tossed into the stove on a cold winter morning as the lobsterman prepares new ones to replace the old.

How much like life is the buoy, and vice versa. The end result is much the same. What it really comes down to is life is a journey, and the end is always the same. To quote Shakespeare from *As You Like It,* "Sans teeth, sans hair, sans everything." In the end, it all goes poof! Then we must choose the trip. Ah ha! There's the rub. Most of us do not have the courage to live life to its fullest and live who we really are. Should we let others tie us to a responsibility, or should we rebel against their efforts to tie us, or should we make our own choices? Is a person happier when tied to the responsibility or free to roam? Each choice has its trade-off. Then the choice is the key.

Responsibility is therefore a joy if it is our choice. Responsibility is a heavy yoke if it merely reflects someone else's idea of what our responsibility ought to be. Every year I re-read Richard Bach's *Jonathan Livingston Seagull.* Where better to read it than from a granite ledge a few scant feet above the waves, surrounded by seagulls.

The tide was high a half hour ago, and it will return to low tide, ebb and flood every six hours for eons. A human life as compared to the age of the tides is less than the snap of a finger. How can I overcome the limitations of necessary responsibilities I've been yoked with since the beginning? Why can't I accept the inevitable ebb and flood of life? Why this restlessness? Go to school, be responsible, get a job, get married, pay taxes, go to work, have kids, don't rock the boat, retire, grow old gracefully, say goo-goo to the grandchildren, become feeble, sans everything, the end.

Be responsible to whom? No one ever said "Remember, be responsible to yourself first, and meet your own needs." Oh, no, put yourself last, and then they won't call you selfish. Yet even the teachings of the Good Book say "Love thy neighbor as thyself." That seems to indicate that before you can give something, you have to have it.

Then love must begin with me loving me. I must not accept limitations set on me by others. And I must not set limitations on others. But sadly this has happened. Then courage must be the backbone of life's philosophy. We need courage to change what we can--courage to reject, without rancor, those messages that are no longer valid. To reject the values of others does not mean to reject the person themselves, simply their values. Of course, this means to question the greatest font of values, the most common source--our parents. To have values set by others is better than having no values at all.

At least with values that do not work, we can take the responsibility of changing them. We can make a slight alteration to tailor our own values and let go of the ones that no longer serve our purpose. But what of the parents who gave you their values. Didn't they offer their values, expecting they be adopted as gospel, never to be questioned but simply obeyed for as long as you live? That's where courage and love enter the picture. No argument, no defense, and no begging, simply live life by the values necessary to meet your needs. Be willing to share your values with others when they see you flying high above the flock with a new freedom. Don't try to sell it to them. Simply live it.

There will not be that many who have the courage to say, "I wish I could be my own person. How did Jonathan Livingston Seagull do it?" First, it seems, I must live with the new values as a fantasy in my imagination, then allow the feelings to issue forth, then accept the isolation from the group. The group is the group because they are afraid to see themselves as individuals. Intimacy is a naughty word. There is safety in numbers. The one who goes off by himself is branded as a weirdo, a loner, a malcontent, with statements like, "Why can't he/she be like everyone else?" Why indeed? Could it be that perhaps we are not on this earth to share mediocrity, to require sameness as a condition for acceptance?

Why can't we love in spite of our differences? Do all women have to be like men before they can be accepted by men, and vice versa?

If we each can excel, grow, express deep thoughts, and meet our own needs at no one else's expense, when we come back together, fire will have been discovered for the second time. I hope my children question the values I gave them. I must remember, without defensiveness, that the values I gave my children are merely what have been handed down generation after generation, and they must be evaluated by each on his path to being who he can be. Perhaps that's the quest sought by the religious, to express values on a higher plane. But alas, the religious are sometimes greedy and hungry for recognition. They seem to be more interested in making you believe their concept of God rather than rejoicing that you have one of your own. Sort of gives one reason to wonder who is right.

Each person, then, must make the lonely trip to his own place of higher value, must rise above his need for clothing, shelter, safety, and recognition. The trip to the "why" of life can best be charted with an acceptance of self.

76
CITIZEN PARTICIPATION

In January 1972 I was transferred to the Permits Section in the Maintenance Office for the Massachusetts Highway Department, but there was no room for me there. Joe McCarthy, the head of the Permits Section, held the same pay grade as I did. He did not ask for me to be there, and he was reluctant to assign me new projects. Actually, he wanted me to leave.

On the other hand, Mr. Kelly, the head of the entire Massachusetts Department of Public Works Maintenance Office, informed me there was no way in hell he would approve a transfer, especially since I had so recently arrived in his section. Herein is a problem within any bureaucracy--no division head wants to see his/her fiefdom shrink in size.

I had to find a way out of the Maintenance Division or go stark raving crazy. In the meantime, I embarked on a new course of studies to become expert at performing hydraulic studies.

I was rescued by two serendipitous events. I noticed that within a short time after stopping the booze, fortunate happenings with no logical explanations frequently occurred. That's when I became familiar with the word "serendipity."

First, the National Environmental Policy Act (NEPA) had been signed into law by President Nixon. NEPA placed great emphasis on Economic, Social and Environmental issues related to the construction of government-funded projects. To assure compliance with NEPA, the U.S. Department of Transportation had to issue guidelines for all the state transportation agencies. In the meantime, states had to do the best they could to respond to the letter of the law.

Under the Social consideration sections, NEPA emphasized the creation of an open and participatory highway planning process involving ordinary citizens. Pete Murphy, a civil engineer, was given the assignment of heading a hastily drawn-up office in Massachusetts called the EAC (Environmental Action Committee). I knew Pete from our days together on construction. He showed me the new law and explained the EAC's role. They were conducting public meetings around the State, finding out what people thought about the new highways that would run through their neighborhoods.

Conducting these types of meetings required a great deal of cool-headedness since the meetings were not governed by Roberts Rules of Parliamentary Procedures. They were modeled after New England town meetings where citizens were allowed to air their concerns with complete freedom to express themselves, and meetings got heated at times. I was really attracted to this sort of challenge.

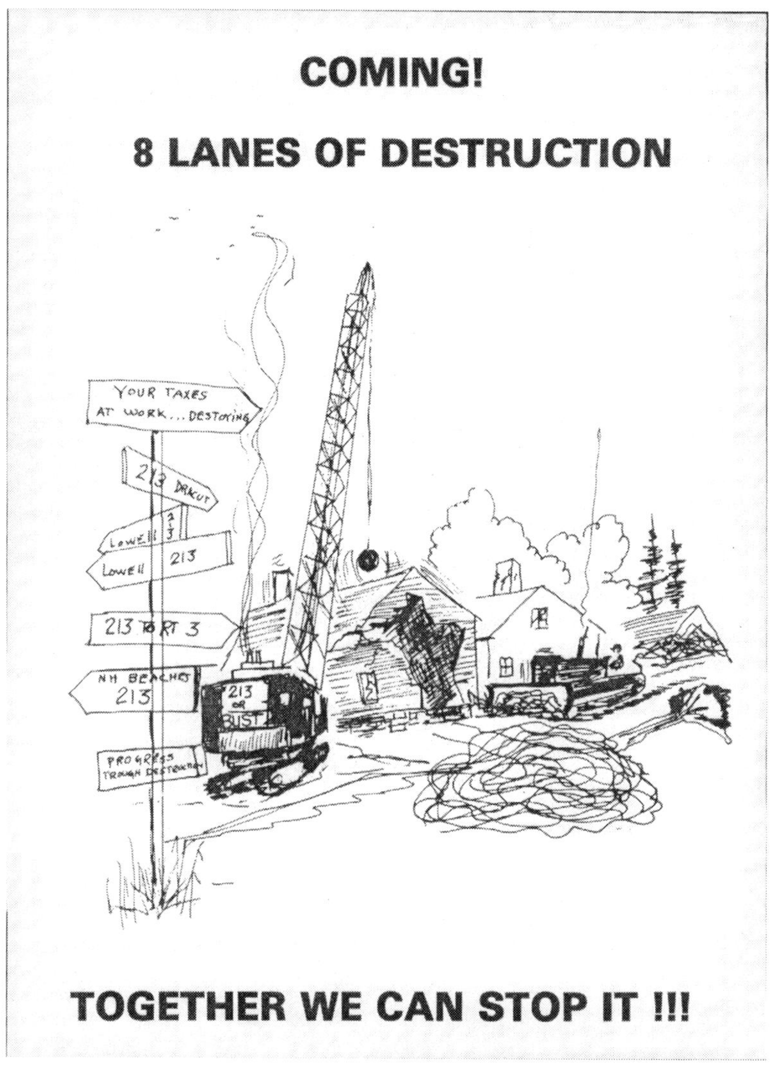

Late 1970s. Posters displayed in Dracut and Lowell, MA, used by opponents to the expansion of Route 213, to rile up citizens before I was scheduled to conduct a public meeting

Second, Bruce Campbell was appointed Commissioner of the Massachusetts Department of Public Works. Bruce was a friend of mine, now at the top of the pile. Pete Murphy informed me that

Jack Hurley, a traffic engineer I knew, was now in charge of the EAC and needed people to fill new positions there.

Murphy, Hurley, and I hatched a plan where Commissioner Bruce Campbell would request my transfer to the new group, now called the Environmental Section. Kelly would have no choice as he could not refuse the Commissioner. Later another old colleague, Bob Horigan, joined us. We were a foursome of engineers assigned to assure that the highway department became sensitive to the new environmental movement sweeping across the country. Our secretary, Sheila McCarthy, dubbed us the Irish Mafia.

I loved this new job. We were on the cutting edge. No one had ever done this before, and we were pretty much given a free reign to do whatever was needed to please the Federal Highway Administration. They had no idea what to do either. Intuitively, we all produced excellent results, in the process making many changes in the way the State Highway Department conducted business.

We all had to study with haste, reading the current literature to learn the basics about archaeology, marine zoology, historical preservation, parkland protection legislation, water quality, fresh and salt water wetlands, air quality, noise analysis, and relocation of people. We had to become skilled at meeting with the public on their turf, as well as making partnerships with federal, state and local agencies that heretofore never communicated with each other.

I discovered that I had a natural talent for conducting public meetings. I facilitated an emotionally-charged meeting in Newburyport, Massachusetts to discuss the widening of I-95 from four lanes to eight. Federal Highway representatives in the audience requested that their presence be kept a secret because they were there strictly to observe our meeting. We had no meeting guidelines, so I decided to proceed by running the meeting by keeping in mind and putting myself in the shoes of the citizens at the meeting who had fears about the proposed new highway. It worked, and I made a big impression on the

Feds. After many other such meetings around the State, I was selected to tour the country representing the Federal Highway Administration, teaching others how to conduct a public meeting. This led me into a contract with the Institute for Governmental Services at the University of Massachusetts to conduct regular seminars for State and locally-elected officials. I also wrote a book entitled *Conducting a Public Meeting*, published by University of Massachusetts at Amherst, which I used as the text for the training seminars.

77
WESTERN MASSACHUSETTS

I spent many years working in the western part of Massachusetts and became well known. I was especially successful in conducting public meetings on the controversial Route 2 highway project, which provided the basic materials for the book published at U. Mass. With the Federal Highway Administration (FHWA) we produced a training film, drawing from 40 hours of videotaping of my actual meetings and training sessions. I thought I was pretty hot stuff, flying around the country "doing my thing."

During the course of the Route 2 meetings, I realized that there *never* would be a new Route 2 through the Wendell State Forest. We were participating in a political game, helping the State politicians give the illusion that Boston was paying attention to the western politicians' desire to promote development. The continuous environmental impact studies were proof of their intentions.

Completing Route 2

Angry Citizens Stand in Way of Highway Construction

February 1977. Typical drawings by opponents to the relocation of Route 2 through the rural community of Wendell, MA, showing exaggerated damage to the community. These would appear before I conducted public meetings. Their cartoons did serve the purpose of getting more people to the meetings.

John Willey, Environmental Engineer with Dept. of Public Works, answered questions from Wendell residents about new Route 2 which may run through Wendell Depot.

At this time, a new engineer from the consulting engineering company of F.R. Harris was assigned to work with me on a public meeting for Route 2 in Greenfield, Massachusetts. Patrick (Paddy) Malone had worked for F.R. Harris in the deep water port in Bantry Bay, Ireland. He made a commanding presence, and together we were an excellent team. We could handle anything that came our way at the public meetings.

I became the "peoples' contact" with the Massachusetts Department of Public Works, and I established a bond with the citizens of Wendell. The reality is that I had actually become a peoples' *advocate.* My thoughts returned to years before when I watched the elderly woman at the West End Project in Boston carried out of her own home, and I remembered the old farmer who committed suicide in Methuen during the construction of I-495.

I began meeting from time to time with Michael Idoine, a very hard-working local activist for the Wendell people. I kept him attuned to the latest plans from Boston and comforted people with the knowledge that the road would never be built. The Route 2 saga continued long after I left the Department, and I have wonderful memories of how I helped the citizens of Wendell to be heard.

78
FEELINGS AND CONNECTIONS

I was sober only about five years when my feelings began to overwhelm me. To put this in context, people who succumb to alcoholism often pay a heavy price in arrested emotional development. I was like Washington Irving's Rip Van Winkle, coming out of a deep sleep and unaware of his new surroundings.

As part of my work, I encountered many professional women who were my peers. A significant portion of environmental/planning studies dealt with relocation of people and economic analyses, areas in which I had no expertise. I found myself heading for the office of Dianne Wood to discuss the contents of the latest report I was writing that covered a wide range of relocation problems. Dianne was part of a new group of relocation specialists the Massachusetts Department of Public Works was required to employ to comply with NEPA. My emotions were emerging, a new facet of recovery for which I was unprepared. Dianne was exceptionally beautiful, well-dressed, educated, confident, soft-spoken, knowledgeable, and a great conversationalist. Our work together was very brief, but I cannot find words to express the confusion, excitement, and elevated feelings that I experienced while in her presence.

As a result of my successes in community involvement, I also met Kathy Stein Hudson, a planner at the Central Transportation Planning Staff (CTPS) in Boston. Kathy was a no-nonsense woman with endless energy who enjoyed high visibility in Washington, D.C. She chaired the federal Citizen Participation Task Force for the Transportation Research Board. Kathy and I shared similar values, and we worked well together. Consequently I was appointed to serve on her committee in Washington D.C. where I was first exposed to the discipline of transportation planning.

I attended my first meeting with Kathy in her office on School Street in Boston. As I approached Kathy's office, I noticed Dianne sitting in an office nearby. I asked Kathy about Dianne being there, and she informed me that Dianne was now at CTPS (Central Transportation Planning Staff). As luck would have it, I had the opportunity to catch up again with Dianne. We occasionally met for lunch, and we chatted about life and its challenges. Dianne liked to discuss Marcel Proust, Freud, Maslow and others. I knew nothing of these philosophers and intellectual giants, so I began to read, just to be able to understand what she was saying. I read Nietzsche, Ralph Waldo Emerson, Victor Frankel and others. I picked up little gems that I could apply to my own life. Dianne motivated me to read books I probably would never have considered.

I always felt a connection with Dianne, and I enjoyed being in her company. She moved on to other responsibilities at a prestigious consulting firm in Cambridge, and then the Regional Planning Commission in Lowell. I visited with her from time to time and continued our dialog. She remarried, and the next thing I knew she was in Casablanca, Morocco, and then she was sent to Russia. We kept in touch for awhile, but then lost touch for a number of years. The memories of the respectful relationship with Dianne served me well over the next 20 years.

Over the years I had talked to my friend Michael Idoine from Wendell about my emerging feelings toward women. He seemed to me to be a free thinker, and I figured free spirits were comfortable with the subject of feelings. One wintry day, long after I had left the highway department, I travelled over 100 miles west to spend a day with Michael with the intent of exploring the subject of feelings. Michael and his wife Karen had a simple unfinished cottage deep in the woods. I had to trudge waist-deep in snow to get to the back door.

Michael greeted me with his self-conscious half smile and welcomed me in. The wood stove was putting out the BTU's, and an aroma of some hearty concoction on the stove turned out to be homemade sausage soup. With a belly full of soup we settled down to good discussions about Joseph Campbell, myths, religion, and my emerging feelings. We had a grand old time and went on to discuss life in general. Soon it was supper time. We ate another bowl of sausage soup, and I left to begin the trek out of the darkening Wendell woods, back home 100 miles to the east.

While I had not solved the "feelings" problem, I had moved one day closer to getting comfortable with the new direction my life was taking. Without being consciously aware, I was learning the importance of making emotional "connections." With Dianne, I thought it was because she was a beautiful woman. Of course, that did not hurt, but it was really about connecting with people on a different level. Then there was the connection of friendship I enjoyed with Michael Idoine.

One day I had an unusual visit from my brother-in-law, Mickey Brown, with his son Jeffery in tow. Mickey had been observing my recovery and knew Jeff was heading down the wrong street. He wanted me to have a conversation with Jeff. Jeff was 16, and I am sure he was about as interested in listening to me as I would have been if the situation had been reversed.

Though we made a good connection that day, we had little contact over the next 15 years or so. One day our paths crossed as I was on my way to work in Boston. The last person I expected to see was Jeff, and I'm sure he did not expect to encounter me. We had a brief conversation, and he told me that as a golf course superintendent, he had to update his license, and he was in Boston to attend a seminar on applying pesticides on golf courses. That chance meeting led to Jeff calling me on a regular basis. For the past 16 years we have been in contact about once a week, each of us learning from the other. He calls me "UJ," which stands for Uncle John.

Being open to new adventures has changed my life. Some adventures were simple and unique, like spending an afternoon baling hay with Bill and Nancy Ames, friends who lived on a farm in Boxford, Massachusetts. Also, I spent many an afternoon with Rory Allen, a man I met on a construction job who was also a lobsterman in Gloucester. I went out with him on his boat, helping him haul in his traps.

79
RAISING THE KIDS

In spite of our often unhappy relationship, Sally and I had plenty of good times, and we gave the kids a strong set of values. We went on vacations to the mountains and beaches, and we picnicked in the State parks of New Hampshire, to name a few of our efforts. At one point we had three kids with morning paper routes, and I learned all the routes in case one of them was sick. When they were younger, I went out in the dark early winter mornings to walk the routes with them. I helped each of the children open a savings account to bank their paper route money. Later they landed jobs at places like CVS, Papa Gino's, and Kentucky Fried Chicken. We made ourselves available to assist with home work.

I imposed constant discipline in the household, which I believe helped keep our large family functioning.

To this day the kids talk fondly about the "Goon Platoon," which was a hold-over from my Navy days. In the Navy, a special barrack was reserved for those who could not or would not follow instructions. Their unit was called the Motivational Squad, affectionately nick-named the "Goon Platoon," a place where special attention was available for those who needed an attitude adjustment.

In our home, all the children were expected to be seated at the kitchen table before the dinner was served. I cooked meals from scratch, and no TV or radio was permitted in the kitchen. On the wall above the kitchen table was a picture of a fish. Underneath it read, "Even a fish wouldn't get in trouble if he kept his mouth shut." I allowed no playing "grab ass" (Navy lingo for inappropriate behavior). If one of the kids violated these simple rules, I would simply point at him or her and say, "Goon Platoon." That meant you picked up your plate and silverware and went to the counter on the opposite side of the kitchen, sat on a stool, and finished your meal alone. No one was allowed to speak to the offender or make fun of them for their banishment.

Unbeknownst to me, one day Sharon pre-planned a "Goon Platoon" episode. Sally's aunt from Canada arranged for her only daughter, Carol, to spend a week with us. All the kids were excited and looking forward to meeting Carol, who turned out to be a well-mannered young woman. Carol was an only child of a single mother, so her visit with us meant she was in for a "Brady Bunch" experience. She arrived with a return plane ticket allowing her to spend a few days with us. Her mother was concerned she would become homesick and would want to return pronto.

It just so happened that at the time of Carol's arrival, the dishwasher was broken. We made assignments for the kids to wash and dry the dishes. When they complained about the lack of a dish washer, I quipped, "You all have one at the end of your elbow." After Carol's first meal, we assigned her to wash dishes.

On about the second evening meal with Carol, Sharon began to really misbehave at the dinner table. I shot her a look, and yet she persisted. With the usually gruff delivery, I pointed my right index finger followed by an order, "Sharon, Goon Platoon." The children began snickering, yet Sharon obediently picked up her dinner and moved to the counter across the kitchen.

Carol was having the time of her life. She enjoyed the mayhem and excitement of being part of such a large family. She adjusted without a problem and did not want to go home. In fact, after a month, her worried mother prevailed, and Carol returned to Canada.

Years later, a few of the culprits, including Sharon, engaged me in a conversation to explain that when Carol visited, they had been bragging about the Goon Platoon and telling Carol how I was an unyielding disciplinarian. Sharon had arranged to show Carole how it worked. I cringed when I thought to myself, "What if I hadn't come through for Sharon and her cohorts?"

For Sunday morning breakfasts, the primary requirement was that everyone would eat breakfast at the same time. Not everyone wanted to comply, but I remember with a smile seeing all the lovely young faces at the same table. In order to get their attention and to awaken the sleepyheads, I played my favorite music at a high volume, usually opera arias with Pavarotti, Domingo, Bergonzi, Tebaldi, Callas and a long list of other greats. Typically I would offer an open menu, including homemade apple cinnamon muffins, French toast, home fries, bacon and eggs anyway you wanted them. Rick held the record for eating the most pieces of French toast slathered with real Vermont maple syrup.

Rick's job was to mow the lawn. We had an old hand-push lawn mower for our small grass plot. When Rick learned that his grandfather had offered me a power lawn mower, he was really excited because now he would have a chance to operate a powered rotary lawn mower. When I refused the new lawnmower, explaining the power mower was a safety hazard for the kids, all summer long he was disconsolate.

80
MARINES AND SAILORS

Rick was surrounded with sisters who loved him, but I think he wanted to escape home, much as I did at about the same age. I was a rigid disciplinarian, a pain in Rick's ass. Without too much ado, in 1975 he signed up for a four-year hitch with the Marine Corp. I am very happy to say that the entire family made the trek to Rick's graduation at the Marine Recruit Training Center in Paris Island, South Carolina. He was a model marine, and we were all very proud of Richard. He looked tall, lean, and squared away, so different from the young man who had left our home just three months previous.

But the trip was not without a major incident. Years before, Cheryl had sewn Linda a little square-shaped doll with floppy ears and legs and arms of unequal length. Made from a towel and stuffed with old cloth, it was possibly the homeliest creature on the planet. Linda named it Bojangles, and she could not be separated from him. How she picked this name I don't know, maybe from watching old movies. The only Bojangles I ever knew was Bill "Bojangles" Robinson, the famous black dancer. He made many movies in the 30's with Shirley Temple, and everyone loved him.

On the return trip from South Carolina we discovered that Bojangles was missing. Linda made it abundantly clear that she could not go a mile further until we found him. We were a long way from the motel where we stayed. Sally told me to pull into the nearest gas station. She called the motel and returned to the car beaming with relief. "Yes," they had Bojangles, and "no," Linda could not wait for him to be mailed home. We turned around with the station wagon full of kids and clothes and returned to the motel. As the housekeeper rounded the corner with Bojangles in her arms, the look of delight and happiness radiating from Linda was well worth the trip back.

In the early months of 1983 Linda made a decision to join the Navy. She joined during her senior year at high school under the delayed enlistment program. That meant that upon graduation, she would be required to leave for boot camp.

Linda and I had been having a running disagreement about keeping her room clean and orderly. After a few warnings and no results, I entered the bedroom one day and emptied her bureau and closet and stripped the bed, dumping everything in the middle of the floor. When she came home, I explained that I wanted her to "square away" her room. When Linda saw the mess, she went ballistic, but she put the room in order.

In the late summer of that year, Linda was in boot camp in Orlando, Florida when a couple of her shipmates were caught playing "grab-ass." The company commander ordered the entire company out on the drill field to perform calisthenics. Upon completion of the calisthenics, the company commander informed the recruits that there would be a barracks inspection in one hour.

As they entered the barracks, Linda's shipmates began screaming, crying and wailing. While the recruits were out on the drill field doing push-ups, the company commander's assistants had been busy "hurricaning the barracks," pulling off the bedding and emptying the lockers into the middle of the floor. The barracks were torn asunder. There were 59 young women in a state of shock, and the 60th (Linda) laughing hysterically as she thought to herself, "That's where the SOB got the idea."

I wanted to send Linda some homemade cookies. I remembered my own boot camp days at Great Lakes and knew if you just sent a small batch, the CPO or the Instructors would gobble them up. Their reasoning was, one for all and all for one. I decided to send enough cookies for the whole company. I set up a baking station at home and made over 300 chocolate chip cookies, and packed them in an empty wine case, averaging 12 to 15 cookies per sleeve. I shipped the whole box to Linda. All her shipmates had five cookies apiece, and she became the hero of her company.

Our whole family attended her graduation in Orlando. Hundreds of recruits were passing in review. The temperature was 102 in the shade. Linda looked really great, and her company of 60 impressed us as they marched by in formation. A dozen ambulances were lined up, ready to carry away those recruits who passed out from the heat. If my memory serves me correctly, not one of Linda's fellow recruits passed out.

A year later she had a rough experience which really tested her character. She was assigned to the submarine tender USS Hunley AS-31, which was stationed in Scotland. She was the first female sailor to serve on that ship. When she reported for duty on the ship, she took the initiation and razzing and survived a lot of abuse including sexual harassment. Linda rose above it, and in time she managed to gain the respect of her shipmates.

81
RESENTMENTS

While working in the Boston office of the Massachusetts Department of Public Works, I met Tom Byron, another man on the same path as I was. Tom is an easy-to-like Irishman, originally from Dorchester. I whined and complained about how awful my life was. One day I said, "Tom, I think I'm going crazy." He replied, "You know, John, sometimes it takes five years to get your marbles back after you quit drinking." I said, "Tom, I've been sober six years." Tom's instant reply was, "With some it takes 10." Rather than feeling discouraged, I felt hope that maybe I was okay, even if a little slow. As it turned out, Tom's estimate of 10 years was pretty close to being on target.

For the first time in my adult life, I was experiencing feelings of all kinds which I suppose had been buried during the years I drank. I was overwhelmed with strong emotions. I felt horribly sad. I felt ripping angry. I was elated with happiness. I was anxious and jumpy. I left home and stayed a few days with Tom and his family in Braintree. Tom and his wife, Martha, tried to calm me down. After a few days Tom pulled me aside and said, "Look, John, ya' gotta' grow up. Stop running. Go home. Face the music. And remember you caused all this shit."

I had been going to therapy, but I could not bear to look at myself. I had a list of resentments as long as my arm, most of them involving my father and my wife, Sally.

I did learn that "a resentment is a negative remembrance of a past event kept alive in the present moment." I was concentrating on the past, and that robbed me of the present. Maintaining these old resentments was using up my energy and keeping my mind in a negative place. I learned that nurturing old resentments was a death knell for a relationship, and could eat me up alive.

My relationship with my father was not getting any better. I continued to try to gain his acceptance. Every time I visited him, I could feel the tension build between us. I was always uncomfortable in his presence. My sisters visited too, looking for Daddy's approval, much as I did. We always hoped that one day he would be in a good frame of mind. Those times when my father was happy, he was marvelous. He had a winning personality and a great sense of humor. However, when the switch was thrown, he could instantaneously become a nasty monster, saying things that would curl the hairs on a longshoreman's head. While my father held Inquisition-like sessions, my mother sat there playing her fingers game. I found out years later that when my sisters Barbara and Joan visited my father, they took Valium to numb themselves, in an effort to protect against his verbal insults and condemnations. Taking drugs was not an option for me because of my fear that drugs would lead me to picking up a drink.

My youngest sister, Norma, took the full brunt of his meanness for the greatest length of time. She was the only child living with my parents after I ran off to join the Navy. My sister, Barbara moved to Boston where she was a nurse at Beth Israel Hospital. Joan was married and living in New Hampshire. Norma became the caretaker of my parents and their home, but often her hard work was taken for granted or criticized.

82
WHAT ANNIVERSARY?

My parents' 50th wedding anniversary was approaching, and my sisters and I wanted to mark the occasion with a celebration. However, we were not sure of the exact date. They did not talk about their anniversary nor had they ever celebrated it to the best of our knowledge. Of course we all had our suspicions, including that they were never married and we were a bunch of bastards, or that something was amiss that they did not want uncovered.

However, we decided to make an attempt at family normalcy. None of us were in a financial position to send them off on a vacation to the South Seas, but we certainly could host a celebration at one of the function halls in Haverhill. I thought, "I'll get their acceptance one way or another; they'll be really impressed." I approached my father and mother about having a party. My mother was fidgety and nervous and began to count her fingers and look at my father with fear in her eyes. I knew then I was on thin ice. My father exploded, with a warning for me to mind my own business. He was irrational, and threatened a law suit!

I knew they were married in Hampstead, New Hampshire, and I decided to go there and get their marriage certificate. I was one angry man. I approached the Town Clerk and demanded to see the records, and she tried to delay me. In retrospect, I believe she saw the fire in my eyes and hoped I would cool down a bit. I read her the riot act, threatening to go to the attorney general if she did not make the records available. I got the record. My parents were married in March of 1930 and I was born in August 1930. My mother was pregnant. They had to get married.

Big deal, I thought, the same thing happened to me and to my grandfather.

I confronted my parents and watched them squirm as they were forced to face their worst nightmare. Until much later, I did not understand the fear, hurt and anger that they experienced at my hands.

Once their emotions settled, my sister Norma arranged for a very nice celebration at Sailor Bill's, a popular function hall in nearby Salisbury, Massachusetts. The entire family showed up, including grandchildren, cousins, and spouses. A really good time was had by all. Dear old Dad behaved wonderfully that day, and both he and Mom were obviously very happy.

I do remember a twist to this story. The following year when March came around, I did not know what to do about the upcoming anniversary. Should I send a card, offer to take them out to dinner, or say nothing as had been the routine for all my life? I knew they did not want another celebration, so I elected to ignore the newly-recognized anniversary date. My father went ballistic about me forgetting their anniversary, and all returned to normal.

83
EXPLORING OPTIONS

The Massachusetts Department of Public Works was becoming a chaotic place to work because over the years the Governor had tried to dismantle civil service rules governing employment. He wanted to get rid of rules like requiring people to pass exams to get promoted rather than appointing politicians' best buddies, guaranteed employment without layoffs, a generous benefit package and pension at retirement. As engineers, we were all members of the A.F.S.C.M.E (American Federation of State, County, and Municipal Employees), the largest public employees and health care workers union in the United States. For more than two years, Democrat Governor Dukakis had refused to sign our union contract. We were all fighting for our jobs, and we had to become political. I remember participating in a strike. Everyone was on edge. Since the engineers and scientists were a small percentage of the larger union, they formed their own organization called M.O.S.E.S. (Massachusetts Organization of State Engineers and Scientists). MOSES banded together in a campaign to "Dump the Duke."

Michael Dukakis lost the election to the Republican, Ed King. Much to our chagrin, the new Governor hired a hatchet man named James Kerecieotis as Assistant Secretary of Transportation. He continued the annihilation of civil service employment rules.

My buddies, two career engineers, Edward Fitzgerald and Peter Murphy, both left the Department to work for consulting engineering companies. Many others followed. They urged me to join them, but I did not have my professional engineering license (P.E.) and was anxious to protect my investment in the pension system. Although Kerecieotis was making our lives uncomfortable, and I really wanted to leave, I was afraid to let go of the security of civil service.

My mind was scattered. I was at odds with my job, my wife, and with myself. A short time later I decided to explore the option of resigning from the State and opening a restaurant. I visited SCORE (Service Core of Retired Executives) at the Small Business Administration. I presented my plan to a small business counselor who had been a successful restaurateur before retirement. He gently reminded me of the restaurant lifestyle which required long hours, nights, and weekends. He compared owning a restaurant to being a civil service engineer for the State. He figured out how much a restaurant would have to gross in order to equal my engineer's salary and benefits. I will always remember that he said to me, "If it don't figure on paper, son, it don't figure." He suggested I go back to work in a restaurant, observe and learn the full range of operations, and see if owning a restaurant was what I really wanted.

I talked to my friend Donald Basiliere, who owned Captain Chris's Seafood, a large restaurant with a function room and seafood market. I told him about my plan, and he jumped at the chance to hire an experienced chef who did not drink (an oddity in the business). My first day in the kitchen instantly brought me back to the familiar routine. I worked a double shift, helping to turn out as many as 500 meals a day. I was off on a new adventure. However, in less than a year at Captain Chris's, I could see this was not for me. I gave up the idea of owning a restaurant.

However, during that year, I had plenty of energy for new pursuits. Besides working as an engineer for the Department of Public Works in Boston, and as a chef at Captain Chris's Seafood restaurant in Haverhill, I was an active member of the Mayor's Crime Task Force in Haverhill, and the president of the Millvale Citizen Group. In September 1981, I catered an outdoor dinner for a 200-person wedding party for my next-door neighbors, Dave and Shannon Hewey. Sally, Shannon, bridesmaids, and friends all chipped in to make it a memorable occasion.

84
U.S. COAST GUARD

The morale at the Massachusetts Department of Public Works (MDPW) was "lower than whale shit." I had been appointed an Associate Environmental Engineer Grade 6A, which was close to the top of the engineering ladder. The new administration was bent on dismantling civil service rules, and they made their goals abundantly clear.

I could not ride out the storm. One day in a fit of rage and confusion, I quit the permanent civil service position at the tender age of 52, an unheard of thing to do. Every engineer's goal at the MDPW was to get as close to a Grade 6 as possible before retiring after 30 years. Here I was, quitting after 21 years, at a relatively young age, holding a permanent Grade 6A.

1982. Party at Joseph's Aquarium Restaurant in Boston, MA celebrating my retirement from MA Department of Public Works. My colleagues "roasted" me, and I had fun responding. Two good buddies, Bob Horigan at left, and Tom Byron at right.

Mom and Dad Willey were really proud of me as I started a new career with the U.S. Coast Guard.

The Department of Public Works is part of the Department of Transportation. I made an appointment with the Secretary of Transportation, James Carlin, and explained what was happening at the Department of Public Works. I was pissed off and I wanted to tell someone off. I closed our discussion by reminding him of a popular song called "Take This Job and Shove It." I shook hands with Secretary Carlin and departed.

As Project Manager at the MDPW, I had been heavily involved with the United States Coast Guard because we needed Coast Guard permits to build or repair our bridges over the navigable waters of the United States. I became friendly with Bill Naulty, the civilian head of the Bridge Branch at the Coast Guard and came to admire and respect the integrity he brought to the workplace. Bill was a rock-solid engineer and a decent person. He was level-headed and lived a respectable life with his loving family. However, in the early 1980's Bill had experienced significant medical problems and was forced to take a leave of absence from his job.

This left Captain David Parr, head of Aids to Navigation, in charge. He was nervous because he knew nothing about bridge regulations or environmental regulations pertaining to bridges. The military segment of the Admiral's staff wanted no part of dealing with the bridges because bridges were a constant source of civilian political intrigue with great potential to hurt a military career. When I approached him for a job, he was delighted, saying the number two position was open and I would be his assistant.

Captain Parr explained the long drawn-out bureaucratic process required to advertise the job and meet all the regulations. I told Captain Parr, "I'm a veteran." He replied, "Great. That will cut the time." I went on to say, "I'm a disabled veteran." Captain Parr's problem was solved. My name went to the top of the list, and I was hired without delay.

In 1982, I started as a GS 11 in the Bridge Branch at the First Coast Guard District Headquarters at 150 Causeway Street, located adjacent to the Boston Garden at the North Station. My salary was $23,565, a bit lower than my State salary of $25,844. However, after I turned in my letter of resignation to Rita Berry in Personnel at the State Department of Public Works, she explained that I was eligible for a small retirement pay of about $6,500 a year. The result was that I grossed $30,000.

My position was solid, and I loved working at the Coast Guard, dealing with navigational and environmental issues related to new and existing bridges. However, we learned in 1985 that the Bridge Branch function in Boston would be closed and moved to Governors Island in the Hudson River off the tip of Manhattan.

No way would I move to New York City and have to travel by ferry to work. The thought of living in New York City was frightening. I decided to leave the US Coast Guard, even though I liked the unique nature of the work and the rapport I had developed with some top-notch people, both military and civilian. At a well-attended goodbye dinner and testimonies from Bill Naulty, Admiral Bauman, and the Chief of Staff, I was presented with a nautical clock which I prize to this day.

Rear Admiral Richard A. Bauman, Commander of the First Coast Guard District, presenting me with an achievement award at the Headquarters Office, Boston, MA.

85
BARBARA'S WEDDING

My first wife, Rita, was obviously very happy with her new husband, a German/American named Paul Griesbach. While visiting my kids in Michigan, I could see that Rita really loved Paul. Although I did not know Paul well, I did understand that he was providing a good home for my children.

Sally and I traveled to Michigan in June 1983 to attend the wedding of my daughter, Barbara. As her dad, I was to have the honor of giving her away. I told Sally I felt like a phony, traveling to Michigan to give Barbara away, when Paul had been more of a father to her than I. I sat down to talk with Barbara. I told her I felt uncomfortable walking her down the aisle when Paul had been there for her all these years in Michigan. She said, "Dad, there's no way I'm going to have Paul walk me down the aisle while you sit there and watch." I thought to myself, "This is a hell of a problem to dump on my daughter a day before the wedding!"

After some more thought, I approached my daughter and asked her if she would mind if we both walked her down the aisle. She said, "Oh! Dad! That grouchy old coot wouldn't want to do that." I asked her to talk with Paul to see if he would consider walking with us down the aisle, Paul on one side, and I on the other. Within the hour Barbara came back to me with a smile on her face. She said, "Dad I asked him, and he started to cry." The three of us made a picture never to be forgotten. Paul walked straight as a soldier and smiled at all his friends as we made our way to the altar. I couldn't help notice that Rita had turned in her pew. She and Sally held hands as we three passed by. Rita said to Sally, "We did a good job." Without anger, we had created a winning experience for everyone.

86
RUNNING AWAY

Our marriage was progressing steadily downhill. However, Sally and I did connect sometimes, and we could do great things together. One example – My son, John Jr. and Pamela Fiala, decided to get married in the summer of 1988. I do not recall why Rudy Fiala chose not to host the wedding for them. Anyhow, the kids' budget was tight. Sally and I suggested they get married in our spacious, well-groomed back yard at 530 East Broadway, in Haverhill. Jim Dever, a friend of John's who was a professional singer, agreed to sing *a cappella* at the wedding ceremony. I made a wooden archway leading into one of our many gardens, where he and Pamela could stand for the ceremony. We catered the wedding with help from many friends and family. The party was lovely, and Sally and I proved we could achieve spectacular results together. On those occasions, I always wondered why we could not do the same thing again. Why couldn't we repeat a great day together?

Unfortunately, our beautiful "dream house" in the woods did not improve the marriage. One morning on the way to work, my mind snapped, and all I could think to do was run. Without any planning or forethought, I found myself in the office of a large real estate office. Within the hour I had rented an apartment in East Hampstead, New Hampshire. I called a couple of buddies, John Torrisi and Dave Ringland, and the next day they helped move furniture and belongings from our "dream house" into my apartment. The suddenness of this move stunned Sally. She was bewildered, frightened and deeply hurt. I was off on my new adventure with my head in the clouds and my feet planted firmly in mid-air.

I went to see a lawyer in Ipswich, Massachusetts and told him my plight. He asked on what grounds I wanted to get divorced. I could not come up with anything except that I was tired of fighting and tired of being a miserable bastard. Actually I was embarrassed, and I did not want to tell the lawyer or anyone how I really felt about our contentious life together and the anger and resentments I felt towards Sally.

Within a few weeks we decided to get back together. We were going to return to our love nest in the dream house and live happily ever after. Our first "date" was a nostalgic drive along the ocean to York, Maine where we found a romantic-looking restaurant with an open deck overlooking the ocean. We ate a lunch of seafood and lobsters with an undercurrent of anxiety. I knew that economic fear, not love, was bringing us back together. We actually got into an argument on the drive home, right back where we started. Yet we continued on our course, both knowing no other way to proceed.

Another 15 years would pass before we both gave up on the marriage. Sally and I spent a lot of time and money trying to learn how to live in a warm, happy relationship. We realized the reasons for our failure to live in harmony, but understanding was not helping us apply the knowledge. Sometimes Sally and I would arrive at the therapist's office in pretty good spirits, yet we would leave an hour later in a bitter argument that would last for days.

I recall that 1985 was the last year we spent at Bailey Island, and our differences seemed too great to surmount. We did not have our usual large July family gathering at Bailey Island that year as the kids were scattered around the country.

87
ACTOR, ENGINEER, OR WHAT?

After leaving the Coast Guard, I started a new position with the United States Environmental Protection Agency (EPA). I was a manager of the Mobile Source Enforcement Program in the Air Management Division. My office was about four feet square, on the 24th floor of the JFK Building in Boston. The elevators were frequently out of order. People who just started working there soon began planning what they were going to do when they retired.

A year later I resigned from the EPA and signed on for one year as a private engineering consultant with the Massachusetts Department of Environmental Protection (DEP). My most interesting project was preparing repair plans for the historic Long Wharf in Boston Harbor, built in the 1700s. I also designed piers for the Boston Harbor Island Park. Often I traveled out to the Boston Harbor islands on a DEP boat to evaluate park shelters and piers. This was the best part of my job.

One evening in late 1987 while talking with Rudy Fiala, a well-to-do retired advertising executive from New York, and the father of my daughter-in-law, Pamela, the conversation turned to show business, advertising, and TV commercials. Rudy suggested I should give show business a try. Soon after, I met Dida Hagen, who worked in the contract office of the MBTA in Boston. She was a very attractive woman who later was crowned Mrs. Massachusetts. Dida also owned an acting school in Malden. I decided to sign up for acting classes.

At Dida's direction I went to the Ford Model agency on Newbury Street in Boston to see about getting a "head shot" for my actor portfolio. I was introduced to Vivian Williams, a fashion model who would be my contact person at Ford's. Vivian told me where to get the head shots taken and accompanied me on a couple of auditions for TV commercials. Vivian alerted me to the casting studio of Collenge-Pickman in Cambridge. I introduced myself and let them know I was available for auditions. This was heady stuff, working with models, auditioning, taking acting classes, and meeting people with totally different outlooks on the world than the conservative, stodgy engineers who populated my other world.

When the movie world discovered John Willey, I would make it big! Should I change my name? Take advanced classes? Quit engineering? The squirrels in my mind were now running in all directions, bumping into each other.

Meanwhile at the acting school in Malden, I played the lead role in *The Dining Room* by A.R. Gurney, a humorous and compassionate play with 18 different scenes, perfect for an acting school. The actors move around the scenes rather than the scenes being changed. We presented the play live on public TV. I was the Dad trying to get my disinterested son, Tom, to listen to my plans for my funeral. We did a credible job, Tom and I, especially in the scene where I looked him in the eye, paused, let our eyes meet, and finally said in a fearful questioning tone, "You do love me, don't you?" There were tears in the eyes of my fellow students.

I was getting audition calls from Ford and Collenge-Pickman. I landed an all-day gig as an extra in a TV movie called the *Fitzgeralds and the Kennedys.* We were filming in the Harvard Yard in Cambridge. At supper one night, I sat close to Charles Durning, a famous actor who played the part of Honey Fitz. After that day-long stint, I realized acting was not going to support my family, and that I had to concentrate on engineering.

September 1988. Shooting the movie, The Fitzgeralds and the Kennedys, *on location in Harvard Yard, Cambridge, MA. In this movie, I played the "Professor" (at left), surrounded by "students."*

I was ready to leave the Department of Environmental Protection. I was upset with the unacceptable political/bureaucratic nonsense. I remember working hard to design repairs for the historic Long Wharf. Various sections of the Revolutionary War-era pier were failing. My work included research in dirty old archives strewn with rat turds. After discovering a perfectly good set of complete repair drawings that were produced by a very competent engineering firm 10 years prior to my tenure, I became disgusted, and started searching out other opportunities.

88
VANASSE HANGEN BRUSTLIN

In October 1988 I excitedly looked forward to starting a new position with Vanasse Hangen Brustlin, an engineering design company. I knew one of the owners, Jim D'Angelo, having met him when he worked a few years for the Massachusetts Department of Public Works. I also worked for his father, Joe, in previous years during my drinking days.

As luck would have it, I was assigned to the roadway design division at VHB. I worked for Ron Thompson. Ron had a saying framed on the wall behind his desk for all to read: *THE BEATINGS WILL CONTINUE UNTIL MORALE IMPROVES.* Ron was young enough to be my son. He had a masters degree in engineering, was a very hard worker, and a principle in the firm. He was also impossible to please.

On November 26, 1991 after only three years with the firm, I received a commendation from the Board of Directors accompanied with a cash bonus for bringing in the biggest job to date which netted the company several million in fees. The commendation reads as follows:

Dear John:

The Board of Directors of Vanasse Hangen Brustlin, Inc. wishes to offer its strongest commendation in recognition of your efforts pursuing project assignments with the Massachusetts Bay Transportation Authority. As evidenced by the Firm's recent notification of our selection for the Fall River/New Bedford extension of the Stoughton Commuter Rail Line, you have helped to establish VHB's presence as a major player in the Public Works market.

Your efforts are notable and have yielded great results. We all thank you for your efforts.

The commendation was signed by the Chairman and ten Board Members (including Mr. Thompson).

89
MASSAGE THERAPY

When I landed the new job at VHB, Sally gave me a party and a card with a gift certificate for a body massage. So we could go together, my daughter, Sharon, had also given her husband a gift certificate. However, for reasons of his own, her husband decided not to get a massage. So off I went to "Massage Only" in historic Newburyport, for my first body massage ever. I was really nervous, but I went anyway.

"Hi. I'm John Willey, here for an appointment." I tried my best to act nonchalant and cool. The studio was typical of spaces in Newburyport, with its Federalist architecture, and a bumpy, uneven brick sidewalk approach. Inside were distressed wood floors laid in about 1815 but newly sanded and finished, exposed brick walls, heavy wood beams, white trim, and green potted plants. In the background I could hear new age music playing softly. Coming from somewhere in the recesses of this quaint space, I smelled a faint hint of incense burning.

A very pleasant, trim woman greeted me with a smile and said, "Susan will be with you in a minute. Please sit down and be comfortable." I sat down and was, of course, uncomfortable. I was certainly not prepared for Susan. When she appeared, I saw a drop-dead, gorgeous woman, with a trim figure, wearing a well-fitted white tee shirt. When she smiled at me, I could feel my sweating hands and an eagle flying around in my stomach with his wing tips scraping my insides. All I could think was "Oh my God, she's going to put her hands on my body. Yikes!"

Susan, a recent graduate, was about 20 years old, very professional and extremely understanding about my nervousness. When I tried to tip Susan at the reception desk, Jackie, one of the owners, reminded me that Massage Only meant exactly that, and they preferred not to accept tips.

I visited once a month for a massage. At Christmastime I was in Jordan Marsh buying presents, and I spotted a sweater that would look good on Susan. I bought it and had it gift wrapped. At my next appointment, I openly presented the gift to Susan. She very nervously declined and set it aside. After the massage, she asked me to see Jackie. I guessed I had screwed up and was going to get an ass-chewing and be told not to come back.

I had no idea the owner, Jackie, was also a psychotherapist. She invited me into her office, and I followed, feeling quite intimidated. Jackie was soft-spoken and explained in a very gentle manner that sometimes a massage and being treated with nurturing kindness could overwhelm a person who lacked that kind of attention in daily life. Bingo! Jackie hit the nail on the head. Ending our meeting, Jackie quietly handed me the present without a word spoken.

Conversations with Susan had become as important to me as the relaxing effect of the massage. I realized that I had become comfortable having a woman as a friend. My next appointment with Susan, I thanked both her and Jackie. Susan and I remain good friends today, over 20 years after first meeting.

In 2007, Susan decided to close out her business and to attend school to train as a physical therapist. Along with many of her other clients, I felt a sense of loss. We were like an extended family. After about a year, one of the clients called Susan and insisted that Susan make an appointment with her for a massage. Apparently Susan wanted to reconnect with her old clients too. She set up a room in her home and made occasional appointments with past clients. It was a good idea and an instant success.

90
EMBRACE THE WORLD LIKE A LOVER

During a therapy session in Andover, Dr. Joseph Harrington handed me a quote from Morris West's novel, "The Shoes of the Fisherman." As a discussion-starter, we focused on this one paragraph:

> It takes so much to be a full human being that there are very few who have the enlightenment or the courage to pay the price.... One has to abandon altogether the search for security and reach out to the risk of living with both arms. One has to embrace the world like a lover. One has to accept pain as a condition of existence. One has to court doubt and darkness as the cost of knowing. One needs a will stubborn in conflict, but apt always to total acceptance of every consequence of living and dying.

I wanted to be "a full human being." I was willing to pay a price in order to live a life I loved, rather than continue my past chaotic lifestyle. The actual financial price was steep. At times I worked two jobs to pay the bills, but still gave priority to seeing psychologists and therapists I consulted along the way. I also accepted the emotional pain of taking an inventory of my past and present behaviors and making course corrections necessary to "embrace the world like a lover."

In 1989 my mother wrote in her poem, "To feel loved and wanted, that is the greatest reward." I understand now that my loving mother planted this desire within me many years ago. She hoped I too would achieve her goal. For years when I read and re-read that poem I felt empty, because hadn't she failed, spending her life desperately looking for love from a man who had none to give her? Now I understand I missed her real message because I was blinded by my own anger toward my father. My mother was not desperate. She had a vision. She saw through my father's angry armor and depression, and in her 80s dared to write about her lifelong dream. Frances Chase Willey, with all her quiet endurance during my conflicts with my father, had given me a gift of understanding about the importance of love.

A long time ago I met a man named Doug Cole, who ranted and raved and screamed about his inability to manage life. He said, "Nobody gave me the Goddam rules. No wonder I'm fucked up!" I identified with Doug. I too did not know the "rules" about how to live an orderly life. Once sober, I began a lifelong insatiable quest for knowledge about how to live a good life, devouring books on human behavior, psychology and philosophy.

91
WATCHWORDS

Not too long before he died, my father gave me a book published in 1891, the only material possession I have from my father, and I prize it dearly. *Watchwords* is a book of poems by John Boyle O'Reilly, an Irish patriot who lived in Boston for awhile. The particular poem I like is called "The Hidden Sin."

Who hides a sin is like a hunter who
Once warmed a frozen adder with his breath,

And when he placed it near his heart it flew
With poisoned fangs and stung that heart to death.
A sin admitted is nigh half-atoned,
And while the fault is red and freshly done,
If we but drop our eyes and think, ---'tis owned,-
'Tis half forgiven, half the crown is won.
But if we heedless let it reek and rot,
Then pile a mountain on its grave, and turn
With smiles to all the world, --- that tainted spot
Beneath the mound will never cease to burn.

I believe the hidden sin O'Reilly refers to is what I call "resentments." I buried my resentments and let them reek and rot so they continued to burn. My resentments toward my father, and then Sally, caused endless grief for my family and me. I was not aware how much I paid to hold onto those resentments.

92
DENISE

In July 1989 I was returning from a week's conference in Breckenridge, Colorado, and my plane landed in Chicago before continuing on to Boston. I stayed on board during the layover. I was alone in the main cabin of an enormous DC-10, reading a book, when I sensed movement and looked up. Way at the far end of the auditorium-sized cabin was a beautiful, tall, slender, young blond crossing the plane from left to right. She reminded me of the movie actress Kim Novak. I sighed, dropped my eyes and continued to read.

"Pardon me, sir. I'm sitting in the window seat." said the young lady. This plane holds 300 passengers, I thought, and she is sitting next to me! "My name is Denise Arrell from Minnesota, and I'm going to Cape Cod," she announced. I immediately put the book away and said, "Hi. I'm John Willey heading for Boston." "Do you live in Boston?" she asked. "No, I live in a city about 35 miles northeast from Boston," and the conversation went on non-stop until we arrived in Boston. At the time, Denise was a college student traveling to Woods Hole in Falmouth, Massachusetts. I was old enough to be her father, but for two hours we talked non-stop about our lives, our hopes and dreams.

When the plane touched down, I was amazed at the feeling of loss I experienced as we bid each other goodbye. She went her way, and I went mine. Two weeks later I received a post card from Denise, thanking me for the information I had given her about the Cape. Our correspondence began with that post card and has continued to this day. Over the past 20 years we've written hundreds of letters and talked by phone numerous times.

The next time I saw Denise was nearly 10 years later in October 1998 when my wife, Barbara, and I flew to Minnesota to visit with Jan, a friend and colleague of Barbara's. We arranged a get together over dinner. Jan and a friend of hers, Barbara and I, met Denise's new husband and her father and mother for supper. We enjoyed a wonderful dinner together.

Today Denise is a happily married mother of two children. We continue our letter and telephone friendship. I hope we will see her again someday. I learned through the correspondence with Denise that age is not too much of a factor when people communicate honestly from the heart. An 80-year old has many of the same feelings and needs as a 40-year old. A peer relationship with Denise was easy and natural. Her insights are as valid as mine. Maybe we have our answers from day one, and we simply need a safe place to express them and share them, to learn we are all pretty much the same.

93
LANDMARK AND THE FORUM

In 1990 I was seeing a therapist named Ann Condon. Her office was in a historical section of Cambridge, Massachusetts, not too far from Harvard Square. I loved walking around Harvard Square, the brick sidewalks, quaint old buildings, and tiny patches of creative landscaping. Sitting on a bench set among the shrubs and flowers in the garden behind her office, I could peacefully wait for my appointment.

Ann is a very talented, experienced therapist who believes in the effectiveness of transformational education. She is straightforward and honest, and I always knew she was truly interested in my wellbeing. She suggested I attend the Forum, a program of Landmark Education.

Attending the Forum was a significant turning point in my life, second only to achieving sobriety. The Forum, a transformational education program, had its beginning in California where it was known as *est*. An intense, confrontational series of interactive lectures, the Forum's classes sometimes attract upwards of 100 people.

Our Forum leader was Roger McDonald. He was instrumental in helping me break a mental log jam which had been holding me back all my life. He made an observation that I could not deny. "John," he said, "You have a belief system that doesn't work and you're defending it." I decided my goal would be to attain a new belief system that did work. After completing the Forum, I was so excited that I offered to pay the course fee for any member of my family who wanted to go. Six or seven of my children attended.

Subsequent to the Forum, for several years I attended other classes offered by Landmark Education. At a follow-up Forum seminar, I met Lynette Reisner. Like most of us, she was having relationship problems. Lynette was divorced and lived in Marblehead. She was an attractive woman, with sparkling eyes and dark brunette hair. Lynette was someone you would notice in a crowd, vivacious, and a great conversationalist.

Lynette had her own circle of friends. Our relationship was reserved for discussing the challenges of life and their solution. In truth, many times I wanted to cross the line and be more than a friend. I envisioned being her lover and living a life of joy and happiness in picturesque Marblehead. However, a cooler head prevailed (hers), and we continued to be friends. We called each other to talk about our mutual challenges, and occasionally we got together for dinner.

During one particularly stressful time, I called Lynette early on a Saturday morning and exclaimed, "I'm going out of my mind and I don't know what to do." She told me to meet her at 10 A.M. at the church just after you cross the town line in Marblehead. I drove down from Haverhill and arrived at the church, where I joined her at a 10 A.M. weekly support group for members committed to helping each other meet their problems head on.

After the meeting I was feeling better but not great. Lynette said, "I usually go to Marblehead Center for lunch. Do you want to join me?" I drove her downtown, and we talked over lunch. We drove to the beach and walked and talked until the sun went down. We went to dinner and back to the beach and continued to talk. At 10 P.M., when she asked, "Are you alright?" I replied, "Yes." I dropped her off at her house and returned home.

Lynette saved my life that day with 12 straight hours of compassion and kindness. I will always remember that unselfish act on Lynette's part.

94
THE LAST MILE

Though my parents' health was deteriorating, Mom and Dad were living in relative comfort in a manufactured home in a well-run park in Merrimac, Massachusetts. They were friends with many of the neighbors. My father tended the lawn and his own vegetable garden. The house had a screened-in porch and a patio in the backyard, which was surrounded by mature white pines.

However, my dear father never recovered from his traumatic childhood. His depression and anger were the fuel that kept me away from my parents. He played me and my siblings against one another, and sad to say, for much of my life I was estranged from my father as well as my three sisters.

My youngest sister, Norma, called me to explain that Mom was failing, as was Dad. She said that they had to be relocated to a nursing home. Norma pulled us all together. We met at my parents' home in Merrimac so we could accompany them to the nursing home. Mom seemed dazed, and Dad was quietly resigned to his fate. We all felt great sadness as we left their beloved little home. I promised my mother that I would dig up every one of her Hosta plants and plant them at my home where I would see them every day when driving up the long driveway. All my past anger and hatred dissolved in that afternoon, realizing that they had always done the best they could against great odds.

They made the transition as well as they could, and bravely we all tried to extol the benefits of the new arrangement. Each time I visited them, I was shocked to see them sitting in a single room with a bed and two chairs.

Mercifully they were not at the nursing home too long. In early December 1994 my Dad became ill and was taken to the hospital. After a short while, he passed away. Before he died I had the gift of a quiet conversation with him and an opportunity to tell him I loved him. My mother was in a very frail condition and was not able to attend the funeral nor did she understand her beloved John had died.

Upon returning to the nursing home after the funeral, I wheeled my mother into the dining room. She turned around in her wheel chair and looked at me with frightened eyes and asked, "Where's John?" Her words broke my heart. She looked so childlike and lost. They had been together over 60 years. We were all there, and we explained to her again that John had been called to rest.

A week and a half later while we were all visiting her in the hospital, I could see that her time was short. A burly hospital attendant standing in the room motioned me to one side. He said, "John, I've been through this many times. You need to tell her it's OK to let go." I returned to her side, leaned over and whispered into her ear, "Mom, it's OK to let go. John is waiting for you on the other side." Within 45 minutes she breathed her last breath, just a few days before Christmas, a scant 10 days since her beloved John had found his peace.

Peggy Lee sang a song, *Is That All There Is?* I looked at my life and reviewed my parents' life and asked myself, "Is that all there is?" Work, struggle, drama, fear, hurt, pass it on, and then die? My motivation took on a new urgency. I was determined to clear the wreckage of the past, to re-invent myself, and never quit. I thought about The Pilot House story I wrote not too many years before, and I vowed to make each day a celebration of life.

95
NO POSSIBLE AMENDS

To celebrate Valentine's Day, I invited Sally to dinner at Jimmy's Harborside Restaurant in Boston, a very romantic venue. We were seated opposite an enormous window with a view of the tiny inner harbor, the fishing boats nestled in a little cove just beyond the window. Sally looked absolutely stunning, and I too was dressed for the occasion. The food, service and setting were perfect, and we looked like a couple who should have been featured in an upscale magazine for "Good Living"

Outside appearances can be deceptive. After we ordered desert, Sally softly asked, "John, do you love me?" I paused. I stuttered. What followed reminded me of the scene in the movie *Moonstruck*, where the lovely young co-ed jumped up in the restaurant and dumped her drink in the lap of the sleazy professor before she stormed out of the restaurant.

Sally jumped up, threw down her napkin, made some very uncomplimentary comments about me, and stormed out of the dining room, leaving me to face the startled patrons and the embarrassed waiter. The rest of the evening was anti-climactic; the damage had been done, and the truth stuck out like a sore thumb.

The years flowed by and we were still together. Sally and I grew apart, and we had great difficulty being civil to each other. The kids had long since left the house, and we had to face our demons alone. We developed a façade for the well-situated folks on East Broadway. We had some pretty upscale parties at our dream house in the woods, and our guests used to utter oh! and ah! after seeing our beautiful house and gardens in our private little nature preserve.

We both played the game of the happy couple living in our dream house. Neither would admit that the end was in sight.

96
STONE & WEBSTER

My promising career at VHB was fast coming to an end. I was unable to manage a good relationship with the head of my department. I really liked working for VHB because the company was well-run and profitable, with lots of promise for me. I was the project manager for the MBTA on the Big Dig contract. The Big Dig was the largest public works project in the United States at the time. The project involved putting the Central Artery underground and extending the Massachusetts Turnpike across Boston Harbor to the North Shore. I was responsible for assuring that the MBTA's subways, buses, commuter trains and boats were protected against adverse effects due to construction of the Big Dig. I had a team of seven sub-consultants of various disciplines available to help me respond to the proposed actions of the design consultants and the building contractors. Things were going very well on the job. My team was performing admirably. We never missed a deadline, and we were under budget, magic words in the consulting business.

A sub-consultant, Stone & Webster was one of the oldest and most prestigious engineering firms in the U.S. I had interviewed with Stone & Webster when I was graduated from Wentworth Institute in Boston back in 1956. I let it be known to the Director of Engineering at Stone & Webster that I was unhappy at VHB, and he gladly made me an offer I could not refuse.

1995. A specialized excavation bucket used for digging slurry walls. Without the use of slurry walls to hold back the earth, the Big Dig tunnel could not have been built.

In early January 1996, I went to work for Stone & Webster. My client, the MBTA, insisted that I continue on as the Project Manager (even though VHB was the prime consultant). To keep me on the job, the contract was subsequently awarded to Stone & Webster, where I happily continued as Project Manager. I was with Stone & Webster for 12 years, and this was the most responsible job of my career. Stone & Webster was a highly-regarded engineering company, and I was proud to be on their team.

97
LEARNING TO DIVE

Ralph Moxey of Winthrop, Massachusetts was one of the early pioneers in scuba diving as a sport. With the intention of enrolling me as a dive buddy, he excitedly described to me the wondrous underwater world. He suggested that I try skin diving, just to see how great the underwater world looked.

Skin diving is simply diving by holding one's breath, wearing fins and a face mask.

I donned Ralph's mask and fins at the Winthrop Yacht Club and dove down about 15 or 20 feet. Once down, I pulled up my head to view the underwater world. My long hair was swept over the mask. I freaked out at the sight of this unknown dark brown stuff before my eyes, and shot to the surface, scared stiff. This was my entire diving experience until 1989, except to watch the adventures of Lloyd Bridges in the TV series, *Sea Hunt.*

More and more people were becoming divers. Towards the mid 1980s, Sally expressed a growing interest in scuba diving. She excitedly approached me one summer day in 1989 and asked, "Would you like to take scuba diving lessons?" I told her "No", and explained that years previous I tried skin diving and had a scary experience. Sally went off by herself to take scuba diving lessons with a Portsmouth, New Hampshire dive shop, which I thought was pretty gutsy. She purchased a full set of scuba gear. After several classes and a couple of pool dives, she seemed to be enjoying her new sport.

When I arrived home the afternoon that Sally made her first ocean dive at Nubble Lighthouse at Cape Neddick, Maine, she was discouraged and thinking about quitting scuba lessons. Apparently the water had been very cold, visibility was about five feet, and the surge in the shallow bay was heavy. At the end of the dive as she climbed ashore, she was washed off the rocks by a wave. I felt terrible for her. Forgetting my earlier scary incident, I tried to be supportive by offering to learn how to dive. Sally continued on with her classes, and I went to Portsmouth to begin my classroom studies and ocean dives.

During the third lesson, my class gathered around the pool. We were going to begin by skin diving, using only fins, snorkel and a mask. The Dive Master teamed me up with a dive buddy named Amanda Lockhart. She caused the class and me a great deal of disruption as she approached the pool in her skimpy bikini. The entire class made a skin dive, and then a scuba dive with full gear. All went well.

Our first ocean dive in a protected bay in Newcastle, New Hampshire was a disaster for me. After suiting up, I attempted to walk through the surf into the ocean. I was promptly knocked on my ass by a little wave. I could not recover my balance, and I was flailing around in the surf. Without realizing what had happened, I landed on my regulator, pressing the valve, which resulted in about 600 pounds of air being wasted. Amanda was already in the water and thought my behavior was really funny. After I yelled, “Hey, you’re supposed to be my dive buddy,” she came to my rescue and helped me get up and into the ocean. We swam out to the circle of other novices, in about 20 feet of water.

The Dive Master lined us up in a circle, bobbing on the surface. He made it very clear that we were going to descend together to the bottom where we would practice a series of exercises. “If you begin to panic, don’t head for the surface. Get your act together on the bottom," were his last instructions before we submerged. During one of the exercises, I noticed that Amanda's air pressure gauge read 2,700 PSI and mine read 2,100 PSI. I panicked. We were under the ocean, I was sure I was going to run out of air, and I could not "get it together" on the bottom. I shot up to the surface, a sure way to get the bends if we had been in deeper water. The Dive Master followed me to the surface. He was giving me hell, when suddenly another diver popped to the surface, both of us stiff with panic. He pushed us ashore, told us to get out of our dive gear, and wait for the rest of the class to return to shore. Now what the hell was I going to do? Here I was planning to help Sally, and I had panicked worse than she had.

Upon their return from the dive, the Dive Master told the two of us who shot to the surface to report the next day to make another dive. He said that we should dive again right away, or otherwise we could lose our nerve. We both turned up the next day and had no problems completing the underwater exercises.

Slipping into unknown waters, feeling weightless, and knowing we are visitors in a foreign realm, makes diving exciting. Diving in the North Atlantic where the plankton is abundant means that visibility is sometimes less than a body length. That, coupled with the cold water, can make diving a real adventure. Recognizing that a boat dive would be far easier than shore diving, the entire class pitched in to rent a dive boat for our certification dives. To avoid landing on a torpedo ray, the dive master told us to keep our eyes on the bottom as we descended. Torpedo rays, which can discharge from 8 to 225 volts depending on the species, use their electricity to stun their victims. We encountered no torpedo rays, and on 26 October 1989 off the shoreline of Appledore Island, Maine, everyone in our class was certified.

Now it was time to join Sally as her dive buddy. As two newly certified divers, this was akin to the blind leading the blind. With a few new friends, we dove at Folly Cove in Gloucester, Massachusetts in about 30 feet of water. I started to panic again, but another diver came up to me and calmed me down. I proceeded to "get it together" on the bottom, and I have been a pretty cool diver ever since.

Over the next six years Sally and I dove off the coast of Maine and Massachusetts, as well as in Bermuda, Key Largo, Bonaire, Little Cayman, and La Paz, Mexico. Our first Caribbean location was the island of Providenciales in the Turks and Caicos Islands. We had many exciting and beautiful adventures, especially in the Caribbean. There were some scary events, including one in the Sea of Cortez off the coast of La Paz, Mexico where we dove on a wreck of the intercoastal ferry, *Salvatierra*, sunk in about 100 feet of water. Sally glided in one window of the pilot house and came out the other side with no problem. I followed, aimed too high, and caught my tank on a loose rope hanging from the overhead. I was stuck on the rope, about 80 feet under the ocean. I remembered what the dive master said years before, "Get it together on the bottom." Before Sally realized I was caught, I had calmly backed up, rolled to the side, and disengaged the rope. I swam out through the other window. By 1996 we had made about 100 dives, and I was hooked. Though Sally dove less as the years passed, I continued to dive without her, finding other people to be my buddies.

In February 1996 on the island of San Salvador in the Bahamas, I met Walter Brust and his wife, Eileen, while diving at the Riding Rock Inn. Walter and I spent many hours together on this isolated island. He listened to my fearful stories about how my marriage was unraveling. Walter was a sympathetic listener, and it felt good to express myself in what I considered a safe environment.

As is the custom on the last night of a dive vacation, on the last night in San Salvador, all the divers met at the bar for a going away party. I had been diving with Kathy Coffee and her husband, Greg, and I could see they were in the same boat as I was regarding their marriage. Kathy and I had a long conversation on that last night. We said our goodbyes, and agreed to keep in touch in the future. Kathy went home to Alton, Illinois, and off I went to Haverhill.

Soon after arriving home, I knew our marriage had unraveled, and I was scared. We continued living in the same house, maintaining distance and indifference. Toward the end of 1996 I came up with a plan. We would take a beautiful vacation to a romantic south sea resort and put it all together.

By coincidence, Walter Brust called one day extending an invitation to go on a dive vacation with the American Littoral Society (ALS), a coastal conservation group based in New Jersey. The destination was the island of Bonaire in the Netherland Antilles, just off the north coast of South America. Following Walter's instructions, I called Barbara Greenberg in New York City to make arrangements for Sally and me to join the group. Barbara was the co-leader of this dive and snorkel trip to Bonaire.

Sally and I embarked upon this journey with a great amount of fear and misgivings. We both were willing to give our marriage another try, but neither of us knew what to do. We figured this trip would be the magic bullet that would save our marriage of 28 years. However, we both knew this was probably the twentieth attempt at salvaging our marriage by doing something or going somewhere special. We hoped an outside adventure would change everything.

To begin the trip, we met Walter and Eileen Brust at their riverside apartment in Fort Lee, New Jersey. We drove together to meet the American Littoral Society (ALS) group at Liberty Airport in Newark. We observed Barbara Greenberg as she was making sure that everyone was ready to go. She was tall, beautiful, high cheekbones with almond-shaped eyes, and reddish hair. She looked like a Celtic maiden. Barbara was dressed in the typical fashion of ALS members, e.g. light olive green, wrinkled, dry-fast shirt with pants to match, and hiking boots—a fashion statement if ever there was one. When Barbara walked into a room, there was no mistake about who was in charge. Sally and I nervously introduced ourselves to Barbara. She was very gracious and apologetic, explaining that the plane was going to be delayed and we would land in Bonaire at three o'clock in the morning.

As it turned out, this was the vacation from Hell. Early on Sally said, "If I could get a plane out of here tomorrow, I'd be gone," and I felt the same way. Here we were in a tropical paradise, warm, crystal clear waters filled with colorful tropical fishes and corals. We fought, we quibbled, and it was truly awful for both of us. To make matters worse, Sally had difficulty diving comfortably, so I hired a private dive master to work with her to no avail.

Shortly after our return from our "dream" vacation to our "dream" house in the woods, we decided I should move out because we were each furious with the other.

98
MOVING DAY

On Patriots Day, 19 April 1997, my friends Dave Ringland, John MacDonald, and John Torrisi, showed up with a pickup truck to move me to my new apartment at View Point at 170 Washington Street in downtown Haverhill. I never felt like such a looser in all my life. My only thought was, "What did I do to deserve this! I lost my dream house and my dream workshop in the woods, and now I am living in an apartment in a converted shoe factory!"

Coming from my parent's lifetime of poverty, they drilled into our heads that the poor lived in tenements and apartments, and the well-to-do own their own homes. I had built my home with my own hands, and now I was back to being a loser in a rented apartment. After my buddies left, I sat on the boxes and cried as I looked out the window at the cold rainy day. I still had thoughts of getting back with Sally, believing that somehow we could make everything all right. I was afraid. What would happen to me?

Soon after I moved in, I realized I needed some cabinets and book cases. I called Sally to see if she would allow me access to my complete carpentry shop to build the cabinets. She agreed and said to come on Saturday because she would be gone all day. My father's dream for me was that I become a tradesman. That dream came true when I became a finish carpenter/cabinet maker. Carpentry, my tools and my workshop were really important to me. To think that I had to ask permission from Sally to use my own workshop and tools was a bitter pill to swallow.

On that appointed Saturday, I was busily completing my bookshelves and cabinets within the time allotted by Sally. I noticed a Haverhill police cruiser coming up the driveway. The car stopped, and out stepped Dave Hall. Dave was a neighbor. I figured he heard about our separation, and he was just stopping by to say hello. I walked over to Dave and said, "Hi, Dave. What's up?" He apologetically handed me a divorce summons and said he was sorry. That felt like a sucker punch to the breadbasket. I was stunned, but I put on a bravado face as though I knew the summons was coming. Dave had been on the receiving end of a divorce summons, and I knew he understood.

In that one six-hour day I managed to build two book cases, a TV cabinet and a storage cabinet for my bathroom. That was the last time I ever set foot in my dream workshop. Only a tradesman can appreciate such a loss.

99
ROATAN, HONDURAS

In June, 1997, Walter Brust called from New Jersey to invite me to go diving in Roatan, Honduras. He encouraged me, suggesting that getting away would be a good idea. Walter and his wife, Eileen, and Barbara Greenberg were planning to dive in Roatan, and Walter said I could be Barbara's dive buddy. I declined because I was attracted to Barbara, and I knew she was already in a relationship. The idea of being with her seemed too complicated.

However, Walter was right. I wanted to get away from all the unpleasantness. My marriage of 30 years was close to an end. I was a bundle of nervous energy, feeling rejected and a failure. I decided to call Kathy Coffee from Alton, Illinois, whom I knew had just gotten divorced. I asked her if she would like to join me on a dive vacation in Belize, and she said yes. She was in the same frame of mind, and she thought a trip to Belize would be a good idea.

During that telephone conversation, I mentioned to Kathy that I had signed up for another class at the Forum to help me move forward. I suggested she take a course in St. Louis the same weekend I was to complete the course in Boston. Kathy had no idea what the Forum was, but she said, "I'll go because I trust you." We decided this would be a common experience we could spend time discussing together. We agreed to check in with each other after the Forum and finalize our plans for the Belize trip.

When we completed the Forum we were both excited and grateful for the new possibilities the experience opened for us. I suggested to Kathy that we should get moving on the travel arrangements for Belize. Her reply staggered me. She said, "John I'm not really ready to go to Belize at this time, since I'm still dealing with my divorce." I asked, "Why did you agree to go a couple of weeks ago?" She said, "John, all my life I've never had the courage to say no. Thanks to you and the Forum, I can do so now." I chuckled to myself and muttered, "Well, you screwed yourself this time with your good intentions." I recovered and respectfully acknowledged her new strength and wished her well. We have been friends ever since.

Now what to do? I really wanted to go diving but did not feel comfortable going alone again. I called Walter and asked him if there was any more space on the trip. "Yes," was his answer. So in late July, off I went to meet Walter, Eileen, and Barbara in Miami. Barbara seemed to be sincerely glad to see me; however, she reminded me she was in a relationship and that she was pleased we could be dive buddies, but that was all. Things were real clear upfront.

We enjoyed the diving in Roatan, Honduras. I was drawn to Barbara, but she did not even have a clue. Besides her pleasant demeanor, I loved her long shapely legs which were driving me crazy, especially when she wore the black bathing suit which was every day. I was a true dive buddy and behaved like a gentleman.

The diving was excellent, mostly along walls, through gigantic canyons, caves, pass-throughs and chimneys. Barbara was a good diver and was not even intimidated with the chimneys. We entered a chimney formation about 4 feet in diameter at about 40 feet deep on the edge of a wall. We swam down one at a time, each following the other, exiting at a horizontal opening about 100 to 120 feet deep. The deep blue ocean that greeted us upon leaving the horizontal section of the chimney was magnificent. We were suspended in endless space at the top of a wall that ran 6,000 or 7,000 feet deep, swimming with barracuda, sharks, turtles, and schools of fishes all around us.

During the middle of the week Barbara asked me if Gail, the resort manager, could join our table for dinner, since Gail told Barbara she was interested in me. I was so nervous. Here I was in my 60s, and I did not know how to behave. I was getting divorced, Kathy changed her mind, Barbara was oblivious to me, I really liked Barbara, and now I had a date with Gail.

Towards the end of the week, we were decompressing from a deep dive, hanging on the rope under the boat at a safety stop of 15 feet. My hand accidently on purpose slipped down and touched Barbara's hand. A shot of electricity ran up my arm, and I am sure something registered with Barbara too.

On the day we were leaving the resort, the three of us, Barbara, Gail, and I, were standing awkwardly saying our goodbyes. Over the past few days, Gail and I had a couple of close encounters, enough to cause Gail to have tears in her eyes as we stood there waiting for our ride to the airport. Barbara looked perplexed. I was a basket case because I was feeling stronger and stronger about Barbara while I was giving a good bye hug to Gail. It was all too confusing, and I was glad to leave Honduras.

Barbara and I landed in Miami and only had a few minutes to find our connecting planes. Barbara was heading for Newark, and I was off to Boston. We grabbed our luggage at customs. I hugged Barbara, gave her a big kiss, and waved goodbye as I ran to catch my plane.

100
THE DREAM HOUSE

For years Sally and I had dreamt about building a brand new home in a secluded wooded setting. We drove the rural roads in Haverhill, searching for the perfect lot, where we imagined we would build our country place. Our favorite rural road was called East Broadway, which ran parallel to the Merrimack River. The area was sparsely settled and forested with white pines and mixed hardwoods, mostly oaks. While this was our dream, we really did not think we would ever be able to afford to buy a lot and then hire a contractor to build the house.

Sally was quick to remind me over and over that I could build the house, since I was by trade a carpenter, and had built houses before I became an engineer. After strong urging by Sally as well as my friends, I mustered up the courage to take on the role of a general contractor. While I was working full-time as an engineer on the construction of the interstate highway, I figured I could build a house in the evenings and weekends.

East Broadway had no housing developments. Private lots were sold to individuals, and each house was custom-built by the owners for their own use. This gave the neighborhood a more stable, up-scale appearance. Also, most of the houses were built well back from the street, which helped to maintain the rural feeling, which was another reason why we loved the area.

Sally worked in the district court in Haverhill. In a discussion with a colleague, she found out about a large parcel of land on East Broadway that was being subdivided into lots, and would soon be coming on the market. I was at home that day, having taken a day off from work. Sally rushed home at mid-day, and she excitedly told me the good news. She explained that we could get the jump on everyone, since it would be a couple of weeks before the City zoning board approved the division of the parcel into lots.

We immediately set off to see the lots, and to our amazement we discovered they were located in the area that we had admired for years. We walked around the whole area not knowing exactly where the individual lots were. The location we liked best had an open area about 250 feet from the street, exactly where we would site the house. The rest of the lot was covered with white pines and oaks, which would give us the seclusion we desired. We hurried home to begin a search to find the owner and to learn the price of the lots. We could not figure out who owned the land, but we did learn that the surveyor who laid out the lots was a man named Billy Barr, a former state engineer with whom I had worked in the past.

The next day Billy and I walked the entire 14-acre parcel. I discovered the lot Sally and I liked was Lot # 2. It was 2 acres, abutting protected conservation land around the Millvale Reservoir, and it was only a 10 minute drive to downtown Haverhill. Billy suggested we should not delay in making our bid for the land, since he did not think the lots would last long at the rock bottom price of $10,000.

We put our Minot Avenue house on the market, which we had bought in 1968 for $16,000. Sally managed to sell the house for $35,000 to a friend at the court house. Now we were homeless. Serendipitously, Sally's mother and father decided to spend the winter in Florida. They offered us their condo in Londonderry, New Hampshire for the winter. On the day they left for Florida, Sally and I and our 12-year old daughter, Linda, moved in.

I called on my many friends to help build the house. We wanted a beautiful Lindal cedar home, but the cost of a Lindal lumber package was prohibitive. I contacted Murray Hewey, a building contractor with whom I had attended trade school many years before. He was a fine craftsman, and he had designed and built many houses in the Haverhill area. Murray designed us a house that replicated the Lindal home we loved, but that could be built using locally-purchased materials. Jake Feenstra, a contractor and friend from the old neighborhood, served as the foreman of all the volunteers who helped me build the house. Ed Fitzgerald, a close family friend and fellow state engineer, became the project surveyor and staked out the house and sewerage system. Another friend in heavy construction loaned me a bulldozer and operator to excavate the cellar hole. We had a lot of fun building the house. Sally and I made heaps of food for all the workers, and we enjoyed many a mid-construction picnic with friends and their families who lent us a hand.

My Dad, who was then in his 70s, was really excited about my building a new house. He helped me pour the concrete for the foundation. At the end of each day, he kept the worksite neat and squared away. He gathered up scraps of wood left by the carpenters and stored them out of the way for future use in the fireplaces. When my cheap old chain saw failed, without saying a word to me, my Dad turned up the next day with a brand new top-of-the-line Stihl chain saw. It worked like a charm. He also helped me plant my 400-tree nursery.

Dad and I worked together at clearing up the back of the lot where a fire had left dead trees years ago. We started big bonfires to get rid of the old dead trees, leaves and brush. While tending those bonfires, I had my closest conversations ever with my Dad. I learned more about my Dad's childhood and early married life than ever before. Our bonfires reminded me of the times when as kids at our Main Street house we helped the grownups burn leaves in the fall.

By the fall of 1977, we got the house closed in so we could turn on the heat and work inside during the cold months. When the huge February 6, 1978 snowstorm hit, the Governor of Massachusetts closed the highways for an entire week. I hired a man with a front loader to make a path through the snowy woods to the house, and I spent the whole week there working on the house.

1978. Under construction, the house I built at 530 East Broadway, Haverhill, MA

We were able to move into the main part of the house on St. Patrick's Day, 1978. The house was roughed in. We had heat and water and necessities, but the floors were not finished, and there were no drapes on the windows. We lived in the house as I continued the building, first the garage, then the breezeway, a solarium, and a workshop. By the end of the winter of 1979, the house was in pretty good shape.

Then I began the landscaping. On nights and on weekends, I worked seven days a week, paving the driveway, and planting seedlings around the lot. I built many gardens in the back. One was a replica of an old English garden, with geometrical designs and raised beds made from discarded bridge planks from a nearby construction project. If my memory serves me properly, I paid for the planks with two cases of cold Budweiser. I built and placed wooden benches around the garden. Also, I created a Japanese sand garden with a tall, angular, gray granite rock in the middle. My coniferous garden had many species of evergreens, including native white pine, Colorado blue spruce, Sitka spruce, and Scotch pine. I built a big picnic area behind the house where we enjoyed many meals. Our son, John, was married in our gardens. Over the years, we hosted numerous parties in the house as well as barbeques outdoors for family and friends.

Sometimes at night I would take a walk alone through the woods and look back towards the house with all the lights on. We had three fireplaces, a solarium, and large windows throughout. From the woods I could see the brick walls inside and the amber lights casting a warm glow on the random-width pegged oak floors I had installed. The woods were quiet and peaceful, and not one other home was within view. I could hardly believe I owned and lived in this beautiful house.

One day Herb Dever said to me, "John, you have a beautiful house, but there doesn't seem to be much love here." He was right. The house was gorgeous and the setting spectacular. However, like Edgar Guest said, "it takes a heap o' livin' in a house t' make it home." One of the things we found out was that no matter how much decorating or landscaping or entertaining we did, the beautiful house did not result in a happy life together. After a party, when our guests left, we hardly spoke to one another.

In our divorce settlement, Sally got the house. I could not imagine how I was going to leave 530 East Broadway without experiencing some dreadful resentments. I sought out the services of a counselor and explained my situation. She gave me some sound advice which I followed.

One afternoon I arrived at the house when no one was home and no neighbors were around. The counselor had suggested I take a couple of hours and say good bye to everything that was near and dear to me as a way of clearing my mind so that I could go on with my life. With tears in my eyes, and looking over my shoulder for fear someone might throw a net over me, I commenced to talk to the trees and say good bye.

The 400 seedlings which I had planted many years before were now 10 to 15 foot trees. Some of my trees had names. I planted a weeping white pine near the solarium that I especially liked. Because of its bent limbs, Linda named the tree "Bently." Everyone remembers Bently, including our friends. Jimmy D'Angelo gave us a dogwood tree as a thank you for the clam bake I hosted in the backyard for the VHB golf club. I planted that dogwood in a prominent place in the English garden. Even those trees which did not have names had significance to me, and I knew I would miss them all.

I saved Bently for last and by then I was emotionally depleted. I said goodbye to the trees, the gardens, the workshop and the house in general. The dream house chapter of my life was closed.

101
VIEW POINT

When I realized I was going to be divorced, my first thought was to convert my new bachelor pad into a den of uncommitted sex and fun time. I would cook exquisite meals and have a string of beauties available for whenever the mood struck me.

The apartment overlooked the Merrimack River, a romantic retreat with floor to ceiling windows, wall-to-wall carpeting, a full kitchen, and an attached garage. I was planning to catch up for all those years of misery. Yippee! I was free! No grounds to keep, no lawns to mow or trees to trim, no household things to fix, and no one to whom I had to report.

I could not stop thinking about Barbara. Here it was July, and I had been out of the house three months, and I was already getting wobbly and gaga over another woman I hardly knew. I did not dare dream that at age 67 I could have a real, committed, loving relationship.

I did not think there was much chance that she would be interested in me. After all, she was quite a bit younger, owned her own business in New York City, and she was in a relationship. Then there was my divorce to deal with, and I still had thoughts about going back to Sally. The vision of the bachelor pad started to evaporate, and it was comforting to think about Barbara instead.

Life was confusing. I was in a state of emotional upheaval. I needed to be alert since I was entering a very highly charged divorce process. Sally and I had friends who did not know which one of us to talk to or what to say. I did not know how to communicate with the kids, as each was going through his or her own grief about the divorce and trying to maintain a neutral attitude.

Several days after returning from Honduras, I called Barbara and asked her if she arrived home OK. We decided to meet. As it happened, our first date was a surprise graduation party for her niece, and I met her entire family that day.

For the next six years, every weekend Barbara and I made alternate trips between Haverhill and New York City. We used every conceivable method of transportation. Sometimes I drove to New York City. More often we took Greyhound and Peter Pan buses, and Amtrak trains, sometimes delayed several hours.

After about three months, I was hesitant to acknowledge that some of the old problems I had experienced with Rita and then Sally were once again appearing with Barbara. Only this time, I was not drinking. My first thoughts were, "I have to get out of this mess, and it's time to run." It took a great deal of courage to stay to face my fears.

Barbara was also a bit apprehensive since she had already experienced the agony and turmoil of divorce. She was pondering the wisdom of becoming involved with a man who had recently left a marriage of 30 years and was not yet divorced. That's when I informed Barbara that I was in counseling to deal with the problems that had resurfaced with our relationship. Barbara was visibly moved and especially supportive of my efforts. During one of my conversations with Susan Murphy where I was sharing my fear about seeing the same old issues arising in the new relationship with Barbara, Susan had recommended a talented and effective therapist from Newburyport named Christine Flaherty.

During the first session with Christine, she asked me the question. "John, what is the common factor in all three relationships?" I knew the answer was "Me." Barbara Greenberg was the third serious relationship I had in my life up to that point, and I understood this relationship would have a familiar outcome unless I changed.

I could hear the stern notice from Ann Condon, a therapist I had seen in past years. "John," she said, "You must stop taking Sally's inventory. Everything you say about her may be true, but how does that help you?" I had to stop the blame game and face the music, concentrate on my own actions and no one else. Christine Flaherty made the same point, and with her coaching, I made a lot of progress towards a loving relationship with Barbara.

Christine said I had attracted a healthy woman, and she would not stick around too long with my poor self image. She helped me to see that if I kept telling Barbara that I was a failure and "less than," that constituted an insult to Barbara, and she would begin to feel like she was settling for a ding bat. I had some growing up to do, and it had to be done with haste. 1997 closed with the sure realization that I still had a long way to go in taming my anger and resentments.

102
THE COUPLES COMPANION

On the New Year's weekend of 1998, Barbara suggested we start the year with a New Year's Day walk in the Jamaica Wildlife Refuge on Jamaica Bay in Queens, New York. Barbara also invited Susan Nobel, her hiking buddy from the American Littoral Society, to join us on the wintery walk. When we arrived at the refuge, I was pleasantly surprised because the Wildlife Refuge reminded me a lot of Plum Island, Massachusetts. Even though it was bitterly cold, we all enjoyed the afternoon.

We hiked around the perimeter of the Wildlife Refuge, chatting with Susan. I learned that Susan was a therapist. I told her about my experiences with therapists over the years.

On the return trip which takes a good hour, with Barbara at the wheel of her old Peugeot, Susan and I became engrossed in a serious conversation about human behavior and how early childhood development affects our whole lifetime. We discussed ways of managing our neuroses and hang-ups. I had been searching 25 years for answers to life's challenges, and I became quite excited about this fascinating conversation. Susan mentioned that she frequently used in her counseling practice a book called *The Couples Companion* by Harville Hendrix and Helen Hunt.

Serendipity! Here was Susan showing up in my life at exactly the right moment, making her important contribution. We arrived in the City after a most excellent day, dropped off Susan at her apartment, and drove home. Upon arriving home I said to Barbara, "I'm going out for an errand. Be back in 15 minutes." I trotted my buns right up to West 82th Street and Broadway and bought two copies of *The Couples Companion*. I saw it as a good omen that Susan's last name was Nobel, so I went to Barnes & Noble to buy the books.

Upon returning to the apartment and without any preparation, I presented Barbara with the book and suggested we study it together. Her reception was less than enthusiastic. She said, "John I'm not into those self-help books. I can't stand to read them." I backed off and later made a more low-profile pitch. Barbara agreed that she would go along with my plan. The book was set up with 365 lessons, and the idea was to read one lesson together each day on the phone, and then have a brief discussion.

On weekends when we were together in Haverhill or New York, we would read face-to-face and discuss the day's meditation. We started off slowly, but within a short while we could see the book addressed situations we had already faced. We read the book together every single day for a year. When the year ended, we agreed to repeat the readings for the second year. By December 1999 we had read it together twice.

The Couples Companion was a blessing. The book arrived at just the right time. All the counseling sessions I ever attended pointed towards unmanageable anger as the basic cause of my problems. I also had learned that when problems are small in the beginning, they are a lot easier to correct.

103
TWO WORLDS

Life at 170 Washington Street, Haverhill was going quite well. I learned to enjoy the ease of apartment living. A good friend, Dave Ringland, moved into one of the other renovated shoe factories a couple of blocks from me. John and Juanita Torrisi lived a short walk away, and I ate many a delicious Italian dinner in Juanita's kitchen. Both Dave and John were good friends who helped me over many a rough spot.

Barbara and I saw each other every weekend. One weekend I would travel to New York City, and the next weekend she would travel to Haverhill. Sometimes on the weekends while I was in New York, my daughter Linda and her two friends, Kim and

Susan, used my Haverhill apartment. The three of them racked up a lot of pleasant memories in their little weekend get-away pad.

I soon learned that Barbara loved any activity related to water--ocean, marshes, rivers, ponds, lakes, and waterfalls. We spent our Haverhill weekends taking full advantage of all the outdoors had to offer. Barbara and I introduced my daughter, Debi, and her husband, Bill, to kayaking, and we enjoyed many wonderful weekends of paddling and picnicking in the quiet waters around southern New Hampshire and coastal Massachusetts.

Barbara introduced me to a new way of life. Her New York City apartment was at 60 Riverside Drive and West 78th Street, a one-bedroom on the 16th floor with a small porch. The apartment had an unobstructed view of the Hudson River. We were regular patrons of the New York Philharmonic, attended a couple of operas at the Met each year, and took in lectures all over the City on every subject under the sun at such places as the Museum of Natural History, The Armory in Central Park, the New York Historical Society, the Metropolitan Museum of Art, and other venues too numerous to remember. We ventured into the neighborhoods of all five boroughs, hearing a multitude of languages, tasting interesting foods foreign to us, and seeing new sights.

In 2000 Barbara had an opportunity to sell her apartment to a next door neighbor who wanted to expand, and we moved to a two-bedroom apartment in the Schwab House at 11 Riverside Drive at West 73rd Street on the 6th floor. I took a week off to serve as the director of the move, supervising the packing, moving, and unpacking. We were exhausted, but we worked well together.

104
NINE ELEVEN

Since 1992, I had been the Project Manager for a team of seven engineering/architectural firms that provided consulting services to the MBTA on the Big Dig. Because the project was winding down, most of the other firms had been released, and I was the lone survivor. I had experience in solving problems relative to foundation and tunnel construction, and I also had the historical knowledge from 1992, making it impossible to replace me. Every few years, we had to re-bid and re-compete for the job. I am proud to say that we were selected every time we competed until the contract finally ended in 2008.

I had been making a lot of noise at Stone & Webster about moving to New York City. In the summer of 2001, as my project for the MBTA was slowing down, my Chief Engineer secured me some spotty assignments in the New York Office. At one point, I was assigned to help one of the New York Project Managers collect around $2.0 million in unpaid invoices from the New York State Department of Environmental Protection. This situation had developed due to accounting problems in 2000 when The Shaw Group bought Stone & Webster.

I also helped to prepare proposals for new work. One such assignment was for me to attend a project briefing in Queens, New York for a proposed Long Island Railroad maintenance facility. On September 11, 2001, while I was waiting in Boston for a train to Penn Station in New York, I heard the news that the World Trade Center had been attacked by terrorists in two hi-jacked planes. The twin towers were destroyed. The terrorists had also hi-jacked two other planes, one they crashed into the Pentagon in D.C., and another diverted by courageous passengers who crashed the plane in a field in Pennsylvania.

All Amtrak trains from Boston were shut down. I tried to reach Barbara, but telephone service in New York City was spotty. The next day I managed to catch a 3:00 P.M. Amtrak train from Route 128 in Westwood. Trains were stuck in front of us, and we arrived in New York City at 8:00 P.M. When I emerged from the station, I was confronted with the constant wail of sirens from police and fire vehicles, and ambulances, and the helicopters hovering overhead. The streets were empty, the subways were closed down, waiting lines for taxis and buses were blocks long. I walked north, hauling my suitcase behind me, covering the two and a half miles from Penn Station to Barbara's apartment on Riverside Drive and West 73rd Street. At last I arrived. Barbara was upset and frightened, and I was so grateful to be there to comfort her. The most memorable thing was the acrid smell in the air, a mixture of humans and buildings. Fire and police sirens continued to wail, day and night.

I reported to my New York Office on September 13th. From the 32nd floor of One Penn Plaza, I had a clear view downtown. I could see the hole in the skyline and the smoke pouring up from the remains of the World Trade Center buildings.

Three thousand people were murdered. The wailing of sirens did not let up for days, and the acrid smell of the smoke lasted for weeks.

105
DIAMOND TIME

Shortly after the 9/11 disaster in New York City, Barbara and I (and many others as we later learned) longed for certainty amidst the uncertainty that faced us all. In early December 2001, we talked about making a more permanent commitment to each other. We decided an engagement ring would suffice for the time being. We were nervous about the "M" word.

Years before, my friend, Gene Petrillo, had taken me to the Diamond District in Boston and introduced me to one of the owners of the DiPrisco's jewelry store on Washington Street. I knew where to buy a diamond for Barbara. I decided to visit DiPrisco's to look for an engagement ring.

I picked out a diamond with the thought that Barbara would choose a setting. I called Barbara in New York City that evening. She was feeling overwhelmed with the news, but very excited. The next weekend Barbara was scheduled to be in Haverhill with me. She arrived at Route 128 in Westwood, Massachusetts on

Friday the 7th of December. I picked her up from 128 station, and we drove to Needham to take Dot, Barbara's mother, to dinner. Dot was very pleased to learn that I had picked out a diamond for Barbara.

Saturday we drove from Haverhill to Boston to visit DiPrisco's. On the way through the store to see the solitaire diamond I had selected, Barbara's eyes lighted up when she saw a three diamond designer ring in a display case. Saying nothing, we continued to the office to view the diamond I had picked out. Soon I realized a solitary diamond was not what she had in mind. She wanted to try on the designer ring. It was beautiful, and she was delighted! She walked out the door wearing her new ring. I was really pleased that I could buy her exactly the ring she wanted.

Later that evening, we attended the annual Stone & Webster holiday party in Boston. We had the opportunity to show off the new ring to my colleagues. Everyone, including the CEO, congratulated us. Barbara and I were beaming with our decision.

106
NEW YORK HERE I COME!

By 2003 Barbara and I had more than enough of the travelling between Haverhill, Massachusetts and New York City. I acted on a plan: I had contacts in Boston, but none in New York. I would find a job with another Boston engineering firm with the proviso that after a while in Boston, they would send me to their New York Office, and I could live with Barbara.

I was 73 years old, and I succeeded in landing another six figure position at URS, a company of about 24,000 people. I took the letter of acceptance to Gerry Doton, my Chief Engineer at Shaw/Stone & Webster, and gave my notice.

I had dreaded going to Gerry because he was the best guy I ever worked for, and I really liked and respected him. The Chief exclaimed, "No way. Hold on until Wednesday." Gerry called the Baton Rouge corporate VP and told him I'd taken another job so I could move to New York City. The VP said, "Well, hell, if that's what he wants, give him a moving allowance and move him down there." Shaw did not want to lose me because they needed my experience as Project Manager for the MBTA on the $15 Billion Big Dig. Sure enough, on Wednesday Gerry Doton called me into his office to tell me that I was moving to New York City.

The next day I arranged a breakfast meeting at the Suisse Hotel in Boston and invited Gerry Doton and the two executives from URS who had hired me. I figured I did not want any animosity among these people with whom we would be working in the future. I explained to them that I was going to stay with Shaw/Stone & Webster and would be moving to New York within two weeks. It turned out we had a wonderful breakfast together.

107
COLD WELCOME AT STONE & WEBSTER

I now resided at 11 Riverside Drive in the Upper West Side on the 6th floor overlooking the Hudson River. I no longer entertained the thought that I was an "also ran." Barbara was introducing me to some interesting people, and I was secretly excited about my new life in New York City. I loved standing on a street corner and putting out my hand and having a yellow cab come swerving to the curb just like in the movies. I did it, and it worked! Walking hand in hand with Barbara down Broadway to Lincoln Center to attend the opera at the Met, or Avery Fisher Hall for a performance of the New York Philharmonic, still gives me goose bumps.

At the tender age of 73, I reported for full-time work at the New York Office of Shaw/Stone & Webster at One Penn Plaza in New York City. I was one scared puppy, because the reception I received at the New York office was less than cordial.

I did not understand this at the time I arrived, but the New York office had been operating in survival mode for many years. I was perceived as a threat or even a stooge for the Boston Office to which the New York office reported. At one time Stone and Webster had 10 full floors at the 60-story One Penn Plaza office building. Many hundreds of engineers worked there during the days when Stone & Webster was the premier firm to go to for the design and construction of nuclear power plants.

By the time I arrived on the scene, Stone and Webster had been reduced to just the 32nd floor, where the president and CEO used to have his office. He had since moved to Boston. Most of that enormous space on the 32nd floor was vacant, and only 25 people worked there. As the old saying goes, "I was about as welcomed as a skunk at a lawn party." Of course, true to corporate culture, no one took me aside and explained the situation.

I approached a guy who looked like he was in charge and said, "Where's my office?" He replied with an attitude of disinterest, "Take any one you want." I promptly moved into the former president's 900 square foot office. In retrospect, I imagine that must have pissed them off. The office was 30 feet square, located in the southwest corner of the 32nd floor with a direct view of the Hudson River, New York Harbor and the Statue of Liberty. I had the high back president's chair, two couches, an enormous credenza, four stuffed chairs, two conference tables, a closet, and 60 feet of floor-to-ceiling windows with drapes. I lasted almost a year before they kicked me out.

Apparently no one explained to them that the only reason I was still working was to keep the MBTA happy, and that the only reason I was in New York is because I quit when they would not transfer me to New York. I was perceived to be powerful, even though I did not realize it at the time. My motivation was not to make a lot of money; I just wanted to be with Barbara. Eventually they understood that I was in New York only because the Chief Engineer, Gerry Doton, wanted me there.

Whenever I was needed by the Project Manager from the MBTA in Boston, I hopped the train to Boston, and popped by our Stoughton office. I kept my 2000 Camry stored at the Stoughton office parking lot. While I was at work in Boston a few days at a time, I could drive to Haverhill and visit with relatives and friends. I had a support team at the Stoughton Office. Jim Horan took care of my car in my absence. Janice Orcutt and Gail Reed processed travel reimbursement paperwork for me.

For the meetings in Boston, I left the car at the Stoughton office, and took a cab to Stoughton Center to catch the commuter train to South Station in Boston. My routine was that I would arrive at South Station and walk across Atlantic Avenue to One Financial Center in time for a healthy breakfast, followed by a short walk to 185 Kneeland Street for the meeting. After the meeting I walked back to South Station and hopped the train back home to Penn Station.

I was also intimidated by having to find my way to meetings and visits with prospective clients in Manhattan, Brooklyn and Queens. This was not Boston where there are five subway lines and one commuter railroad and some busses connecting to the relatively quiet North and South Stations. This was the Big Apple, with 24 subway lines, and five railroads, and zillions of bus routes, and 13,500 yellow cabs, all connecting to the mad houses at Penn Station and Grand Central, which were moving 6,000,000 people daily.

I remember the time when one of the former Stone & Webster executives who survived the Shaw merger with Stone & Webster made a comment to the entire group about me. He loudly announced how Stone & Webster was, "Supporting John Willey's love life." I wanted to say, "F--- you Tom." But instead, the new John Willey responded by looking him right in the eye, and loudly saying, "Thank you, Tom."

108
NO COUCH POTATOES HERE

Barbara does not consider age an excuse to become a couch potato. We average about 30 kayak trips annually in upstate New York, New Jersey, Connecticut, Rhode Island, eastern Pennsylvania and western Massachusetts. We hike in upstate New York and New Jersey whenever we can find time. We enjoy "waterfall weekends" in the Catskills and the Delaware Water Gap. Our passion for scuba diving has not lessened. Since 1997, we have dived 25 locations in the Caribbean and made a couple of trips to the Pacific side of Costa Rica.

Shortly after my permanent arrival in New York City, I found the World Yoga Center at West 72nd and West End Avenue, about one block from our apartment. I knew one of the secrets to aging well was to remain flexible. I am determined not to become an old man, tottering along taking baby steps. There is no better way to stay agile than to practice yoga.

I introduced Barbara to yoga. She injured her back many years ago when she was run over by a truck. I was so pleased when Barbara trusted me enough to attend her first class of Restorative Yoga. The first few practice sessions left her sore but not in pain. Gradually she has seen her back problems disappear. Now she hates missing a class. This is another happy memory to add to the bank. She has become dedicated to the practice of yoga, and she is a good motivator to keep me going to classes.

109
TRIANGLES

I made some basic mistakes handling the conflicts that arose within my original family in Michigan. I wanted so badly to see peace and happiness in the family, and to be able to be part of the solution, rather than part of the problem.

For instance, a cranky son-in-law would call me and tell me stories about one particular daughter and how she was disrupting the family. Then I would get upset and fearlessly pick up the phone and call the particular daughter, and read her the riot act and tell her to get herself together. Then she would call someone else and tell them what an asshole I was for sticking my nose where it did not belong. Then the cauldron would boil over, and the whole family would point the finger at this one daughter.

Sorry to say, I could not seem to utilize my years and years of therapy, reading, research, and behavioral seminars to help my family. Finally, I called Rita, and we agreed to seek a solution. My daughter, Barbara, talked to more than one family counselor to see if they would meet with the family; but there were no takers. I wanted so badly to help my family. Constantly lurking in the back of my mind was the knowledge that I had abandoned my family. I looked for ways to make amends.

Barbara Greenberg suggested a book by Edwin H. Friedman, a family therapist and ordained rabbi. The book's title is *Generation to Generation*. I struggled through the second chapter, "Understanding Family Process." A rather scholarly work, most of the book was over my head, but I did retain some basic information.

I called my dear friend and therapist, Ann Condon, and she heard my story. She said, "John, there's no reason why you can't go out there as a loving father and have a conversation with your family within some boundaries." I told her about what I had read in Friedman's book and she followed up with a suggestion.

"John, invite those who are willing to meet in a neutral place, and ask them three questions as a way of generating a powerful conversation. Do not vary from the three questions, since they are the boundaries." On 11 April 2003, Barbara Greenberg and I flew to Michigan. Rita arranged for us to meet in a private dining room at the airport.

We experienced an enormous victory in our family, showing the power of sustained dialogue. The entire family was invited including the grandchildren. Those who accepted the invitation were Barbara and I, Rita and her husband Arnold, daughters Barbara, Laura, and Patty. We met in a private room at Brownstones restaurant at the Muskegon airport on Saturday 12 April. I asked the three questions that Ann had recommended:

What is it that we do as a family that works?

What is it that we do as a family they does not work?

What is it that we can do to make a difference?

Each person had an opportunity in a round-robin format to respond to each of the three questions. We were together four hours. Everyone participated and offered their views. We enjoyed a feeling of accomplishment when we ended.

Personally, I felt extremely grateful for the opportunity to feel more a part of my family. Also, I was grateful for Barbara's willingness to fly to Michigan to support my efforts. As a result of this encounter, we all agreed that we must not allow communication triangles to develop in our family. If A has a gripe with B, then A must talk directly to B, and not complain to C, who then tells everyone, and B gets ganged up on, and nothing is resolved.

The next morning when the family gathered for breakfast at a local restaurant, some of the grandchildren asked us what we learned at the meeting the day before. We explained the "triangle" and how to diffuse it. They understood immediately. One granddaughter shared a recent experience in which she and her girlfriend had participated in a triangle which had caused problems in their friendship.

110
INVESTMENTS

Barbara is comfortable with investing. She spends significant time reading and learning, and investments are tangentially part of her consulting business. She offered to teach me about investing, which seemed to me a mysterious business. I knew that stock brokers were not my friends, but rather they were salesmen, who earned their salaries by buying and selling stocks.

I wanted to learn about sound ways for me to invest. I remembered the words of my colleague, Louie Wax, "John, in America, you should be earning money while you sleep." Having grown up in the Depression, I am sensitive to the importance of having enough money. I understand I must invest in order to live well. Living in capitalistic America and not investing, seems a crime of neglect. Here was my opportunity to learn how to bypass the commission-seeking brokers and learn how to invest my own money.

When I am frightened, I use anger as a cover up. I'm not happy to note that Barbara's efforts to teach me about investments over several years were met with angry outbursts. She stuck with me. With her coaching, I developed an Excel spread sheet for my asset allocation, and I simplified the management of my assets by consolidating them all in one good institution, Vanguard.

My investments grew. In spite of the financial setback my divorce caused, I have managed to accumulate a solid portfolio of equities and bonds in mutual funds. I review my assets quarterly now. I plan to continue the philosophy of being an accumulator, as opposed to being a consumer.

111
THE DONKEY DIED

Unbeknownst to me, there was a power struggle going on as to how the New York office of Shaw/Stone & Webster would be run in the future. Companywide, there were three major sections, Environmental, Infrastructure, and Power. While Power was the strongest sector companywide, in the New York office we had just Environmental and Infrastructure. I was in the Infrastructure sector.

Being present in the office was really stressful, and I needed all my resolve to continue to keep working. This time I did not quit. I just laughed at the corporate games. I could see in 2004 that the Environmental guys were going to gain control sometime in the near future, and I suspected the first order of business would be to can Willey. I was a high salaried employee they would not likely keep on the payroll. I said to Barbara, "I'm riding a dying donkey." She said," What are you going to do?" I replied, "I'm gonna' ride the bastard 'til he dies."

In late September 2005, the donkey died. I was canned on the first day of the Environmental takeover with no advance notice and five weeks' severance pay. I had known the end was coming, I was financially okay, Barbara and I were secure in our relationship, and I was calm. I was ready for whatever was coming.

On the same day I was canned, my boss, Gerry Doton, called from Boston and said, "What the hell are we going to do about the MBTA?" I felt like saying, "Where do you get the "we" shit, white man? I didn't lay me off." But I really like and respect Gerry and said, "I don't know."

Gerry called back within the hour and asked if I would continue working part-time casual, which means no benefits. I would only have the one client. My funding would be from a contract I negotiated with the MBTA. In effect it was a win/win situation. Shaw/Stone & Webster kept the client and I had a client to serve, with no "bullshit" at the corporate level. I was my own boss. That sounded great to me, and I said, "It's a deal." The most I have worked in a week since then is about 16 hours, and I love this arrangement!

I have an attitude of gratitude and have capitalized on every move that has been made. The MBTA is happy, Shaw/Stone & Webster is happy, and more importantly I am happy. All I can say is, life is good!

112
A BIRTHDAY PARTY FOR MY SISTER

Visiting my sister, Barbara, cooped up at the nursing home, always made me feel sad. My sister, Norma, and her husband, Arnold, usually accompanied me at my request. In 2007, I asked Norma what she thought about having a big surprise party to celebrate Barbara's 75th birthday. Norma was all for it and worked tirelessly to make the arrangements, including a special van to transport Barbara. We hired a room at DiBurro's restaurant in Haverhill, and in July of 2007 we had a great old-time reunion. The entire family showed up, including my former wife, Rita, and daughter, Barbara, from Michigan. My mother would have been overjoyed to see such an outpouring of love and celebration.

As a result of this wonderful party, I learned another facet of my past life about which I was unaware. My daughter, Barbara described how her Aunt was always there for her as a young kid growing up. My nephew, Jeff Brown, who has made his living as a golf manager professional, described how his Aunt Barbara gave him his first set of golf clubs. I heard my son, John, make glowing remarks about his Aunt Barbara, saying how important she was in his young life. John was an avid race car enthusiast, and he related how his interest began because his Aunt Barbara took him and his friends to the Norwood Arena in Norwood, Massachusetts to watch the races. On more than one occasion when young John was "acting out," his Aunt was there to give him some pretty strong guidance.

These revelations about how important Barbara was to my children during the 1950s were important for me to hear. During that time my sister, Barbara, was looking after my family in my absence. I was off in a world of booze, resenting her "interference" as she became a surrogate parent, helping Rita with the task of bringing up the four children. Barbara actually moved in with the family for awhile, and she was a big help to Rita during a very difficult time.

Observing my sister, Barbara, I saw that she was happy and feeling a warm rapport with my children and former wife, Rita. My step-daughter, Debi, served as the "official" photographer recording this historic event. My son, John, was having a private talk with his daughter, Colleen; from whom he had been estranged for many years. All these gifts were way beyond anything I expected.

113
THE DESERT

Many times I explained to Barbara that I had always wanted to spend some time alone in the hottest western desert. Barbara is definitely a water person, and the thought of being in the desert was not even slightly appealing. She said, "John, lets Google the hottest desert and see if we can find you a place there." Within an hour or two she found a casita for rent in the Sonoran Desert just west of Tucson, Arizona.

In May 2007 I arrived at the Casita Nopalito. Outside was a hot tub where I practiced yoga every morning and spent time in meditation. I was free and one with the incredible expanse of desert stretching in every direction. The sky was bright blue, the air was dry and clean. I felt like I could soar over the mountains. While May is not the hottest month of the year in the desert, the temperature did manage to hit 106 pretty much every day. I loved the heat.

Hiking alone in the desert is like being in a small boat in the middle of the ocean. I felt just how insignificant I was in the scheme of things. A short drive from my casita was the Saguaro National Park. I walked along the center of the dry river beds, which are called "washes," avoiding rocks where rattlesnakes sought shelter from the heat. Among all the beautiful cactus plants, my favorite was the three-story high saguaro (sah-wah-ro) with its white, pie plate-sized flowers with bright yellow centers.

As I drove the roads near the casita, in locations where washes crossed the road, signs read "Do Not Enter When Flooded." In these spots, so much water could suddenly flow down the wash that you and your car would be swept away with the current.

I drove through Grant's Pass, up to Tucson Mountain Park and beyond, to see the natural stone monuments at Mount Lemmon. Signs in some of the canyons read, "Danger: High Mountain Lion Country. Enter at Your Own Risk." At first, the mountains were barren, nothing but Palo Verde trees and low-growing cactus, including teddy bear, prickly pear, and cholla. One strange phenomenon on Mount Lemmon was that as I drove higher up the mountain to about 9,000 feet in elevation, the trees grew larger and larger. I would have expected the trees to become smaller and squat as they do in alpine areas here in the northeast. These enormous and regal looking trees were Ponderosa Pines.

I felt closer to Barbara because of her support of my solo vacation in the desert. Actually I was not alone in the desert, because I called Barbara every day. I knew she was happy because I was living out my dream. I did manage to get to Tucson and purchase some beautiful, turquoise Native American jewelry, and of course that added to the excitement of my happy return home.

114
77TH BIRTHDAY PARTY

On 19 August 2007, Barbara and I drove north to visit Fred Allen and Nancy DeMarinis in Groton, Connecticut. We love southeastern Connecticut. The kayaking along the shoreline and in the marshes is excellent, there are isolated sandy beaches for picnics and swimming, and water temperatures are easily tolerable. At least once a summer, we make the trip to visit Nancy and Fred.

Soon after we arrived, Fred described the bridge renovations underway on the Thames River in New London, and he offered to take me for a ride on his boat to check it out. Off we went, without Nancy or Barbara, to check out the construction of the new bridge over the Thames. I enjoyed being out on the water. When we arrived at the bridge, I explained to Fred the various pieces of equipment being used and the stage of work going on at that moment. We motored back down the Thames and east to the Shennecossett Yacht Club, where Fred keeps his boat. We tied up, made everything ship shape, and headed back to their house on Shennecossett Road.

Fred and I entered the front door and greeted Nancy. Suddenly, Angela Cristini and Bob Lazell, Debi and Bill Osgood, and Barbara jumped out from behind a closed door shouting, "Surprise!" This was a 77th Birthday celebration for me, only Barbara was tricky and made it the week AFTER my birthday, so I never suspected a thing. After I caught my breath, Debi presented me with a 50-page photographic memory book, an incredible book full of photos and writings from family, friends, and colleagues.

Barbara announced that we were all going to the Fishermen's Wharf restaurant in Noank for a delicious seafood dinner and a birthday cake to celebrate my 77th birthday. We had a wonderful time. I really like this shoreline restaurant because the food is good and the ambiance is old New England.

The next day another surprise was in store for me. We all boarded the high-speed catamaran in New London and zoomed out to Block Island for three days.

Barbara was extremely generous in taking the eight of us to Block Island and renting a large apartment where we all hung out together. We went grocery shopping for various foods, and Bill Osgood cooked a supper for us the first night we were there. We walked atop the cliffs I had seen from my Navy destroyer when the ship's home port was Newport. We walked the trails throughout the island and enjoyed a picnic lunch on the route.

I had been oblivious to all the planning. After all, this was not a "zero" number birthday, and who would expect such a special birthday celebration the week AFTER my birthday. Without my knowledge, during the early part of 2007, Barbara and Debi worked together to produce the photographic memory book for my 77th birthday. Debi did all the design and art work, and Barbara contacted scores of my friends, asking for photos and messages from them to be included in the book. This was truly a labor of love and a beautiful gift.

Barbara had called my office in Stoughton, Massachusetts and talked to the Chief Engineer and explained to him about the surprise birthday plans. Apparently she motivated him to call a meeting of his group, and together they also produced a very clever book to accompany the one Debi produced. I was really pleased that the Stoughton office responded so fully, since I had been stationed at the New York City office for some time and saw the Stoughton office people only once in awhile.

Many years ago when I first met Barbara, I told her the story about the days when I was a young sailor on board a destroyer stationed in Newport, Rhode Island. I mentioned, more than once, that I had fantasized about going to Block Island, R.I. and walking the 200 foot high cliffs that I observed whenever we left Newport for training exercises.

I figured Block Island would become one of those places I would like to visit, but somehow just never get there. Once before I met Barbara, I had planned to go there to scuba dive with the New England Aquarium Dive Club, but that plan failed to come to fruition.

Barbara's surprise birthday party overwhelmed me. We have built so many wonderful memories together. Since that time I have spent many an hour viewing the photo album and book marking my 77th. The journey continues, as we have added many other adventures together, but the 77th was so unexpected, it will always stand out.

115
STRENGTHENING OUR FUTURE

My relationship with Barbara Greenberg provided opportunities to have open conversations that I had never had in my previous marriages. I could honestly tell her about things that were on my mind, or about subjects that had been forbidden in the past. These conversations were alright with her, but disarming to me. I was always waiting for the other shoe to drop. For example, when I explained that I wanted to do something I had never done before, she would reply, "OK." We treated each other with respect and acted as adults, but I began to think that maybe I could not handle it.

In 2007 I noticed a change taking place between us that was not pleasant, and as a matter of fact, it was quite disturbing. We were getting on each other's nerves. We were finding fault with each other, nit-picking, arguing over senseless issues. I decided to reread *The Couples Companion* to find answers. We were living a good life but something was off, and it did not make sense. After a year, this became too big to ignore. I said to myself, "Don't tell me at this stage of my life that I have to go back to see a shrink!"

We decided that we were not likely to be able to figure out how to resolve the problems by ourselves. Towards the end of 2007 I said to Barbara, "What do think about going to see a pro to find out what's going on?" Without hesitation Barbara replied, "Yes!"

I talked to a lawyer friend here in the City, asking him for a recommendation. He gave me a name, and I called. The therapist explained that she was not taking any new clients, but she gave me the name of Patricia Zorn. In my Haverhill days, I used to hide the fact that I was seeing a therapist, but in New York City it seems not having a therapist makes one suspect. I just plain knew I needed to have more education in the tricky subject of human interactions.

Before I called Patricia Zorn, I had a conversation with Barbara about what credentials we wanted in a therapist. I said, "You know we had a lot of success with the book *The Couples Companion*, by Harville Hendrix and Helen Hunt." Barbara agreed and said, "Why not ask Patricia if she is familiar with the teachings of that book as a requirement?" We both agreed, and I made the call.

When I asked Patricia if she was familiar with the book, she explained, "John, not only am I familiar with that book, but I was trained by Dr. Hendrix." Bingo! We made an appointment for the 16th of January 2008, and from the minute I made the appointment, Barbara and I breathed a sigh of relief.

Barbara and I were a little bit apprehensive as we walked the 22 blocks north on West End Avenue from our apartment on West 74th to Patricia's office on West 96th Street. We each were having thoughts about what the nature of the problem was that we could not see or deal with alone. In my own mind, I knew my part was centered on my old nemesis – anger. Fortunately, we started this counseling with a great deal of mutual love and respect, and that carried the day when things got sticky. We were certain Patricia was not going to "fix us," but that we both must be willing to do some serious work. We were encouraged with the idea of submitting to a coach, since we realized that all great performers have a coach, even Tiger Woods.

At the first meeting with Patricia, we each needed to build trust. We both connected with Patricia from the moment we sat down. We started off by explaining to Patricia that a friend with whom we had become very close had mentioned that Barbara and I were bickering and that it was not pleasant to be around when that was going on. The use of the word "bickering" was a hot point for Barbara as well as for me, and we both reacted badly to it. This was a signal to me that I was a failure because I thought I had already conquered anger.

Patricia was skillful in helping us to see that while we had read *The Couples Companion,* we had probably progressed over the last eight years to a point beyond the book and would need more input to go further. We learned about "triggers" and how to manage anger. We learned that one does not get rid of anger, but rather manages anger. We learned how to breathe and to take deep breaths when things got sticky. We learned how to use a signal so that when either of us became emotionally "elevated," we would walk away until we calmed down.

The first thing that had to be expunged from our minds was the concept of blame. This was not about blame, but rather about the workings of the human mind. We learned that the present conditions sometimes "trigger" a remembrance of the "feeling" from the past, and we react as we did as a hurt little child. Our minds do not always connect with the actions from the past, but rather with the feelings produced by the past incident.

During times when our "triggers" were activated, we learned that the next thing that would happen was that our little five-year olds would come alive and start to fight their ancient battles. We had mistakenly thought it was caused by the present incident. I always wondered why we experienced reoccurring events that never seemed to get resolved. No wonder. We were simply replaying the old hurts from our childhood, and no resolve was possible. We had to give up all hope of having a better past, but we had high hopes of seeing the future differently.

Being a typical American like the guy seeking Zen enlightenment, I figured a few lessons and we'd be all set. However, that did not turn out to be true. We will not ever forget one of Patricia's most memorable statements following a heated discussion where I was ready to bolt. Patricia said, "John! If this were easy, it would be easy!"

During another time when the discussion was getting tense, I noticed a bright pink plastic wand about two feet long with colored ports and strange shapes, almost like something from Star Trek. I growled, "What the hell is that thing?" Patricia playfully picked it up and pushed a button. Sparkling lights turned on, and it beeped, bopped and whistled as she waved it over our heads and announced, "You're both cured." We all started to laugh, and a great lesson was learned. Patricia was comfortable with humor and used it in such a way as to allow both of us to see its value. The unspoken message was clear, "Don't take your self so seriously."

Our last appointment was about one year later. The improvement has been phenomenal. We had the willingness to follow through, and we both felt victorious. We agreed to adopt this new way of communicating we were taught. We came through our year of training much stronger than when we started.

Patricia gave us a parting gift that was meant to drive home the idea that we must not take things too seriously. She presented each of us with a kazoo. Whenever we feel a grouch coming on, we simply approach the other and play a tune on the kazoo. No one can resist a smile or a laugh out loud when someone plays the kazoo.

This is a very simple summary of the lessons we learned from Patricia, but the main point I want to make is that Barbara and I showed a willingness to correct a very difficult situation. We both wanted to improve our relationship. We learned to maintain a sustained dialogue. We cannot solve differences if we withhold and withdraw into our caves of fear and misunderstandings.

116
MENTORS

In spite of his wretched childhood, my father knew how to work hard. He instilled in me the importance of work. As a 10-year old, I thought nothing of shoveling snow, or planting and harvesting our large WWII garden, or jumping into the many other odd jobs my father found for me as a youngster. Without his gift of such a strong work ethic, I could not have gone to college while working two jobs to support my wife and children.

As of 2010, I have been working continuously for 62 years. I have never collected unemployment compensation. My current Big Dig contract ends December 2011, which will be in my 81st year on the planet.

I have described my bosses, foremen, and supervisors who were nasty, petty, and vindictive, but here I want to tell you about three men I respect who taught me many important lessons about life and work.

Bill Naulty was the civilian chief of the Bridge Branch at the First Coast Guard District in Boston, Massachusetts. I worked as Bill's assistant engineer for four years. Bill took his responsibilities as an engineer seriously. He was totally dependable, always present when needed. He kept his word, and did what he said he would do. He based his decisions on engineering principles, and he would not back down, not even for an admiral. He was respected by all who worked for or with him. He was a living example of integrity in action.

The second is Gerry Doton, the chief engineer of the Infrastructure Division at Stone & Webster in Boston. For 10 years I reported to him when I was a Project Manager on various assignments within his Division. Gerry kept our Division on track during a very difficult transition period when 111-year-old Stone & Webster went bankrupt and eventually was acquired by the Shaw Group. In spite of the confusion, lay-offs, rumors, and uncertainty, he kept us competitive and focused during this stressful time. I never saw him panic, no matter what happened (and plenty happened).

The third, John Favorito, is a Senior Project Manager at the Massachusetts Bay Transportation Authority (MBTA). For nearly 20 years I have worked with him in an engineer-client relationship. We manage the MBTA's efforts to protect its infrastructure in the wake of the Big Dig construction project, dealing with some complex and state-of-the-art engineering designs and construction aspects. Our efforts have been focused on keeping the MBTA whole, and we have enjoyed extraordinary success. The MBTA survives unscathed through this nearly two-decade period while its commuter rail system, subways, bus routes, commuter boats and power distribution system have been continually adversely affected by the Big Dig construction.

The first concern of the MBTA is safety, and the second is running on schedule. During times of conflict when the builders of the tunnels were not taking MBTA's safety and infrastructure damage concerns seriously, I wanted to attack and start a war that we probably could not win. John was my client, and I had to listen to him. In a detached way, he would take me aside and squelch my anger by saying, "John, let this one go," followed up with, "We'll only pick battles that we can win." In all these years I saw him lose his cool only once, and even then he recovered and his point was made. We are an effective partnership.

My working relationship with John is the best I have ever experienced, and it can very well be classified as unique. John knows how to bridge the gap between political administrations and the private business world. We have worked together through changes in elected officials and MBTA general managers. We have learned from each other. I brief John on engineering problems, and he briefs me on political realities. We have worked together as a team, and there has been no competition between us. Never have we had a cross word with each other. Certainly we have had heated discussions and disagreements about job-related challenges, but the relationship is worthy of note, especially in the context of the complex heavy construction problems we have faced and resolved together.

John and I have become close friends over the years. We have shared many personal events in our family lives and yet have managed to maintain a professional relationship on the job. I take my hat off to John for his ability to separate the personal from the professional.

117
GUILT

The nagging feelings of guilt about abandoning my own family to take on the responsibility of another family, come and go. Several years ago I sent out Thanksgiving greetings to my nine children. I was not prepared for Sharon's e-mail response. I read the note with a lump in my throat:

Dear Dad

I was thinking of you the other day as I was driving down Rte. 110 along the Merrimack River (off to get my nails done), and I flashed back to evenings where we would finish dinner, literally pile into the station wagon, and head to Wasmacco's for an ice cream. You would then drive us down to the rest area at the river, and we would run around and eat our ice creams. It was a nice flash back to a happy "family" moment ... one of many. We had our crazy challenges, but there were fun times as well.

So for this Thanksgiving, I am grateful for the fact that you took us on like we were your own when you married Mom. And while you may have been somewhat strict, you contributed toward a strong family foundation for us with some fun "family" times, and you instilled some strong values as well.

I realize this is more the exception than the norm as my sons did not have that blessing when John and I split, so all the more appreciative I am for your being a "Dad" to us.

May you have a Happy Thanksgiving as well.

Love,

Sharon

118
FEBRUARY IN THE SUN

With 2008 coming to an end, I made a presentation to Barbara about how I wanted to find a way to escape the cold Northeastern winter. Here was another dream that had been on my mind for 50 years, ever since I declined the job opportunity with Pan Am in Florida. I realized "I can't wait until I'm old. I am already old. I want to go to Florida. If not now, when?" We settled on one month, February, definitely the coldest of the winter. Similar to the Tucson trip, when I told Barbara about my dream and she jumped in to find me a casita in the desert, Barbara said she would help me find a place in Florida.

Barbara remembered that her friend, Beth Collins, was leaving her condo in Tampa at year's end to return to Houston, and she suggested that Beth's Tampa condo might be an option to pursue. I called Beth and made a deal to rent her condo, a loft in a converted cigar box factory in the Ybor City section of Tampa. In 1900 Ybor City was the cigar capital of the world, and it is now designated a historic section of Tampa.

Barbara has a business to run, and she could not be away a whole month. On 26 January, I left for Tampa on my month-long adventure. I had no trouble filling my days alone in Florida. I hiked in Florida's beautiful parks and walked on beaches. I wrote sections of this book. I visited with three retired state engineer friends, as well as with John and Juanita Torissi, formerly from Haverhill. Also, I met my daughter Cheryl in Sarasota for lunch one day.

Even though I was alone in Ybor City, I was not. I called Barbara every day, and Barbara flew down for two long weekend visits. We packed picnic lunches and spent time amongst the noble cypress trees festooned with Spanish moss. We hiked in state parks, discovered beautiful sandy beaches, and collected shells.

The next year I repeated my "February in the Sun" adventure, this time staying in a condo Barbara found for me in Key Biscayne. However, as our relationship grows stronger, I no longer have the need to spend a month alone anywhere. I fulfilled the dream. Now I am pleased and comfortable to be here in New York City with Barbara, even in the cold!

119
FAMILY REUNION

In January, 2009 I called my former wife, Rita, who lives in Muskegan, Michigan, to discuss with her my idea of a July family reunion in Muskegan. Her enthusiasm was instant, and we began the planning. Barbara, Rita and I worked together to make the reunion a reality. Imagine--another first—much like the 50th wedding party for my folks, the 75th birthday party for my sister Barbara, and now a family reunion in Michigan.

Barbara and I, and Rita and her husband Arnold, had the wonderful experience of seeing our family having a big picnic on the shores of Lake Michigan. How good it was to see my children, John Jr., Patricia, Barbara, Laura, and Linda, all together for the first time since my stepson Rick's wedding about 16 years before. Also, our granddaughters, Colleen from Massachusetts, Lea from Nevada, and Alexandra from Lansing, were there to make the event a special pleasure. Granddaughter Olivia could not come to the beach since she was in a nearby hospital recovering from serious injuries resulting from a car accident. We took turns visiting her and kept her company day and night over the long weekend.

The next day we all gathered again, this time at the new Saugatuck home of my daughter, Barbara, and her significant other, Joe. Their lovely new house is set back in a grove of red oaks. Some of us poked around downtown Saugatuck. With the Kalamazoo River winding through the town and boats berthed at marinas, Saugatuck reminded us very much of Cape Cod. Barbara and Joe prepared a delicious cook-out feast in their backyard. We took group photos, told stories, hung out together, and built another powerful memory.

120
WEDDING RAINBOWS

For years Barbara and I had talked about getting married. In 2009, we decided to take this major step. We wanted a low-key, private ceremony. Our dear friend, Nancy DeMarinis, who lives in Groton, Connecticut and is a justice of the peace, agreed to marry us. We chose a spot on the shoreline near the Avery Point Lighthouse in Groton, in view of Pine Island, where we love to kayak. Our close friends made up the wedding party: Nancy's husband, Fred, as well as Angela Cristini and her husband, Bob Lazell.

A week prior to the wedding, Angela and Bob, Barbara and I, packed kayaks atop our cars and headed to Prudence Island, in the upper Narragansett Bay area near Bristol, Rhode Island. We rented cottages there for a week, enjoying the sun, sea, and many days of paddling as well as digging clams and quahogs. At the end of this most excellent kayaking trip, we headed for Groton.

Our wedding day was 22 August 2009. We drove to Nancy's and Fred's house to get our act together. The day had been rainy off and on, but we were fortunate the sky cleared up a little in the late afternoon. We drove to Avery Point, a distance of less than a mile. Angela served as maid of honor, and she made Barbara a beautiful wedding bouquet to carry. Fred walked Barbara across the wide lawn, down to the shoreline. Bob held the rings for us. Nancy had prepared a special marriage ceremony tailored just for us. We stood as bride and groom, within a stone's throw of Long Island Sound. Miraculously, a beautiful rainbow appeared in the sky. A second rainbow appeared as we drove to our wedding dinner, and a third appeared as we arrived at the Inn at Mystic, the restaurant where we celebrated.

In the next several months, we celebrated our marriage two more times. At the Rialto in Harvard Square, Cambridge, Barbara and I hosted a dinner for my sister, Norma, and her husband, Arnold, and Barbara's brothers, Larry and his wife Sally, and Dick and his wife Jan. That was the first time our siblings met each other. And our dear friend, Starr Tomczak, hosted a third wonderful party for us at her New York City home, attended by 10 good friends from New York City, as well as Jan Schwarz from Minnesota.

22 August 2009. Barbara and I were married at Avery Point, Groton, CT.

121
KAYAK KHRONICLES

Early in the book I wrote about the wonders of Plum Island, the joy of my youth in the Little River area, my love of the Maine coast, and in general, my passion for the great outdoors. I am not a famous naturalist like John Muir or John Audubon, but immersing myself in the natural environment brings me a feeling of great peace.

My first kayaking experience was with Barbara Greenberg in mid 1997. We were on a scuba diving vacation on the island of Roatan off the coast of Honduras. After a day of diving, Barbara invited me to go paddling in a two-person, sit-on-top kayak. Reluctantly I agreed, and off we paddled across the small bay. About half way across Barbara said, "John, let's stop paddling for a moment, and just listen." We paused, enjoying the sounds of nature, water lapping on the side of the kayak, a gentle breeze, tropical birds calling in the distance. This felt like a spiritual experience, simple, yet so memorable. We paddled further across the bay and found an opening in a mangrove thicket. We slipped our kayak into a small channel. The water was mirror smooth and black as midnight. Suddenly we arrived in a round-shaped clearing, about 30 feet in diameter. The knotted and twisted mangrove branches arched overhead, giving the illusion of a grand natural cathedral. We sat there quietly for a few minutes, admiring the mysterious beauty of this space.

In later years, one weekend in New York City, Barbara asked me to join her for a paddle in the two-person kayak she stored in Jamaica Bay, Queens. Within minutes, we were gliding through salt water marshes, breathing in the fragrance of the ocean, paddling past tall grasses, and hearing the sweet song of red wing blackbirds. We saw blue crabs feeding, schools of small fishes darting here and there, blue herons stalking fish, and sea gulls squawking and shoving each other aside, competing for food.

For years, Barbara and I traveled back and forth each weekend between Haverhill and New York City. Weekends when we were in Haverhill, we had no kayaks, and eventually we decided to go ahead and buy kayaks to use in the Haverhill area. Debi and Bill offered to let us store them in their barn in East Kingston, New Hampshire. Debi and Bill fell in love with kayaking too, and they bought their own kayaks. They sold their horses, demolished their horse barn, and went kayaking instead! Bill said, "We have a lot more fun with the kayaks, and you don't have to feed or take care of them when they are not in use." Bill and Debi expressed wonder at the natural places just a stone's throw from their home on the Powwow River. They had never seen its beauty until we all kayaked its upper length right up to Country Pond.

When Barbara and I go kayaking, I pack a picnic lunch, often roasted chicken thighs and legs with onions and peppers. Debi and Bill dubbed it "Kayak Chicken." Sometimes I added Italian sausages to enhance the culinary delight. Soon Bill asked for the recipe, and we took turns bringing the picnic lunch.

I cannot think of a better picnic spot than a grove of Eastern Hemlocks on the banks of a river or pond, soft and fragrant hemlock leaves as a cushion, enjoying our Epicurean delights, observing the beautiful natural environment, and taking a snooze.

One of our favorite spots was Labor-In-Vain Creek. Feeding directly into the Ipswich River in Massachusetts, this tidal creek has an eight to nine foot tidal exchange. At low tide there are gorgeous, clean sand bars to play on and explore. We paddled up the Labor-in-Vain Creek on an incoming tide, and at the top of the Creek, hung out until we could ride the outgoing tide all the way back. Sometimes we "rafted" our kayaks together, leisurely turning and twisting with the currents, gently floating back downriver. Great fun!

Our paddling goals are to be peaceful and to enjoy nature in remote places only accessible by kayak. We oft times go to the same lakes in Harriman State Park in upstate New York. We love to observe the natural evolution of flowers and trees from May to October. In the spring we inspect the beaver dams and see what streams the little fur-bearing engineers have blocked off, and figure out ways to get around or over them. In late May the abundant white blueberry blossoms give way to the showy splash of gorgeous white and pink mountain laurels. We enjoy observing the first arrivals of the yellow water lilies followed by the intricate white water lilies. We never seem to be able to remember all the various plant life that we admire, even though every year we look up their names in the field guides.

In case anyone thinks this sport is for sissies, I have news for you. In the last several years I have begun recording each trip in a document on my computer, which I call *The Kayak Khronicles.* The following is from 2 August 2008 on our 19th trip of the year. Please bear in mind that lightening strikes the highest object, which means if you are on a river, you are the highest object. Yikes!

2 August, Saturday (Paddle # 19) Barbara and I met Debi and Bill at the launch site of the East River in Madison, Connecticut by the Route 1 Bridge. Bill and Debi arrived from New Hampshire at 11:00 A.M., and Barbara and I arrived from New York City at 11:05 A.M. The East River is a tidal marsh river, six miles long from its mouth at Long Island Sound.

We ate our lunch at a picnic table at the launch site, in constant sight and sound of fish jumping out of the water on an incoming tide. Two ospreys were in action, along with a cormorant or two. Thanks to Bill, we had an abundant supply of kayak chicken and Bill's famous tomato salad. We brought quantities of melon and cherries.

Under a cloudy sky, we launched and started paddling upstream with the incoming tide.

The River was beautiful, but within an hour, the clouds darkened, and we heard rumblings of far-off thunder. Barbara said with conviction, "Let's turn back." Barbara and Debi did so immediately. Bill and I grumbled and said it was nothing to worry about; however, we all headed back downstream. Soon a woman on the Guilford bank hollered at Debi, telling her to come ashore and into her house immediately because a "severe thunder and lightning storm" was predicted to hit within a half hour. Bill and I said, "Thanks, but we can make it."

Within 10 minutes by the clock, lightning began to strike, followed immediately by thunder that sounded like a 16-inch coastal cannon. Strikes were close at hand and in rapid succession. The rain was coming down so hard we could not see the shore. We all were paddling at breakneck speed, Bill's kayak was planing, Debi was leading the pack with a rooster tail off her stern, and John and Barbara were pushing their wide, short kayaks to the max. Debi headed for a private dock and scrambled ashore.

Although the owner beckoned for her to come into the house "now," Debi waited and helped each of us pull our kayaks ashore. We each arrived, soaking wet, with the kayaks half full of water. The severe lightning continued, and the rain actually caused the river to overtop its banks. Mr. and Mrs. Peter Mumola were most gracious, offering us their covered porch as shelter. After an hour or so of raging storm, Peter drove Barbara and Debi to our launch site to retrieve the cars. We loaded our kayaks at their house and drove off to the Sandpiper Inn in Old Saybrook.

With great gratitude, we ended the day with a delightful meal at the Dock and Dine at a corner table overlooking Long Island Sound. We were glad to be alive, and we all agreed that extreme adventures would be better saved for others.

Everyone who goes kayaking with Barbara quickly becomes committed to searching along the shorelines for fishing bobbers to add to her abundant collection of over 200 bobbers and counting. She has every shape and color imaginable, piled high in a huge basket in the living room.

I can truthfully admit that I would not be kayaking--something I love to do--if it were not for the tenacity of my wife, Barbara. There is a lesson here for me about further developing my character: When you want something, do not let anything stand in your way. Barbara has always been willing to go to any length to overcome the enormous obstacles facing a city dweller who loves to kayak. Finding places in New York City to store and easily access a kayak is a formidable task. Barbara was insistent that we find a better solution than driving all the way across the City to Jamaica Bay to store and use a kayak.

I was prepared to give up kayaking entirely because it was just too hard, but Barbara persevered. One day, I jokingly remarked, "Why don't you get a storage locker?" Bingo! Within a few days she had found and rented a 4 x 4 x10 foot high storage locker on the second floor of the Storage Post in Yonkers, New York, a city just north of the Bronx. From November to April, our kayaks are stored, standing on their noses in this narrow storage bin. In May we install the roof rack on the car, hoist up the kayaks, and off we go to paddle lakes, rivers, and marshes. We keep the kayaks on top of the car until November. I dare say we own the only car in Manhattan with permanently attached kayaks for six months every year. The good news is we are ready to go kayaking at a moment's notice all season long.

We also love kayaking with our friends Nancy DeMarinis and Fred Allen along the coastal waters and marshes near their home in Groton, Connecticut. And we frequently kayak with our dear friends, Bob Lazell and Angela Cristini from Valley Cottage, New York. We have enjoyed many a trip with them throughout New York, Connecticut, Rhode Island, New Jersey, and Pennsylvania.

Our kayak adventures continue, and we never cease to be amazed at the pristine rivers, lakes and marshlands we can reach in our kayaks. We average about 32 paddling trips per year. We are always planning trips to new locations. Even though the places we "explore" have likely been visited by thousands over the years, they are new territories to us, and we figure that qualifies us as "Great Explorers."

August 2006. Barbara and John kayaking on the Poultney River near the Vermont border in Whitehall, NY

122
RELIGIOUS INSTITUTIONS

Not too long after I arrived in New York City, I was introduced to Malachy McCourt. He was a well-known personality in the entertainment world long before most people ever heard of his now famous brother, Frank, the author of *Angela's Ashes*. Malachy invited me to attend the October 2009 memorial for Frank McCourt, along with about 1,000 others at the Peter Jay Sharpe Theatre on Broadway and 95th Street. Frank's book was noted for how truthfully he told his story, especially regarding his religious upbringing. As described in an October/November 2009 article in the *Irish American*, he "loathed the institutional church that he grew up/in under..." In the same magazine, "With characteristic modesty, Frank said his book came out because he wanted to get it out of his system."

I feel the same way in regards to the churches I was required to attend, and I want to get it out of my system. The first religion to which I was exposed was the Unitarian Universalist Church. My mother took me there, but neither my mother nor my father ever attended. I really liked this Church. The people were friendly and warm. We had fun, singing in the choir, learning roles and acting in plays, pouring maple syrup on the snow and eating the freshly made candy. I loved being part of that welcoming and kind community. Then, my uncle, Benjamin Lester Chase, insisted I be baptized at age 12 at the Winter Street Baptist Church in Haverhill. To impress my first wife, Rita, I later converted to Catholicism at a big ceremony by Bishop Wright at the Cathedral of the Holy Cross in Boston. I studied Catholicism for a long time, investigated Judaism, the Eastern Orthodox Church, and Buddhism. Buddhism left me bewildered, trying to pronounce Sanskrit words about 30 letters long. I also bought a copy of the Koran (Qur'an) and tried to make sense out of that collection of mysterious writings. I was completely snowed with the Koran, but at least with Buddhism I got the general idea and it made sense to me.

I spent years reading and studying the Bible, both the Old and New Testament, and even studied the Book of Mormon. I learned about the Angel Moroni, keeper of the golden plates of Mormonism and other characters I did not know existed. Sally and I both attended the Course in Miracles. I saw many places in the New Testament that related to living an exemplary life. Two stick out: the 13th Chapter of First Corinthians, and the Book of James. But in every case, it seemed to me that religious zealots or fundamentalists mucked up the Good Word and exercised power over the religious lemmings who did not take the time to read the words themselves and form their own opinions.

Many years ago when I re-established a good relationship with Rita, I found out that in her new location in Michigan, she had embraced the Lutheran religion. I had a chuckle thinking how I had become a Catholic to impress her.

Since 1992 I worked with a gentleman I admired greatly for two reasons. His name is Thomas Chang, Ph.D. He was part of the consultant group that I managed as the Project Manager representing my client, the MBTA, on the Big Dig in Boston. Tom was calm, well disciplined, and a family man. He had the respect of everyone who came in contact with him. He is also the most knowledgeable geotechnical engineer I have ever met.

On one particularly difficult problem, I approached Tom. "Tom, I know it's Friday but we really need to complete the report on the isolation caissons for the north tower of the cable-stayed bridge. Can you stay late?" Politely Tom replied, "John I attend classes every Friday evening at the Temple." But he went on, "I'll be happy to come in on Saturday or Sunday to complete the report for Monday morning." I said, "I'll see you on Saturday."

With the report out of the way, I asked Tom about the Temple. He explained, "John, I've been a Chinese Buddhist all my life, and am committed to the study." I began firing questions at Tom that had been in my head for years.

Tom quietly explained that Buddhism does not have a God, nor is it a faith-based religion, but rather a system of training the mind. This information set my mind on fire, like I had discovered gold. Later, Tom gave me a book titled *Fundamentals of Buddhism* by Peter D. Santina, and off I went on a new learning tangent.

After years of studying a small collection of Buddhist literature, I realized that I was not going to become a Buddhist. However, I liked the philosophy. I also liked the way Tom handled the fact that there are thousands of religions or sects. He told me, "John, we're all climbing the same mountain." That philosophy really resonated and gave me comfort. Buddhism is the system of training and of teaching people how to live a good life that makes the most sense to me.

Somewhere in my travels, I picked up a magazine article written by Robert Fulghum about an American seeking enlightenment in a Zen Temple in Japan. Of course the American wanted the miracle to happen in about six weeks. I have kept this little story for years because it spoke to me. The American was in the temple a short time and realized he did not have the patience to get properly Zenned. Before going home, the Zen Master invited him for a chat and brought him into the temple. Reaching for a scroll, the master first read it in Japanese then translated it into English:

> There is really nothing you must be.
> And there is nothing you must do.
> There is really nothing you must have.
> And there is nothing you must know.
> There is really nothing you must become.
> However, it helps to understand that fire burns,
> And when it rains, the earth gets wet …

"Whatever, there are consequences. Nobody is exempt," said the master. With a wink, he turned and walked away.

This little presentation of my views on God and religion is important to me because I have taken the time "to get it out of my system." I have attempted to attain a neutral attitude about the many Gods and the thousands of religions that are available if one chooses to discover them.

The greatest peace of mind came in later years after all my searching, when I realized that it did not matter if there was a God or not. I cannot bring myself to adhere to any particular religious guidelines. I feel comfortable not adopting any institutionalized religion. I believe that a better approach to life is to just deal squarely with the difficulties of living, and rely upon the strength inside me. In any case, I believe that man invented God and not the other way around. After all my experiences with religions, I close out this vignette with the belief that the substance of all of them together can be summed up in two words: Love and Service.

123
SCUBA

In previous chapters I wrote about the thrilling sport of scuba diving, how I got involved, and my many fun-filled underwater adventures. However, scuba diving has made an enormous contribution to my life on a whole different level. In the early years of diving, my life and my diving were enveloped in a constant soap opera. I was so busy surviving the chaos that I did not have an opportunity to examine the bigger picture. From 1997 until the present, a whole new scuba diving experience has unfolded. Now I can see with clarity what was heretofore hidden by my own confusion and the drama in which I lived.

Scuba diving is an opportunity to face fears, build character, and improve self-confidence. I greatly admired Ralph Moxey for his courage to dive in the North Atlantic, and I had fantasies about my doing the same thing. Dive shops did not exist, and wetsuits could not be purchased anywhere. Ralph made his own wetsuit by tracing outlines from a paper pattern onto a roll of neoprene. He cut out the pieces and cemented them together to fashion the wet suit. Ralph cast his own weights by pouring molten lead into homemade molds.

Back in the 60s, Ralph talked me into trying skin diving with his equipment at the Winthrop Yacht Club. My skin diving ended with my fright and flight to the surface at the sight of my own hair falling over my mask. That attempt at skin diving left me feeling a humiliated failure, much like the time when I left the first grade at recess time and went home early. Not so deep down, I really wanted to dive, but I was too scared. The idea of walking into my own fears and coming out the other side a better man never occurred to me. In 1989, close to 25 years later, I rose to the challenge to save Sally, the fair maiden in distress. Because I wanted to rescue her, I volunteered to do what I was otherwise afraid to do. Sally was going to quit her dream for the same reason I quit free diving many years earlier --- Fear.

Today, from a position of self-confidence, I can see how this lifelong romance with scuba diving has benefitted me. I conquered my fears because I was motivated to do something for someone else. With the goal of impressing Sally and being her champion, I was forced on every dive to walk into the unknown.

Diving has been one of the high points in my life, not only for the adventure, or the feeling of weightlessness in the foreign world of the sea, but for building my self-confidence. Diving, like life, is never routine. The possibility always exists that a challenge will show up unexpectedly which will require rising to the occasion or drowning. One time I was approaching the boat's ladder after a long 50-minute dive, and wham! I was caught in a rough current that swept me back out to sea. Another time I was ascending to the surface to climb on the boat and discovered that a squall had blown through, there were eight foot waves, and the dive boat's ladder was dancing around in erratic patterns. These kinds of experiences taught me to be calm, assess the situation, and take appropriate action. I realize now how important it is to have a partner I can trust and respect while at depth. In addition, I now realize how important it is to have a partner I can trust and respect when I am not diving.

On our last dive trip, I completed my 406th dive, with Barbara not too far behind at 300+ dives. Over the past 12 years, Barbara and I have taken about 25 dive trips throughout the Caribbean, the Bahamas, and the Pacific coast of Costa Rica. We have covered thousands of miles in our quest for diving adventure, sometimes returning to our favorite places a half dozen times. While we often talk about other kinds of vacations, when push comes to shove, we almost always decide on diving.

At this point in time, a typical dive vacation for us is focused on the overall adventure. We spend weeks planning the trip together. How can we get the most out of our frequent traveler miles? Where is the best weather for diving even in the winter months? The anticipation and planning are of equal importance to the actual trip, and these can only be enjoyed in the absence of my former life's pattern of unending drama.

For example, we have traveled to very special isolated places in the Caribbean. In Belize we stayed at Lighthouse Reef, an uninhabited island inside an atoll. The only signs of life on our island were the small dive operation and the cabins where we lodged. We flew from Belize City in a six-passenger plane, landing on a 20-foot wide paved strip that ended a scant few feet from the ocean. The island has no roads, and our dive luggage was delivered to our cabins with a front-end loader. Two brothers, who lived alone on an adjacent island of only a few acres in size, delivered fresh fish each day for our meals. Staying on the island with us was a total of about 20 divers and snorkelers. A staff of equal size took turns staying out on the reef a week at a time, then returning home to Belize City for a week, etcetera.

Barbara and I dove in the Blue Hole, discovered and made famous by Jacques Cousteau in the early 50's. The Blue Hole is a flooded limestone sinkhole about 1,000 feet in diameter, 400 feet deep, rising from the ocean floor to about 40 feet from the surface. At about 140 feet, the Blue Hole is the deepest dive we have ever made. We glided around stalactites and enjoyed the company of many reef sharks.

A recent dive trip during Thanksgiving week of 2009 was a return trip to Bonaire, a favorite place of ours in the Netherland Antilles, about 45 miles off the coast of Venezuela. Barbara found a neat apartment with cooking facilities, close to a good dive operation. Off we went, confident we would meet new friends and have great fun.

We also discovered a little-known location on the southwest coast of the island of Puerto Rico, where the weather is perfect. The diving is good, and there are many isolated, sandy beaches, as well as great hiking paths along the shore, and little towns to explore.

We plan to continue diving for as long as we are physically capable. In the 1980s I could dive 18 times during a one-week dive vacation. My ears have gradually become sensitive to the undersea pressure. On the last vacation, I made 9 dives in a week and felt completely satisfied.

Both Barbara and I are comfortable knowing that change is constant, and we can adjust to life as we grow older. We now spend as much time exploring on shore as we do diving underwater. I can see the day when diving will be a pleasant memory, but I am grateful that even at my 80 years of age, we are still planning dive vacations. What remains with me are the powerful lessons I have learned about life as a result of scuba diving.

March 2000. Barbara and I relaxing in between dives at Scott's Head on the island of Dominica.

January 2003. Barbara and I in Washington Slagbaai Park, Bonaire, Netherlands Antilles, taking a day off from diving to explore the island.

124
THE DEMON UNCOVERED

In September of 1982 my friend, Tony, introduced me to "Recovery, Inc, " one of the earliest self-help groups, which had been founded by Abraham A. Low, M.D., at the Neuropsychiatric Institute of the University of Illinois Research and Education Hospitals.

Tony gave me a copy of the basic text called *Mental Health Through Will Training.*

I began attending meetings on a regular basis, soon realizing that I had to learn how to deal with my anger which had been a destructive force throughout my life.

I had not had a drink in over 10 years, yet I had continued making illogical decisions. I believe now that when I began to drink alcoholically as a young person, my normal maturing process halted. Naturally, I continued to grow older, but when I quit drinking at age 41, I had the emotional maturity of an angry 15-year old. I came to realize that alcoholism was merely a symptom of deeper underlying causes that had led to my self-defeating behavior. Anger blinded me to my own liabilities, and I could not get free.

I also have come to understand that "injustice" triggers my anger. I wrote earlier about my reaction to the Rape of Nanking, the Nazi's persecution of the Jews, and my father's dictatorial approach to parenting. Any "injustice" caused me great anger and feelings of powerless. On more than one occasion I abruptly left a movie during a scene about the Holocaust or other presentations of gross injustice. I would leave my companions sitting in the theatre, go for a walk, or sit in the lobby.

The gang I grew up with in Haverhill had a banquet every two years. My old buddies traveled from all over the country for the get-together at the Rod and Gun Club. I decided to attend one of these gatherings, and I really looked forward to seeing my old friends, catching up with some guys I had not seen in 10 or 20 years. But soon after the party began, the strippers arrived. What I saw looked like a spectacle where the Christians were being fed to the hungry beasts. I saw a frightened look in the eyes of one obvious novice young woman, and I bolted. I felt anger and disgust and confusion as I rushed out, walking alone through the filled parking lot to get in my car and escape. I never answered another invitation.

This deep-seated abhorrence of "injustice" was born in my childhood home. I grew up with a father who had been terribly hurt as a youngster. He was depressed and angry all his life. The "injustice" he caused and I witnessed, affected me, as well as my mother and sisters.

Now as I write this book, I can connect the dots. The anxiety about loss of civil service employment rules we experienced at the Massachusetts Department of Public Works (MDPW) at the hands of the Governor and the Commissioner triggered my anger, and I quit my job without thinking through the consequences. In a promising career in the display department with Sears & Roebuck, I quit my job because my boss unfairly took credit for work I designed.

In an early morning epiphany in September 2008, I realized that such visceral reactions to "injustice" had caused me a lot of grief. I also realized that none of the people involved in the three instances where I quit were the real problem. I created the problem by overreacting to the "injustice." I am grateful now to be able to see my part in my lifetime problem.

On 2 October 2008 while vacationing on Cape Cod, Barbara and I took my former therapist, Ann Condon, out to dinner. I related to her my new awareness about injustice, and she looked at me in such a way that I knew I had missed something. Ann asked, "John, what do you think about what's going on in Darfur? I replied, "It's awful. It's beyond human understanding." Ann said, "That's injustice!" She went on to say that we needed to distinguish between "injustice" and "mean and unfair."

She explained that what happened to me as a child growing up was "mean and unfair," and I could not do anything about it. And then as I grew older, when anything looked like "mean and unfair," I was triggered back to the five-year old, and mistakenly called this "injustice," feeling powerless, angrily running away, or quitting a job. Ann then drove the point home, as she play-acted a frightened little five-year old in a sobbing voice. With her thumb in her mouth, she cried, "You're mean and unfair, and I'm going to tell my mommy, and I'm going to my room."

Sonovabitch, that was me well into my 70s, still sucking my thumb and letting my life be run by an angry, frightened little five-year old! Then Ann asked the big question, "Where did this "unfair and mean" stuff first happen, and when? The answer is all too obvious -- at home when I was a child. After 39 years of not drinking, I can see how anger has manifested itself throughout my life.

Self examination, or as I prefer to think of it, self-inventory, is the key to the whole recovery process. I fondly remember the night in 2004 when visiting my daughter, Linda, we were discussing the challenges of life. She asked me if I had ever read a book by Dr. Seuss called *Oh! The Places You'll Go.* I had not. Linda read the whole story to me. When she came to this passage, it really clicked:

> I'm afraid that some times:
> you'll play lonely games too.
> Games you can't win
> 'cause you'll play against you.

I could see that anger was the lonely game I was playing, and I could not win because I was playing against myself.

During my time with the Coast Guard I was aware of my anger, and this allowed me to see the anger in other people. I observed a young 3rd class petty officer I will call Mary returning from lunch on Fridays after a "three Martini lunch." After a few weeks I called her into my office and talked to her like a friend. I knew she was married and heading down the wrong path. I was trying to do for her what Irving Cleary had done for me so many years before. She listened patiently and thanked me and left my office. Soon after that she was assigned to the west coast and shipped out. Mary experienced some life-threatening events because of her choice to meet life's challenges with the aid of booze. One day in a fit of despair, out of the blue she contacted me from the west coast, and wanted to talk about the conversation I had with her months earlier. Mary and I began a pen pal relationship that was to benefit both of us as the years rolled by. We both gained insight into the damage we had done to ourselves with the misuse of anger. She confessed that in 1985 when I talked to her in my office, she had no idea what I was talking about, but listened because "I was a nice old guy."

I cannot measure the contributions we have made to each other's lives in the last two decades. Mary had many angry incidents that ran parallel to mine, and we supported each other in the attempt to live a better life. Years later, I met Mary in the summer of 2007 in Providence, Rhode Island for our first reunion in close to 20 years. She is a very responsible person, retired from the Coast Guard, and now a consultant overseeing the safety and operations of commercial fishing boats.

At Vanasse Hangan Brustlin, Dave Wilcock was also a target of unfair abuse at the hands of Ron Thompson. Dave's response proved to be a better route than mine. I left. Dave is now a principle with the firm and Mr. Thompson has long since left the firm following a rather unpleasant series of events. In retrospect, Ron Thompson was not the problem, but rather my inability to deal with a problem in an adult fashion. I ultimately went to work for another engineering company. When my contract ended, my client was so satisfied with my performance that he arranged for another engineering and design company to hire me so I could remain as the Project Manager.

This is not to cry over lost opportunities but rather to recognize my part in them and the power of early childhood development. Taking things personally and reacting with anger proved to be my undoing.

125
THE CHEF

My mother was a great cook. She could make delicious, tasty meals from a limited choice of inexpensive seasonal New England foods on a very small budget. She made simple deserts like doughnuts, cakes, bread pudding, or rice and raisins. Her lemon meringue pies were to die for. Every fall she canned a couple hundred quarts of fruits, vegetables, and chicken for use in the following winter.

I think I inherited her cooking genes. Much of my life has centered on cooking. My cooking career began quite by accident around 1945 when I started to work at Ray's Restaurant in Monument Square, Haverhill. I was hired as a part-time dish washer and pot-walloper. In the beginning, I mostly worked after school, scrubbing pots. Little by little, I showed interest and the chef would let me peel vegetables, then mash the potatoes, and use the Fryelator. Pretty soon I was cooking simple things like a hamburger, and then I was serving whole meals. In a fairly short time, they hired another kid to clean the pots. I served as a cook's assistant until I left a year later.

For the next 15 years, all the cooking I did was at home. When we lived in Winthrop, Massachusetts I watched Celina, the French woman who took care of my wife Rita's grandmother. By watching her, I learned how to truss a chicken, cook and carve a leg of lamb, and make French style string beans. I watched her make a Roux as a first step in perfect gravy and sauces, using various pan drippings and sometimes just butter. Celina always had a stock pot simmering, or sometimes two, getting ready to make her soups, gravy and sauces.

In the 60s when I worked at Vicliff's Steak House as a waiter, I observed the various chefs and cooks, and added more to my virtual experience. I saw how to butcher, how to prepare a prime rib roast, cut and cook lobster, prepare vegetables. I learned the 6 P's from one of the chefs, "Prior Planning Prevents Piss Poor Performance." Everything had to be ready in advance of when you needed it. I learned how to evaluate foods as to their freshness, how to give "new legs" to tired vegetables, fish, and meats.

When I started to work as a line cook, I learned nothing must be wasted! I read *The Epicurean* by Charles Ranhofer, the well-known French chef for 34 years at the world famous Delmonico's in New York. The book was a series of recipes that he used at Delmonico's from 1862 to 1894. I found the book in the belongings of Rita's grandfather, who had been the chef at the Hotel Vendome in Boston. I read about the top French chef in the world, Auguste Escoffier. Escoffier's recipes, techniques and approaches to kitchen management have been adopted by chefs and restaurants, not only in France, but also throughout the world.

When ViCliff's owner, Cliff Crawford said, "Get your whites on," I was ready. I soon did what I did in engineering. I learned all positions in the kitchen, and eventually excelled as a broiler man. I loved the attention I got from working a broiler in the dining room. Black and white checkered pants, sparkling white jacket, a red neckerchief, and all topped off with a tall starched chef's hat. I kept a steel steak sizzler on the side containing fat trimmings reduced to liquid. Every once in a while when I was preparing to put out an order, I would tip the sizzler into the coals. A gigantic flame would erupt, accompanied by gasps and ooohs from the patrons. I maintained a serious look, pulled meats off the grill and placed them on the dinner plates, as though the flames were all part of the process.

I broiled on anthracite coal (hottest ever), gas, electric, wood and charcoal briquettes. I learned how to spot range-fed beef, green beef (not aged), and lot-fed beef, and the difference between Commercial, Choice, and Prime cuts of beef. I was called upon sometimes to manage the restaurant in Cliff's absence, to chat with customers, to carve plank steaks at the tables, and to train waitresses.

My next restaurant was The Margery in Ipswich, a fairly upscale restaurant in an affluent location. My job was broiler man in the dining room. Sundays were special days, where the restaurant featured roast beef with freshly made popovers, which I made at the broiler station. I loved to see the patrons' looks of awe as I pulled a pan out of the oven. Popovers are really nothing but simple bread consisting of eggs, flour, milk and a little salt, cooked in cast iron popover pans at high heat for about a half hour. They rise without baking powder or baking soda, but rather by steam trapped inside the batter. I can still remember the first part of the recipe: "Break 108 eggs (9 dozen)."

The Lamplighter Motel in Lawrence was run by Jimmy Costas, a well known Greek chef. From Jimmy, I learned about cooking seafood. Unfortunately, the establishment was owned by a small group of lawyers and businessmen who knew nothing about running a restaurant. Heretofore successful, Jimmy left when they refused to let him run the place, which soon led to the restaurant's demise. Steamed *Clams A La Grecque* (in the Greek manner) was a big favorite there. Over the years I have cooked hundreds of pounds of steamers to wild acclaim from family and friends.

Clams A La Grecque

Choose a large tight-covered pan, big enough for a good size batch of clams. Dump the clean, fresh clams in a big container of water. Get rid of any "floaters" that look tired and are probably dead. Place a steamer pan on the stove with low heat. Pour in some olive oil (prevents the butter from burning), a couple of tablespoons butter, about a half dozen mashed garlic cloves, and a small bunch of basil leaves. Stir them around, and then dump in the clams. Immediately cover the pot, and turn the heat up as high as it will go. Do not be tempted to add water! When the cover is hot to your bare hand, the clams are almost ready. Take a quick peek to be sure the clams have opened and are being steamed in their own juice. Stir them up with a big kitchen spoon. Put the cover back for a minute or two. Then pour off the broth into small bowls for dipping. Dump the scrumptious clams in a big bowl and Buon Appettito! (There are 23 different ways of saying "eat up." I prefer the Italian.)

My next restaurant was The Country Squire Inn in Middleton, Massachusetts. I spent about three years there, and from Chef Sam Rallo I continued to learn about cooking as well as how to manage people. We catered to the function business where large groups were served in addition to the normal restaurant business.

During this period of restaurant work, I had a monkey on my back that at times felt more like an 800-pound gorilla. In recounting the stories about my cooking in the various restaurants,

I should note that this was accomplished while my civil engineering career was progressing. Between highway and bridge construction and cooking, I frequently worked 16-hour days and 7-day weeks. Added to that equation was the fact that my alcoholism was also progressing, and consequently things on the home front were going from bad to worse.

I was also a full-time chef at home with Sally and the five kids, and these skills came in handy and saved us a lot of money. We ate only home-cooked meals, using fresh produce and inexpensive cuts of meat which I turned into tasty meals. Later when we moved to Haverhill, I prepared many enjoyable dinner parties for family and friends.

September 12, 1981. I catered a wedding for 200 in the backyard of our next-door neighbors on East Broadway, David and Shannon Hewey

The saga continues in my New York City life. Here, when people decide to have a dinner party, they often head for Zabar's at West 84th Street and Broadway and load up on all kinds of expensive, cold, prepared foods. People show up for the party and when "dinner is served," they line up at the buffet table. Then the challenge is to find a place to sit where you can balance the meal on your knees and hope to hell you do not spill anything on an expensive rug. Drinks can be a disaster. Using a knife to cut anything is next to impossible and a sure way to tip over the plate. Sometimes there are exotic concoctions to select from the buffet that taste like boiled overshoes. This, I learned, is when you smile, swallow the unidentifiable substance, and gush at the hostess with a rave review of the dinner.

Early on, Barbara announced that she wanted to have a dinner party for about eight people. Barbara said, "Should we go to Fairway's, Citarella's or Zabar's." I said, "I'd like to prepare a sit-down dinner with real food." Barbara was really nervous, and her retort was, "John, people don't cook like that here in New York City. Traditional sit-down meals just won't work here in these small spaces." I made a strong case, and after convincing Barbara to pull out the extra leaf in the dining room table, I proceeded to prepare a real meal.

Everyone seemed to like the idea of a sit-down dinner. We served baked stuffed haddock, and roasted chicken, Delmonico potatoes, string beans with rosemary, ginger carrots, fresh-baked rolls and butter. Barbara was shocked to see her dainty friends asking for seconds. At the end of the meal, there was nothing left to put away in the refrigerator.

We have served many more delicious meals, such as roast leg of lamb, roast turkey, braised lamb shank, braised short ribs, Italian favorites like pasta e fagiuoli, chicken cacciatore, meatballs and Italian sausages, braciole, baked stuffed lobster, sautéed lobster and of course, steamed *Clams ala Grecque.*

Barbara and I have taken many vacation trips to the Caribbean. Sometimes we go with another couple, and we rent apartments, and I cook for the group. When Barbara and I vacation with Angela and Bob, I have a blast in the kitchen. At Prudence Island in Narragansett Bay, Rhode Island, we dug clams and quahogs, and bought lobsters from the local lobsterman. I made *Clams A La Grecque* of course, plus clam chowder, and baked stuffed quahogs.

One time In Florida Bay, we and Bob Lazell and Angela Cristini spent a week together, each couple renting a house boat to explore Florida Bay. We tied the boats together at night, far from land. Angela spotted an unmarked lobster trap chock-filled with spiny lobsters. Barbara encouraged us to take action. Bob dove in the shallow water and fastened a line, and we pulled up the untended trap, liberating most of the lobsters. Several lobsters found their way into a pan of salt water and the result was we had hot boiled lobsters accompanied with corn on the cob and a full order of sautéed lobsters en casserole with toast points. This is one of hundreds of fun times and fond memories I have had because of my cooking skills.

A couple of years back, Barbara and I, and daughter Debi and husband Bill, spent Thanksgiving in the Turks & Caicos Islands. I said to Bill, "Looks like we'll have grouper for Thanksgiving this year." Bill replied, "No way. We're going to have turkey with all the trimmings." Bill had taken an interest in cooking, and he is quite a good cook. He has the basic skills that are required: Like he says, he reads. He is not afraid to ask questions, and he is not afraid to try new dishes. Before we left for the Turks & Caicos, Bill called ahead to a grocery store to be sure we could get all the ingredients we needed, including the turkey.

There we were on a tropical island, having purchased the turkey and all the fixings. "Hey Bill", I called at Debi and Bill's door, "Do you have an oven?" His reply was,"Hell, no!" Thanksgiving Day was one we will never forget. We devoured a perfect turkey dinner cooked inside the gas barbecue, right by the swimming pool, under a small pavilion surrounded by tropical flowers and palm trees. Prepared in our combined kitchens, we had all the fixings.

The tradition goes on no matter where we go and what kind of stove we find in our lodgings. Last year Barbara and I were in Bonaire, Netherland Antilles for Thanksgiving. As I prepared to roast a chicken, I noticed the temperature gauge was in degrees centigrade. Good thing I could fall back on my engineering training and remembered the formula to convert to Fahrenheit!

Now I do all the cooking for us at home. I have a lot of fun with cooking, which has become a full-time hobby. In New York City, Barbara and I have many fans. We are an unbeatable team when we have dinner parties, and we do not resort to Zabar's, Citarella's or Fairway's except for some tasty deserts. I have refrained from baking because we are conscious of our waist lines. However, occasionally I make a cranberry nut bread or a killer blueberry cake using Barbara's mother's recipes. And once in a while, just for old time's sake, I make a batch of my apple cinnamon muffins.

126
CONNECTIONS

I have learned that relationships have their beginnings and endings. Some last for a brief moment, like when you smile at someone as they step into an elevator, say "Hello," and as you leave you say "Goodbye." Some last for months and years and a few for a lifetime. We ought to let people have their exits and entrances. We can be happy when they come into our lives and willing to let them go if the time is right.

As Shakespeare wrote in *As You Like It:*

All the world's a stage,
And all the men and women are merely players:
They have their exits and their entrances;
And one man in his time plays many parts,
His acts being seven ages. At first an infant, ...

I know I am not in the first age and not in the seventh, but I am somewhere in between. I am grateful for all the players who have had their entrances and exits in my life.

Until these later years, I lived my life "unconsciously," without much planning, and frankly, rather serendipitously. I had no known intentions, and I suppose I was like an insect floating down the river on a frail leaf, at the mercy of capricious winds and currents.

I read the words of the Greek philosopher Socrates later in life; "The unexamined life is not worth living," and I have since heeded his words, examining my life on a regular basis. To realize that I have been given a priceless gift by my loving mother at this late date is the grandest gift of all. She gave me life, but more importantly, she gave me her love. She believed in my dreams, and she encouraged me to believe in myself. She planted these gifts so very subtly, so innocuously, that I hardly understood her gifts until I began to live consciously. .

Frequently I am reminded of gruff old Herb Dever who died in 2006, the guy I quoted in the beginning of the book, "All anybody really wants is someone to love, and more importantly, someone to love them in return." Herb would be thrilled to know that I used his words and that they give me strength and purpose.

127
JOHNNY IS DONE RUNNING
3 April 1952 – 29 March 2010

"Hi, Dad. We're having a 92nd birthday party for Bill's mother in Concord, New Hampshire on Sunday the 21st of October 2007. Can you and Barbara come?" After checking calendars, we called Debi back and said we would arrive at their house in East Kingston, New Hampshire on Saturday, the day before. The drive through New England was spectacular with the fall foliage at its peak, and we had a great time at The Cat and the Fiddle restaurant in Concord. Bill's mother, Mary, was really excited that we drove up from New York to celebrate with her.

I was at the wheel on Sunday, driving home to New York City from the birthday party. Somewhere in Connecticut, my cell phone rang, and Barbara answered. "Hi. How are you doing?" Then I just heard bits and pieces, "Uh huh. I understand. That's great. I'll have him call as soon as possible."

Barbara excitedly said, "That was your son, John, and he called to tell you he needs to talk to you, and that he's all done running." My response was a sure indicator that my anger was not yet under control, "Bullshit, he's been rejecting me for the past 17 years," was my surprise reaction. Barbara said, "Look John, he left his telephone number and he really wants to hear from you." She went on to urge me, "John, pull into the next rest area and make the call." "Stop bugging me," was my angry reply.

I did pull into the next rest area. I was an emotional basket case of confused feelings. When I stopped the car, getting ready to step out, Barbara slipped me the paper with John's telephone number. At the same time I picked up some accumulated trash that collects on long drives, with the intentions of tossing it in the waste receptacle before making the call.

I approached a neat little rest area building, the kind for which Connecticut is famous, and threw the collected trash into the little hole in the top of a deep waste receptacle. I pulled out my cell phone and dug into my pocket for John's number. "Shit, the number went into the receptacle," There was no way I could retrieve that number, or so I concluded, not remembering that I could get the number from the cell phone. Back at the car I told Barbara what had happened, and she responded with an angry accusation that this was a sub-conscious reaction on my part. The ride home from that point on is better left unrecorded. Here was my son, John, who was in deep trouble with booze and drugs for most of his life, a son I had never even known, and I threw away his telephone number when he finally reached out to me.

Summer 1983. The days of wine and roses on Padre Island, TX. John F. Willey Jr. at left, and John's cousin, Jeffrey Brown, at right.

The next day on Monday 22 October 2007 I called his companion, Lesley, and she gave me his number. "Hi, John, what's happening?" John said, "Dad, I'm done running, and I need help." He told me he had been fired again, that he was close to being put out on the street, and that he had no money, a car that did not run, and he was a mess. I said, "John, I have a morning meeting in Boston on Thursday, and I'll come up to see you after the meeting." In the meantime, I called Dave, an old Haverhill buddy who lived not too far from John, to ask him to look in on John. Dave was no stranger to the plight of my son, John, and he knew how to deal with him.

On Thursday of the same week, I had a monthly meeting in Boston with a client that I had been providing engineering services to for close to 20 years. When the meeting concluded, with uneasiness mixed with hope, I drove to Sandown, New Hampshire to see John. He greeted me with a warm welcome.

His shoulders dropped, and he breathed a sigh of relief. After a brief hug and a few words of encouragement, I decided we should take a ride to Newburyport to have lunch at The Grog. The Grog is what you would expect in a waterfront inn in old England, with its exposed brick walls, creaking floors, and wooden booths proudly wearing a patina of over 100 years of use. The Grog represented years of pleasant memories for me, and I was counting on the positive energy to color our conversation as we discussed the next steps.

In the back of my mind was a nagging fear about his physical condition. He looked awful, and his grayish complexion spoke of poor health. Several teeth were missing. He was unkempt and needed a haircut. He looked older than his years. His eyes had a look of despair that bored into my memories of guys I had seen over the years who were in trouble. I "listened" to his eyes, because I find eyes do not cover up with clever words or avoidance. Eyes tell me what's happening within. He looked like a warrior who had lost a long hard battle. I realized that he understood he had lost, and no one had to convince him. Booze and drugs had done a thorough job. The war was over, and he was not the victor.

I drove him back to his home in Sandown. My friend, Dave, picked him up that night and drove him to an Alcoholics Anonymous meeting. That Johnny attended an AA meeting made me hopeful, but I could not shake the sadness I felt at his physical condition and the suffering in his eyes.

John's loving partner of 15 years, Lesley Sarchione, was hurting too, not knowing what to do with him. After John and Dave left for the meeting, I took Lesley out to dinner at the 1686 House in East Kingston, New Hampshire. Over dinner I explained to Lesley, whom I hardly knew, about the devastation caused by alcoholism. She was scared and grateful at the same time. She had no idea how much the booze had been affecting John. I could see that Lesley really loved John, a truth that I did not learn from John.

Later that evening when John returned home, the three of us had a direct conversation about what had to happen if the two of them wanted to maintain their relationship. John had to stop drinking. He had to be honest with Lesley about his drinking and losing jobs and lying. He told Lesley he was going to change. After many hours of talking, at midnight John suggested I sleep over. I flopped onto his bed. Lesley retired to her bedroom. He slept on the couch downstairs.

Looking around the room at his scant possessions, I felt anguish that this room and its contents represented all John owned after 55 years on the planet. I noticed the end table I had made during my first divorce, while living in a one-room apartment in Lawrence, Massachusetts. I had wondered whatever happened to that table. I remembered from years ago that he had kept an old coat of mine and my old sea bag from the Navy. I was pained to know that holding onto those possessions was as close as he had come to saying, "Dad, I love you and want to live a life without booze and drugs and be with my daughter, Colleen." At that moment I realized that he had wanted a connection with me and his family, but alcohol and drugs had made his decisions.

I slept fitfully. I fantasized about "what might have been" and about what could be as the future unfolded

The beginning of John's new journey was highlighted by a conversation where he informed me, "All I want is for you to be my Dad." What was left unsaid but that I heard clearly was, "I'll take care of my booze problem." John knew that his mother, Rita Van Nunnen, had practically worn out two pairs of knees praying that he and I would someday get together. I had called Rita many times in frustration at failed attempts that I had made to spend time with Johnny.

Johnny was getting his life together. At his request, I called him every weekday at 6 A.M., and he called me once or twice over the weekends. Within a very short time, John contacted a former employer, Emmett Horgan, owner of Rockingham Toyota in Salem, New Hampshire, to ask him for a job. John had been an excellent worker over the years; however, the booze and drugs always interfered. His work record was not perfect, and Emmett knew that. John talked straight. He told Emmett about his booze problem and described the steps he was taking to make a new life. Emmett gave him a job in the parts department, and until the end, neither John nor Emmett ever had cause to regret Emmett taking a chance on John.

He and Lesley nurtured each other on this new path. It was a joy to behold them experiencing a new adventure. John became very active in AA. From the outset, he was a welcoming beacon to newcomers. When I was in Boston on business, he invited me to attend his regular meeting in Manchester, New Hampshire, which was open to the public. I was so pleased to see how he was interacting with his fellow members. The group held raffles as a way to raise money for rent, books, and operating expenses. Johnny brought zest to the job of selling raffle tickets at the meetings. John's sponsor, Scott, remarked that John had elevated to an art form the mundane job of selling tickets, and used it as a platform for greeting newcomers who oft times were a little shaky. At some point over that first year, Lewis, an active member of the group, anointed John with the nickname of "Johnny Tickets".

Working as a consultant for a Boston-based client gave me the benefit of traveling to Boston every month on business. I took the train up a day or two early and stayed at a hotel in Haverhill. On Tuesday evenings I would meet John in Sandown, drive to a McDonald's, and pick up his friend, Addie. Then off we would go to his Manchester meeting where I could observe him in action.

I helped bring John and his estranged daughter, Colleen, back together. The three of us had dinner and established a dialogue that had been broken for many years. In 2009 I gathered the entire family together for a reunion in Muskegon, Michigan. John's original family laughed and played together at an all-day picnic on the shores of Lake Michigan. He was having the time of his life, surrounded by his family. Things were falling into place.

After a year and a half, we gradually reduced the early morning phone calls to about three or four a week. I was being his Dad, and he was taking care of his booze problem. However, as his Dad, I hounded him about getting a physical since I was concerned about his health after all the years of neglect. He agreed that he should get a physical. However, not until early January, 2010 did he finally pay a visit to the Veterans Administration Hospital in Manchester, New Hampshire. After his first exam, he described for me a host of tests he had taken, and a laundry list of medical ailments that needed attention. His VA doctor had developed a plan of attack.

In February 2010 John hurt his back while picking up a fairly light television set. When the pain became unbearable, he went back to the VA Hospital in Manchester. John called me to say that in one of the visits, his physician informed him that he was pretty sure John had Multiple Myeloma, an incurable form of cancer. On 19 February 2010 John called me with confirmation of the horrible news. He went on to say that he would be examined by an oncologist on the 8th of March. The oncologist took one look at John and shipped him to the VA Hospital campus in Boston, Massachusetts. Unfortunately, the cancer was in an extremely advanced stage.

Visiting John was a painful reminder that his days were numbered. Because of his severe back pain, he was never able to work again. He could no longer attend AA meetings, though every day his AA buddies visited, bringing an AA meeting to him. He looked ashen and haggard, and yet he continued to smile and comfort all who visited him at the hospital. He never whined or complained. He said to me more than once, "I'm okay, Dad. I'm okay with this." In the face of death, I marvel at how he found such courage and acceptance.

With no hope for recovery, John was discharged from the VA hospital and returned home on 18 March 2010. In an attempt to lessen his pain, on 25 March he received his first of two doses of chemotherapy at the VA hospital in Manchester. Dr. Gerald Ghea talked straight to John, saying, "I'm going to do everything within my power to give you all the time we can."

John's 58th birthday was coming up on 3 April 2010. On Saturday 27 March I called Lesley to arrange for my wife Barbara and me to visit John. Lesley informed me that I had better get up to New Hampshire right away since he was at that moment being taken from their home in Sandown by ambulance to the Elliott Hospital in Manchester. Barbara and I drove directly from New York City to the Elliott Hospital, arriving about 3 P.M. One look at John, and we immediately agreed to cancel the trip we had planned to Argentina on the 4th of April. Later that evening, Barbara and I checked into a nearby hotel.

On Sunday morning 28 March, Barbara and I arrived at the hospital about 10:30 A.M. John had barely survived the night. With the hour glass running out, I suggested we talk about what he wanted for final arrangements. I asked John, "Do you want to be buried in your mother's Brugnani family grave site in Haverhill or the Willey grave site in Fremont, New Hampshire? His immediate response was, "I want to be cremated, half the ashes to you, and half to Mom, no funeral, just a simple service, no clergy, no religious stuff. Just my Higher Power—you know what I mean, Dad." We also discussed with John the fact that he wanted no extreme measures taken to keep him alive. Later in the day, Lesley confirmed that they had talked about that too, and she knew of his decision. Even though no official papers were signed, we shook our heads in agreement.

All day Sunday we took turns visiting with John. That afternoon, Barbara and I decided to take a walk to the family room to give Lesley private time with John. John was very secretive about his love for Lesley, and I was not astute enough to see what was obvious. Later, Lesley came to the family room, visibly shaken. She hugged me and blurted out, "Johnny asked me to marry him." On his death bed he had asked Lesley something that had probably been on his mind for years, but booze had kept him from his desire. Physically and emotionally drained, around

6 P.M., Lesley left to return home for the evening. Barbara and I went out for dinner, returning to the hotel about 9 P.M.

Shortly after 9 P.M. Barbara said, "John, we must get back to the hospital." She said it with a firm conviction, but I remarked, "Barbara, the visiting hours were over at 8 P.M." Her response was, "John, we have to go back to the hospital now!" We arrived, signed in with the night guard, and headed to John's room. We were intercepted by an orderly who immediately pointed us to the attending physician. As they wheeled Johnny's bed past us, she explained that Johnny was going to ICU, he was having trouble breathing, and he was close to the end. Barbara and I rode the elevator with Johnny, and I held his hand all the way. I could see in his eyes that he understood what was happening. The doctor guided us to the ICU waiting room while the staff settled Johnny into ICU.

At about 10:30 P.M. Barbara and I were admitted to his room in ICU. John was fighting to breathe. The attending doctor asked if he wanted her to administer a ventilator tube to keep him alive, and he shook his head to indicate no. I said no, Barbara said no. And when we called Lesley to tell her what was happening, she told the doctor she was sure Johnny understood he was going to die, and he did not want to be kept alive on a ventilator tube. The doctor seemed relieved, and ICU began to administer morphine to ease his pain. We asked the nurse in ICU what we could do to help Johnny. She said that touch and voice would be helpful for him. She suggested that massaging his feet would help him relax. For the next two hours, Barbara gently rubbed his feet, and I held him and continually talked to him about how we all loved him. The nurses kept him heavily sedated, easing his pain, and relaxing him. At a few minutes past midnight, on Monday 29 March 2010, Johnny took his last breath. I was there for him at the end, at his side, his head cradled in my arm. I regret I was not with him when he was born – I was a US Navy sailor on a destroyer operating in the Yellow Sea. Weary and sobbing, Barbara by my side, we made our way out of the hospital, back to the hotel.

As the weeks passed, I began to think about the service I had promised John. I enlisted help from my daughter Linda, my wife Barbara, and Lesley. We decided to have a Celebration of Life for Johnny. Our intention was to bring out the good memories of Johnny as a way of enabling us to remember the good times and accept Johnny's death.

On Saturday 24 April 2010, with the entire family and many friends, about 70 of us celebrated Johnny's life at the Atkinson Country Club in Atkinson, New Hampshire. We told stories about Johnny, remembering the good times in his childhood, right through the last two and a half years of his sobriety. I felt pleased and comforted to see so many people there honoring Johnny.

The next day, the Manchester Original Group of Alcoholics Anonymous celebrated Johnny's life. About 80 people attended, and our entire family was invited. Both Rita and I spoke, expressing gratitude on behalf of all our family. Johnny's doctor at the VA was there, as was Emmett, his boss at Rockingham Toyota, Emmett's wife, and many employees. I so appreciated the loving words and actions of the members of his AA group.

Many years ago I read the work of Elizabeth Kubler-Ross, and that has been helpful. Also, soon after Johnny died, I attended a meeting at Gilda's Club (a nationwide organization that helps people grieve the loss of loved ones due to cancer). I talked to a Hospice grieving specialist and to many of my friends who had experienced the loss of a child. No matter what I do or read, the pain goes on.

A month or so after Johnny died, I was reading the latest book by one of my favorite authors, Jacqueline Winspear. She described an incident where the heroine, Maisie Dobbs, was robbed of her leather brief case as she walked through a park. The case had been given to her by friends 25 years ago on the occasion of her going off to college. The old case was scuffed, and a clasp was missing, but it held great sentimental value. As the story unfolded, Maisie sat in reverie, recalling old friends and good memories of places she had been while carrying the case.

Tears suddenly flooded my eyes. I caught my breath, dropped the book, and ran from the bedroom where I was reading. When we had visited Johnny in the hospital, Lesley had informed me that certain papers that we needed were in Johnny's briefcase that sat beside his hospital bed. I had jokingly remarked about the condition of the battered old case with all the racing decals attached and the broken clasp. I realized this was the same case he had with him at the AA meetings when he was selling raffle tickets. Lesley then reminded me that Johnny treasured that case, and that Sally and I had given it to him many years before.

When she told me that, I sat in the hospital room with tears streaming down my face as I realized that he had kept that old case as a memory of happier times. He had wandered here, there and everywhere, and the old case was his connection to a time he valued, a time of promise, a time of sobriety. He did love his family, but the power of alcohol had kept him on the move.

My wife Sally and I gave John that briefcase to celebrate his becoming a businessman. At that time Johnny was living with us for a brief spell between his travels to faraway places with strange-sounding names. Our daughter, Linda, managed to get him a job at a robotics manufacturing plant in Wilmington, Massachusetts. Having been "On the Road" like Jack Kerouac all those years, Johnny had never developed a career path. This was Johnny's first professional job. He expressed his enthusiasm about the opportunity, and we all were excited for him. That briefcase had traveled everywhere with him over the past 30 some odd years.

As the days unfold, unexpectedly, reminders of Johnny hook my emotions, and waves of sadness wash over me, no matter how much I read or talk with friends who comfort me. However, the last two and a half years of Johnny's life were a precious gift. All my life, I had wanted a close relationship with my son. We had some good talks every morning at 6:00 A.M., and he certainly packed a lifetime of service to others at AA into those two and a half short years.

128
LIVING THE LIFE I ALWAYS WANTED

I would like to explain the title of this book, *Living the Life I Always Wanted*. All my life I just wanted to "be happy," but never could I dream big enough to imagine the life I am living now. I wanted to live in peace, without conflict. I never imagined that "happiness" would be living in New York City with a woman like Barbara Greenberg.

Never in my life did I say to myself, "Gee, I wish I lived in New York City." Quite the contrary, I used to think how awful it would be to live in a crowded, noisy, electric metropolis. I envisioned enormous, tall, warehouse-like apartment buildings, with little cubicles into which people were crammed like sardines, the aroma of boiled cabbage and hamburgers pervading the corridors. I envisioned a crime-ridden, dangerous place where pickpockets and shysters would cheat you out of your money, and no one cared about you, and everyone was out to harm you. Pictures in my mind were of scary places like The Bronx; Brooklyn; Flatbush Avenue; Hell's Kitchen; the Bowery; Harlem, and the waterfront where gangsters hung out. The idea of visiting New York City was frightening. Living there was unthinkable.

I grew up in Haverhill. I have many pleasant childhood memories of my hometown. I enjoyed the comfort and familiarity of living near friends and relatives, and of people recognizing me on the street and in the shops. I know hundreds of people in Haverhill. When I walk down Washington Street, I can name every old factory building, what it was used for, as well as how it is now being used. I watched Haverhill transform itself from a mill town, with the Merrimack River full of sewerage and factory waste, into a desirable place to live with decent restaurants and nice apartments in the old factory buildings. All the River banks in Haverhill and neighboring towns were vacant and smelly, and no one wanted to live there. With the infusion of federal money, sewerage treatment plants were added, and beautiful land along the River became a real estate developer's dream. Boat marinas popped up along the River. Now people do the unthinkable, actually swimming in the River. Train service was reinstituted. You can train into Boston to work, and even up to Portland, Maine to vacation.

Years ago I built a house on East Broadway, surrounded by beautiful natural wilderness. East Broadway was a new neighborhood, the place to be, and I was proud to live there. After my separation and divorce from Sally, I moved into a converted shoe factory in downtown Haverhill which I had known as Bixby Shoe when I was a child. My apartment had floor-to-ceiling windows looking over the River and the railroad bridge. I discovered a new way of living, carefree, come and go as you please, with freedom to walk away, close the door, and not worry about the apartment. I had re-invented myself. I no longer lived in the woods, no longer had a workshop full of tools. I began to see a whole new way of living in an apartment. I realize now that this happy adjustment to my Haverhill apartment helped make it possible for me to contemplate moving to New York City.

In the six years from 1997 to 2003, each weekend Barbara and I took turns traveling. One weekend she took the train to Haverhill, and the next I took the train to Manhattan. I slowly acclimated to Gotham. No doubt about it, the City is big and noisy, but it is also exciting! Gradually I made the transition from the Merrimack Valley to the new world. After those many years of oscillating every weekend between Haverhill and Manhattan, Cupid stepped in and said, "Time to make a decision."

It was obvious I would be the one to relocate, rather than Barbara moving to Haverhill or even Boston. Barbara has a well-established consulting business, all of which is based here in New York City. I went to see my favorite therapist and presented my problem to her. After listening for a short while, Ann Condon closed her eyes, and with both palms up, replicating the statue of Justice, raising and lowering each hand, she said, "Haverhill - Manhattan; Haverhill – Manhattan; living in Manhattan with Barbara, or living alone in Haverhill." She opened her eyes and said, "Seems like a no brainer. Move to Manhattan."

In 2003 I moved to Manhattan, scared but happy. My company transferred me to its New York City office and paid the moving expenses. We live in a neighborhood called the Upper West Side. We are right next to Riverside Park and the Hudson River, and Central Park is a 15-minute walk away. The subway at West 72nd and Broadway is a two-minute walk, and my office at One Penn Plaza is an eight-minute ride.

New York City is alive and jumping, the people dynamic. I now count among my friends, actors, writers, musicians, composers, engineers, and hedge fund managers. The neighborhoods take on a small town atmosphere where friends stop and chat about the current events, and people do care about their neighbors.

People come to New York from all over the world, with the intent of "making it." I met a man, originally from Vermont, who arrived here to further his acting career. He is now a successful building contractor. The City is full of colorful characters who have made their mark in one way or another, who are on their way down, or on their way up. Mickey Cohen, a man I've come to admire, is in his 80th year. A biologist, he has led 20 excursions to the Galapagos. More recently he has been leading groups to Tanzania, and he is currently scoping out a new trip to India. Realizing I am somewhat of a character myself explains why I have no problem blending in here in the Big Apple.

Barbara and I work together in our spacious home office, and I have been able to assist her in dealing with her contracts and proposals and in entertaining some of her valued clients. Also, on a personal level, we have fine-tuned our communication skills and are supportive of each other in difficult times.

I am so grateful to live here in New York City. Lincoln Center, a 20-minute walk from our apartment, is where the Metropolitan Opera and the New York Philharmonic are located. The dream of my lifetime came true the first time we attended the Metropolitan Opera. Now we see several operas a year, and we have season tickets to the Philharmonic. After an evening at Lincoln Center, we walk home, often close to midnight, without a worry about our safety.

I love to get dressed up and walk down to Lincoln Center with Barbara, meet some friends at a nearby restaurant, walk across West 65th Street to Avery Fisher Hall to attend a short 7:00 P.M. pre-concert lecture, and afterwards rush to take our seats for the 8:00 P.M. performance. Founded in 1842, the New York Philharmonic is by far the oldest orchestra in the United States and one of the oldest in the world. Last night we attended the 15,010th concert of this wonderful orchestra. Earlier this year I started to attend rehearsals of the Philharmonic, another wonderful way to enjoy Lincoln Center.

A special treat this year was attending a performance of Puccini's *Il Trittico* at the Metropolitan Opera, something I had dreamt of doing for years. More recently we attended a new production of *Carmen*. While sitting with another couple in our excellent seats, I could not help thinking to myself, "Not too bad for a guy from Haverhill. You've come a long way, baby."

Special events surround us year round. We live within walking distance of the famous American Museum of Natural History; the Metropolitan Museum and the dozens of museums on 5th Avenue. Times Square is one stop on the number 2 or 3 train. Ethnic neighborhoods are within easy access by New York City's 24 different subway lines and 50 bus routes. Within one block or so we have our grocery store, bank (open seven days a week) the Beacon Theatre, two drug stores, florist, the subway, numerous restaurants, and the beautiful Riverside Park.

On warm summer nights we walk for miles along Riverside Park at the edge of the Hudson River, or walk a quarter of a mile out on the 72nd Street pier into the Hudson; sit on a bench and view the George Washington Bridge while being caressed by cool summer breezes coming down the River. We can stop at O'Neill's restaurant at the foot of the pier or walk up to the 79th Street Boat Basin and have salad and burgers at the other O'Neill restaurant, while watching the sun set over the Hudson on the New Jersey shore. For that matter, we can take the elevator to the 17th floor of our own apartment building and spend the evening on the roof looking at all the sights from a quiet and private bug-free perch.

A short drive puts us at the Cloisters, a structure made up of original 10th Century French churches taken over stone by stone and erected at the northern end of Manhattan Island. From the Cloisters, we are surrounded by beautifully landscaped grounds with views of the New Jersey shore and the pristine Palisades forever protected from development. A drive of less than an hour takes us to the 55,000 acre Harriman State Park where we enjoy kayaking all summer long in the lakes, a natural environment that we enjoy so much. We manage to get in about 30 to 35 kayaking trips a year throughout the northeast.

Life is good! I have evolved to where I am at peace with my family and see them as often as possible. Barbara and I enjoy vacations to scuba and kayak locations. We have many friends around the city. We spent Thanksgiving 2009 in Bonaire, 40 miles off the north coast of Venezuela. I have logged over 400 dives and Barbara is not too far behind. In my 80th year I am still working a few days a month as a consultant engineer on the Big Dig in Boston. Recently I signed another two-year contract that ends on 31 December 2011.

All this, and the greatest gift of all is to be married to Barbara Greenberg. We have deep respect and love for each other. This good life is truly beyond what I could have imagined years ago. I am living the life I always wanted.

AFTERWORD: LIFE COMES AS IT WILL

Never having written a memoir, I was not prepared for all the revelations and changes in perspective that I experienced as the writing progressed. I also did not expect the pain the writing caused as I revisited all the events of my life. Perhaps that is why so few autobiographies are written. It is too damn hard.

Also, I did not realize the burden I would be placing on Barbara when we decided that she would be my editor. The book stirred up a lot of strong feelings and angry outbursts. We spent years working closely, as she edited my work and made it readable. On vacations in Bonaire and Puerto Rico, and on holiday weekends at home, we spent many a long day together over the computer, digging deeper into what I had written, and establishing a closer bond between us as a result.

I decided that I would not rewrite various chapters again for the umpteenth time, but would offer these last thoughts that have come to me now that I am finished writing.

In my younger years, I was afraid of women, and I invented reasons why I could not be comfortable in their presence. I easily mixed with men of any color, belief system, age, financial status, or occupation. I learned fast, and became "buddies" quickly. They were either good guys you could trust, or they were shitheads you avoided. It was that simple. No mystery. Now as I re-read this book, I can see that my relationships with women started to improve shortly after I quit drinking.

An epiphany arrived a few weeks after completion of my writing. I was reading the 1928 Pulitzer winning novel, *The Bridge of San Luis Rey,* by Thornton Wilder. In the book Brother Juniper witnessed a catastrophe when the bridge at San Luis Rey collapsed, and five people were hurled to their death. Brother Juniper's conclusion was, "Either we live by accident and die by accident, or we live by plan and die by plan." Brother Juniper spent the rest of his life trying to ascertain God's intentions in the everyday happenings of humans.

Brother Juniper's query is mine. What the hell are we here for? In the section, *ABOUT THE AUTHOR*, the following words gave me a jolt. "Although it was never Wilder's aim, nor Brother Juniper's fortune to discover any final answer, there is in his novel a pattern of meaning to the passions and errors and longings of human beings. The meaning is a human one, for although we can never be totally assured of Divine Intention in our movement on earth, the "bridge" of love that connects one to the other gives dignity and purpose to even the lowliest of lives."

I immediately saw the point about the "bridge" of love that "connects." I was excited about the idea that there might be another way of dealing with Brother Juniper's conclusion that, either we live and die by accident or we live and die by plan.

My life has often been influenced by serendipitous events. Accepting serendipity makes life lighter and helps me recognize that life comes as it will. Our task is to take from the events that "unfold on the knife edge of the present," and implement our plan. I do not have to ponder the heavy alternatives like Brother Juniper. It matters not to me whether life was an accident or a plan. Being free from worry about God's Intentions, my life has turned out exceedingly well. My goal is to live free and happy with dignity and respect for others.

"Success is the progressive realization of a worthwhile goal while remaining well-adjusted." Since I adopted that simple and practical definition, and I am now living the life I always wanted, I know that everything in-between had to happen to get me where I am. I am at peace. My goal is not to seek some splendid, far-reaching, earth-shattering accomplishment of magnificent proportions, but rather to achieve the love and caring my mother wrote about in her poem many years ago. I have done that--I live with someone I love, and she loves me in return. That person is Barbara Greenberg.

The pattern has been set for the rest of my days. I look forward to accepting change as a consequence of living. My feeling of completeness is a direct result of having written this memoir.

2010. The author at 80 years old, diving off the island of Utila, Honduras

CPSIA information can be obtained at www.ICGtesting.com
260909BV00003B/1/P
9 781450 290319